The classic novel

MANCHESTER
UNIVERSITY PRESS

THE CLASSIC NOVEL
From page to screen

edited by Robert Giddings and Erica Sheen

Manchester University Press
Manchester and New York

distributed exclusively in the USA by St. Martin's Press

Published by Manchester University Press
Oxford Road, Manchester M13 9NR, UK
and Room 400, 175 Fifth Avenue, New York, NY 10010, USA
http://www.man.ac.uk/mup

Distributed exclusively in the USA by
St. Martin's Press, Inc., 175 Fifth Avenue, New York,
NY 10010, USA

Distributed exclusively in Canada by
UBC Press, University of British Columbia, 6344 Memorial Road,
Vancouver, BC, Canada V6T 1Z2

British Library Cataloguing-in-Publication Data
A catalogue record for this book is available from the British Library

Library of Congress Cataloging-in-Publication Data applied for

ISBN 0 7190 5230 0 *hardback*
 0 7190 5231 9 *paperback*

First published 2000

06 05 04 03 02 01 00   10 9 8 7 6 5 4 3 2 1

Typeset by Action Publishing Technology Ltd, Gloucester
Printed in Great Britain
by Bell & Bain Limited, Glasgow

Contents

Notes on contributors

Jonathan Bignell is Senior Lecturer in Media Arts, in the Department of Media Arts, at Royal Holloway College, University of London. His publications include *Media Semiotics: An Introduction* and essays on postmodernist cinema, semiotics and postmodernism.

Jenny Dennett teaches Literature and Media at Farnham College. She has worked for the BBC and *Times* Newspapers and published on Dickens and Turner.

Robert Giddings is Professor of Communication and Culture at Bournemouth University. He has published on the BBC, imperial and military history, Smollett, Dickens, Twain, Matthew Arnold, *The War Poets 1914–1918* and *Screening the Novel: The Theory and Practice of Literary Dramatization* (with Keith Selby and Chris Wensley).

Fred Inglis is Professor of Cultural Studies in the Department of Continuing Education at the University of Sheffield. He is author of *Popular Culture and Political Power, The Management of Ignorance: A Political Theory of the Curriculum* and *Media Theory*. His biography of Raymond Williams was published in 1986.

A. Robert Lee is Professor of American Literature at Nihon University, Tokyo. His publications include *Designs of Blackness: Mappings in the Literature and Culture of Afro-America*, and the essay collections *A Permanent Etcetera: Cross-Cultural Perspectives on Post-War America* and *Other Britain, Other British: Contemporary Multicultural Fiction*.

Ian MacKillop is Reader in English Literature at the University of Sheffield and author of *The British Ethical Societies, F. R. Leavis: A Life in Criticism* and *Free Spirits: Henri Pierre Roché, François Truffaut and the Two English Girls.*

Alison Platt is Lecturer in Continuing Education at the University of Liverpool. Her doctoral dissertation was on *George Eliot and the Revolution of the Mind.*

The classic novel

Keith Selby is the author of *How to Study a Dickens Novel, Screening the Novel: the Theory and Practice of Literary Dramatization* (with Robert Giddings and Chris Wensley), and *How to Study Television* (with Ron Cowdery).

Erica Sheen is Lecturer in English Literature and Film at the University of Shefffield, and has published on early modern theatre and Hollywood cinema. She is currently completing studies of Shakespearean drama and of the widescreen image in contemporary film.

Neil Sinyard is Head of Department in the Department of English at the University of Hull. He is author of *Filming Literature: The Art of Screen Adaptation* and other publications on adaptation.

Suzanne Speidel teaches Film and Literature in the Department of English Literature, University of Sheffield and is completing a study of the novels of Conrad and Forster and their film adaptations.

Bronwen Thomas teaches Linguistics and Literature at Bournemouth University. Her research focuses on the stylistic analysis of dialogue in comic novels of the 1920s and 1930s and she has published on Firbank and Waugh.

1

Introduction

Erica Sheen

Film has been around now for over a hundred years, so it is surprising that the nature of its relationship to literature is still an open question. Surprising, perhaps, only if we assume that intellectual disciplines evolve according to a teleology of definition. Indeed, definition had until recently seemed to be the issue. Writing in the mid 1980s, Thomas Elsaesser identified a 'war of independence' between film studies and 'English Literature, Mass Communication studies, American Studies, Modern Language Departments'.[1] For a while it seemed as if this war had been well and truly won, but over the last decade or so pockets of resistance have re-emerged in these non-specialist arenas. Their importance to the study of film is considerable, particularly in an audio-visual culture increasingly disposed towards cultural and linguistic diversity: almost all work currently being done on Russian, Asian and Slav film, not to mention the main European cinemas, is done in these contexts. It would be hard now to find a single Department in higher education faculties of art or schools of humanities that does not offer a wide range of courses organised around the study of film. Since in many cases they treat a range of textual forms (film, TV, video) as more or less interchangeable – as we do in this volume – what they do might, from a 'film studies' perspective, be deemed to violate the primary disciplinary directive: to identify and describe the audio-visual text as an object of study. From such a perspective, film is frequently drawn into service to illustrate a notion of 'culture' which is similarly undefined as an object of study. This may well be methodologically problematic, but – at a time when EU audio-visual policy is looking to the generalised notion of culture implicit in the all but discredited concept of public service broadcasting for a concept of community – the indefinition is one of some historical moment.[2]

From this point of view, it is neither surprising nor coincidental that adaptation – the transfer of an 'original' (literary) text from one context of production to an (audio-visual) other – has begun to attract academic attention. In that it articulates a range of competing disciplinary commitments even as it strives for the priority of one such commitment over another, adaptation encapsulates the dilemma of institutional identity I have just been describing. The ideological investments at stake in this process reveal themselves in the central critical category of adaptation studies: the notion of 'fidelity', or 'faithfulness to the text'. All the essays in this volume take the question of fidelity as their primary critical point of reference. Given that Brian McFarlane, in one of the few book-length studies on the subject, has insisted that 'the study of adaptation has been inhibited and blurred' by 'the near fixation with the issue of fidelity', this may require some justification.[3]

As a critical term, fidelity behaves anomalously. McFarlane has shown that there is no reliable equation between fidelity and critical approval, infidelity and disapproval. Even more oddly, the same adaptation can be received by different critics as both faithful and unfaithful. As he puts it in a discussion of Bogdanovich's *Daisy Miller*,

> [F]idelity critics clearly have something other in mind than this kind of scrupulous transfer of the transferable. What their dissatisfaction comes down to seems to be a sense that the illusion of reality created by the film does not coincide with their perception of the illusion of reality created by the novella. They write as though the latter were somehow *fixed* and that it is merely obtuse of the film-maker not to have noticed this and reproduced it in the new medium.[4]

After considering a range of 'representative reviews' he concludes that 'fidelity ... cannot profitably be used as an evaluative criterion; it can be no more than a descriptive term to designate loosely a certain kind of adaptation'.[5] But whilst the term may have a limited use from a formalist perspective, from an institutional point of view there are many more things to be said; the first of which is that an institutional point of view is precisely what it requires. The tendency for 'fidelity critics' to make 'objections, on the basis of fidelity-related issues ... couched in terms of amorphous ill-defined disapproval' is in itself a phenomenon worthy of analysis. McFarlane gets to the heart of the matter when he discusses competing 'illusions of reality'. 'Amorphous' and 'ill-defined' are important perceptions here. The way adaptations produce not just animosity, but incoherent animosity, suggests that what is at stake is institutional definitions and identities rather than textual forms and contents.

Institutions may be, and often are, formalised as legal bodies, like corporations; but their relation to society at large is at its most significant level subliminal. Institutional values and protocols behave as if they are consensual, but they have a relative autonomy within the public sphere, and they work hard to ensure that that autonomy is maintained, even as it continues to be perceived as consensual. In this sense they might be said to behave like the unconscious in relation to the consciousness, and it is with this analogy in mind that we can understand Brian McFarlane's perception that the views he presents as evidence constitute a 'depressing fuzziness' or 'unpondered subjectivity'. 'Fuzziness' is a word used by linguists to describe the failures of logic that psychoanalytical accounts of signification see as symptomatic of the eruption of the Semiotic into the Symbolic.[6] On such terms we might see 'fidelity criticism' not so much as a loss of articulation as an articulation of loss.

Loss of what? As McFarlane indicates, 'fidelity criticism' is very often found in reviews. As I suggest in my own chapter on *Pride and Prejudice*, reviews are not just abstract analysis. They have a force of institutional performance. Fidelity criticism is perhaps most appropriately seen as a rhetoric of possession. The literary text is implicitly assessed, in relation to its adaptation, as what it actually only becomes when it leaves the academy and goes somewhere else, and that is a *property*. To understand the way this works – even in the case of the 'classic' text, which in many cases has never had a copyright, or long since gone out of it – one has to consider the terms on which the literary work is 'owned' by the academy. Unlike filmmakers, critics do not have to 'acquire' the work they subject to their own distinctive version of adaptation. They can treat even works that are still in copyright as if they are classic texts. This statement has a largely circular force: a classic text may on some fundamental level be a 'popular' one, but what makes it 'classic' is a certain implicit relation to the academy. As Pierre Bourdieu has put it, 'classics ... owe their consecration, and therefore their widespread durable market ... to the educational system.'[7] It is in a consideration of this implicit relation that we may find the source of the peculiar passion elicited by the transfer of the literary property to the audio-visual domain.

We can work back to it from the *explicit* terms of some of the most recent copyright laws, the so-called 'moral rights' which came into force in England in 1989. These consist of the right of paternity (the right to claim authorship), and the right of integrity (the right to object to derogatory treatment in relation to the work).[8] Moral rights are unassignable, which is to say that they cannot be transferred to any other person except the creator's heir/s, and when the work falls out of copyright they come to an end. These laws may be relatively new, but they enshrine the humanist ideology that has buttressed the literary property throughout the modern period – though it might be more true to say that literary property has buttressed humanist ideology, not least in the part it has played in idealised models of society such as that of the Habermasian public sphere. The contemporary literary academy – though a better, because more inclusive, term might be Bourdieu's term, 'the literary field' – is the guardian of these values. It provides the institutional mechanisms and procedures that buttress the concept of authorship and structure the changing frames of reference for critical perceptions of textual integrity.

It has not always been thus, and may not continue to be so. Indeed, the study of adaptation is, at its broadest level of significance, a study of authorship in a state of historical transformation. Michel Foucault's concept of 'the author-function' may well be our most useful theoretical tool here, and one of the main aims of this introduction is to suggest how this tool might be used.[9] According to Foucault, 'the author-function is not ... constant': once, 'those texts which we now call "literary" were acccepted, circulated, and valorized without any question about the identity of their author'. Now, they are 'dominated by [authorial] sovreignty', but 'we can easily imagine a culture where discourse would circulate without any need for [this figure].'[10] Something like this transformation has already begun, and it is closely associated with the effect on the literary text of the development of cinema. A hundred years after the rise of film as a mode of narrative founded on adaptation, the sovereignty of the author is fraught with contradiction. As a system of production, film certainly observes the formalities of copyright; indeed, the income of those who work within the industry often depends on it. But it severely tests the ideological values conventionally associated with the concept of literary property. For instance, a typical acquisition agreement will not only grant a producer adaptation and reproduction rights that waive the rights of paternity and integrity, but also assert her or his right 'to use the Author's name, likeness and biography in connection with the exploitation of the rights hereby assigned'.[11] This is a remarkable manipulation of what Foucault calls the 'signature' of a work – to the extent, indeed, that the title 'Author' is now a term reserved for a production's *final* rights owner, and that – at least as far as Hollywood is concerned – is usually a film's *distributor*. Since in most cases all the creative work on a film is done *before* distribution,[12] we would seem to be in the strange situation where a film does not have an 'author' while it is actually being made.

In actual fact, this is not really strange at all. Rumours of the death of Author, as they say, are greatly exaggerated; but not because it is still alive. Rather, because it has never really succeeded in being born. What film makes us realise is that copyright is, and always has been, a mechanism that facilitates the *exchange* of the literary property, not its stabilisation. These are the material realities that underlie the process Suzanne Speidel, in her chapter on Hitchcock's Conrad adaptation *Sabotage*, describes as 'broad, unrepentant adaptation – to which we frequently apply the term unfaithful'. Jonathan Bignell provides a telling instance of this kind of scenario, and of its status as a primal scene in the history of cinema in his chapter on Bram Stoker's *Dracula*. Stoker's widow owned the copyright of this novel after her husband's death, and obtained a court order for the destruction of an early adaptation, Murnau's highly influential film *Nosferatu*. As Bignell records, the film now exists only because copies were made from surviving prints. Given the extent to which the market for this novel has been bound up with the popularisation of an audio-visual Gothic aesthetic, it would be hard to imagine what future her husband's work would have had if Mrs Stoker had succeeded in driving this stake through its heart so early in its career.

What we are concerned with here is what Foucault describes as a 'transdiscursive position':

I have discussed the author only in the limited sense of a person to whom the production of a text, book, or a work can be legitimately attributed. However, it is obvious that even within the realm of discourse a person can be the author of much more than a book.[13]

Foucault describes this kind of author as an 'initiator of discursive practices', and indeed he cites Ann Radcliffe – who 'made possible the appearance of Gothic Romances at the beginning of the nineteenth century' – as an example:

The distinctive contribution of these authors is that they produced not only their own work, but the possibility and the rules of formation of other texts.[14]

But he goes on to make a further distinction between authors whose 'function ... exceeds the limits of [their] work', and those who

not only made possible a certain number of analogies that could be adopted by future texts, but, as importantly ... also made possible *a certain number of differences*.[15]

What he is specifically addressing here is the initiator of a theoretical discourse, like Marx or Freud. But his contrast might be drawn into service as the basis of a discrimination between intertextuality and adaptation 'proper'; that is to say, between a form of productivity that elides the differences between contrasting modes of textual production, and one that foregrounds them. Despite its supposedly deconstructive frames of reference, intertextuality is in some ways always on the side of literature. Since it extends the parameters of the literary field past the point where the interests of competing technologies come into play, and thus evades precisely those issues that come into focus around the question of fidelity, we might say that one of its aims as a critical strategy is to pretend that adapation has not taken place. From this point of view, the second of Foucault's categories is more useful, particularly in its description of the 'return to origins' that attends the process of discursive transformation. I quote this part of his discussion at some length because it raises the question of 'omissions and inventions' – an issue that recurs throughout the present collection of essays:

It is always a return to a text in itself, specifically to a primary and unadorned text with particular attention to those things registered in the interstices of the text, its gaps and absences. We return to

6

those empty spaces that have been masked by omission or concealed in false and misleading plenitude ... It follows naturally that this return, which is part of the discursive mechanism, constantly introduces modifications and that the return to a text is not a historical supplement that would come to fix itself upon the primary discursivity and redouble it in the form of an ornament which, after all, is not essential. Rather, it is an effective and necessary means of transforming discursive practice.[16]

As we have seen, Foucault's argument eventually moves towards a position in which 'we can easily imagine a culture where discourse would circulate without any need for an author'. Clearly, however, his own proposition suggests the extent to which the literary author is paradoxically *reinforced* by its own historical supersession – not least because this 'return' focuses a certain politics of resistance, as Brian McFarlane's chorus of amorphous, ill-defined disapproval shows.

The reason for this resistance is that something extremely important is at stake here. The emergence of the author-function in its characteristic modern form – 'the simple attribution of a discourse to an individual'[17] – also marks the emergence of that defining position of Western European privilege, the *intellectual*. Filmmakers, who work on the more complex terms of the attribution of discourse to an *apparatus*, are not seen as intellectuals – a significant anomaly when, as Neil Sinyard and Suzanne Speidel both suggest, the intellectual quality of the filmmaker's work can be higher than that of the writer he or she adapts. This would be a relatively trivial matter – a mere prejudice of art against popular culture – if it were just a matter of a contrast between the two. But adaptation makes it clear that what we are dealing with is something of a historical crisis. The transition from page to screen articulates a radical discontinuity. It effaces the presence of the intellectual in the production system, even as the text itself effects a switch from invisibility to visibility. The adaptation – particularly the kind of adaptation that flaunts the signature of its own authorial origins – pays lip service to the intellectual, but subsumes it into the general circulation of mass communication. Brian McFarlane, and Neil Sinyard in this volume, both show how this transition is seen as an assault on literary 'subtlety', and it is revealing that it is the word 'subtlety' that surfaces in the critical material to which they both refer. 'Subtlety' carries a range of specifically linguistic connotations; connotations deriving from logic, rhetoric, philosophy. 'Subtlety' encapsulates the values that would come to inform what Martin Jay has called the 'anti-visual' tradition of contemporary theoretical discourse.[18] To be subtle is virtually by definition to be using language, not image.

Foucault suggests that 'a last feature of these returns is that they tend to reinforce the enigmatic link between an author and his works'.[19] In the second half of this Introduction I want to suggest that adaptation provides a system of difference in relation to which the literary work has become, precisely, literary. As we shall see, the return of the adapted text to its literary origin reinforces a link that the literary field is now unable to maintain on its own terms.

In a discussion about the classic TV serial at a recent *Screen* conference, John Caughie suggested that, in the 1990s, producers would be unlikely to take on the adaptation of a text as contingent to the present-day educational curriculum as Evelyn Waugh's *Brideshead Revisited* – arguably the outstanding adaptation of the 1980s, discussed in this volume by Fred Inglis. In a discussion to which I have already referred, Bourdieu identifies a 'total opposition' between '*bestsellers*, here today and gone tomorrow', and '*classics,* bestsellers over the long run, which owe their consecration, and therefore their widespread durable market to the educational system'. He characterises this as 'two completely different ways of organising production and marketing', as well as 'two contrasting images of the activity of the writer and even the publisher'.[20] In an increasingly impoverished educational system, this opposition will collapse, as writer and publisher seek ways of accessing both sides of the market, and authors become increasingly susceptible to the notion that intellectual status depends on media visibility. The result is a process of adaptation that is *prior* to the secondary process of adapting an author's text. In events like the Booker Prize, which is now above all a TV event like the Oscar ceremony, it is the *author* that is adapted, and with it the critics that are its functional prosthesis. Significantly, this process mimics a legal one: the selection of a winner is made by a panel of judges, and that panel is itself validated by a prior process of selection.

Nigella Lawson – a member of the 1998 panel – provided an account of this in her column in *The Observer* in the immediate aftermath of the award. Offering by way of analogy a contrast between Peter Hall's high-concept reasons for accepting his knighthood and Richard Eyre's disarming confession to 'vanity and insecurity', she recorded her own 'breathy affirmative' to the invitation to join the panel. 'Britain's greatest literary event gains its momentum from television,' she deprecated, but then disavowed any involvement with 'blurbs, press releases ... reviews and ... articles'. 'I didn't want my subjectivity sullied', she said.[21]

This dependence of an 'unsullied subjectivity' on the institutional structures it purports to repudiate is precisely the point. Philip Elliott has suggested that 'to a large extent the intellectual space [in the media] rests on notions of public service and journalistic responsibility'.[22] If Bourdieu's analysis of 'the author, the critic' – '[T]he only legitimate accumulation consists in making a name for oneself, a known, recognised name, a capital of consecration implying a power to consecrate objects (with a trademark or signature) or persons (through publication, exhibition etc.)'[23] – is now more appropriate than Barthes's sense of the critic as a reader of myths,[24] then, as Elliott succinctly concludes, 'public service is no longer viable'.[25] Within such a scenario, Anthony Minghella's extraordinarily successful adaptation of Michael Ondaatje's *The English Patient* is highly symptomatic, and it receives considerable attention in this volume, both here and in Bronwen Thomas's analysis in our last chapter. This production demonstrated a remarkable accelerated ageing process in its negotiation of that 'total opposition' between bestseller and classic. The novel was shortlisted for the Booker Prize the day it came out, and made into a film very quickly afterwards. As Ondaatje put it in a recent interview with *The Observer,* 'The merry-go-round began from a standstill, in a way, and just when I thought it was over, a film happened.'[26] His elision of the *agency* of adaptation – 'a film happened' – shows just how naturalised the transition from page to screen has become within the production of the contemporary novel as both bestseller *and* classic. It also shows how appropriate Thomas's choice of stylistics as a critical approach to this adaptation is. Stylistics is an analytical method that presupposes structural equivalence between contrasting language systems. This presupposition is fundamental to the Hollywood approach to adaptation, as the presence of Russian formalist and structuralist narrative theory on the syllabus of production courses testifies. In Suzanne Speidel's words, 'the central assumption behind Hollywood screenplay strategy is the independence of any story from its chosen mode of discourse'. The production of both novel and film became merged, even in Ondaatje's own mind:

It took me about a year and a half to edit *The English Patient* as a novel and even do the filming, actually. One of the things that interested me was to see how a really good editor like Walter Murch can structure something and make a completely different form and shape out of it.[27]

As I said, this is a highly symptomatic notion of adaptation. If the Booker Prize adapts the author, this adapts the adaptation. Its hallmark is the way 'a completely different form and shape' appears to exist as a concrete potential within an organic metamorphosis from the literary to the filmic – to the extent that film editor Walter Murch can be recognised by the work's author as an author of the text.[28] Significantly, this 'emptying out' of the author provides a critical identity to take back into the literary field. Of his new collection of poetry, Ondaatje observed, 'I wanted to remove my personality when I was writing this book'. There may seem to be an opposition between the visibility of the first process and the invisibility of the second, but it is one of mirroring rather than confrontation. The mode of personality he wants to 'remove' – so that the 'removing' is, in effect, what is being written – is the one acquired in becoming, so to speak, the author of *The English Patient*. As in Nigella Lawson's comment about 'unsullied subjectivity', there is a link between this invisible media visibility and T. S. Eliot's notion of 'individual talent' as a catalyst that participates in the production of the work but remains unchanged by it.[29] One might predict that this kind of critical formalism will stage a return in the face of authorial desire to inhabit the space of film, but look back through the looking-glass to the field of literature, and there are signs that it is doing so. A certain literary fetishism is beginning to be associated with the more sophisticated echelons of film spectatorship, ranging from tendency to see the screenwriter as a point of identification *within* the film (Quentin Tarantino, Matt Damon), to the presence within the frame of the literary text (Herodotus in *The English Patient*; W. H. Auden in *Four Weddings and a Funeral*) and the representation of the literary apparatus, rather than that of film, as guarantor of high production value (*The Pillow Book,* rather than *sex lies and videotape*). Clearly, Foucault is right about the way the adaptive return reinforces a link between authors and works. But he is less able to account for the way that return recreates a virtual literary culture in which the quality of literariness – the theoretical El Dorado of those formalist and structuralist thinkers beloved of aspiring Hollywood producers — becomes what we arrive at when we experience the literary work as a decontamination of its audio-visual other. From this point of view it is fascinating to see that Alison Platt and Ian MacKillop — F. R. Leavis's biographer — are interested in what it is about the experience of reading a classic novel that its adaptation *restores* to us. In a new New Criticism, 'restoration' could become a more vital critical term than 'fidelity'.

The English literary canon — from most contemporary critical perspectives as non-viable as public service broadcasting — gains a new interest when seen as an effect, not a cause, of this process of restoration. Accordingly, we have presented here a group of essays loosely clustered around that canon and ordered according to *its* chronology, not that of the films in question. The reason for this is not that literary history has priority over that of film: rather, that such a priority is the history of itself film has insisted on telling. Our adapted canon betrays its audio-visual commitments particularly in its later stages: thus Jane Austen, Dickens, George Eliot, Hardy and Conrad are succeeded by Waugh and Ondaatje. From a literary perspective, both Waugh and Ondaatje have an ironic relation to the English literary canon and its values; but they have been positioned firmly as its heirs-apparent by outstanding TV and film adaptations.

All the writers in this collection approach our topic from what might be described as the literary side of the fence. One of the most striking features of this is that — whatever their position in relation to what Fred Inglis refers to as Theory — they all demonstrate a commitment to the critical activity known as 'close reading'. However unfashionable it may be, close reading is institutionally definitive, and it is not surprising to see it reveal its affinity to fidelity criticism. Significantly, however, it is by no means a general conclusion of the essays that follow that the literary text is superior to its adaptation. The inference we might draw from this is not merely that 'Eng. Lit.' remains a productive frame of reference for the study of film. It is also, perhaps, that the study of film might now derive more benefit from a treaty of union than a war of independence.

NOTES

1 Thomas Elsaesser, 'The New Film History', *Sight and Sound,* 55: 4 (1986), p. 246.

2   I am indebted to Lorna Woods and Jackie Harrison of the Departments of Law and Journalism at the University of Sheffield for discussions of their work on EU audio-visual policy.

3   Brian McFarlane, *Novel to Film: An Introduction to the Theory of Adaptation* (Oxford, Clarendon Press, 1996), p. 194.

4   McFarlane, *Novel to Film*, p. 164.

5   McFarlane, *Novel to Film*, p. 166.

6   For 'fuzziness' see James D. McCawley, *Everything that Linguists Have Always Wanted to Know about Logic* *but Were Ashamed to Ask* (Oxford, Basil Blackwell, 1981), pp. 360–94; Robert de Beaugrande and Wolfgang Dressler, *Introduction to Text Linguistics* (New York, Longman, 1981) *passim;* for the 'semiotic disposition' see Julia Kristeva, 'The System and the Speaking Subject', in *The Kristeva Reader*, ed. Toril Moi (Oxford, Basil Blackwell, 1986), p. 28.

7   Pierre Bourdieu, 'The Production of Belief: Contribution to an Economy of Symbolic Goods', in Richard Collins et al. (eds), *Media, Culture and Society: A Critical Reader* (London, Sage, 1986), p. 153.

8   These definitions are provided by Rhonda Baker in *Media Law: A User's Guide for Film and Programme Makers* (London, Chapman and Hall, 1995), p. 144.

9   Michel Foucault, 'What Is an Author?', in *Language, Counter-Memory, Practice* (Oxford, Basil Blackwell, 1977). Page references to this essay hereafter are to the version in *Authorship: From Plato to the Postmodern*, ed. Sean Burke (Edinburgh, University of Edinburgh Press, 1995).

10 Foucault, 'What Is an Author?', pp. 234, 236, 237, 245.

11 Baker, *Media Law*, pp. 66–8.

12 Of course, the rights owned by a distributor notoriously include the right to make a final cut. The distinction between this cut and the one notionally 'intended' by a director has begun to acquire a significance that is retrospectively invested with a quasi-authorial value, as in the case of Ridley Scott's *Bladerunner*. As an issue of 'sovereignty', this is complicated by the fact that the 'director's cut' is not the 'original' and has not replaced it in any way. Both have their own copyright and there is no basis on which the 'original' could be deemed to have violated the paternity or integrity of the 'director's cut'.

13 Foucault, 'What Is an Author?', p. 240

14 Foucault, 'What Is an Author?', p. 240.

15 Foucault, 'What Is an Author?', p. 241, my italics.

16 Foucault, 'What Is an Author?', p. 243. If at this point we return to *Bladerunner*, discussed in n. 12 above, the conclusion we might now reach is that the 'original' initiated a discursive practice that was powerful enough to produce a transformation (the director's cut) characterised by a 'return' to an 'author' – which is obviously about right. On the terms of my own analysis, this means that 'the director's cut' is an *adaptation* of the original. Despite the fact that there is no obvious relocation from one apparatus to another, I think this is true. It highlights an interesting feature of cinema – the fact that its apparatus is constantly in a radical state of transformation. Cinema of the 1990s *is*, effectively, a different apparatus to

Introduction

cinema of the 1980s. On these terms, Gus Van Sant's controversial shot-for-shot 'remake' of Hitchcock's *Psycho* is also an adaptation, just as his earlier *My Own Private Idaho* was. And – from a queer theory perspective – it is a very interesting one, because, by effacing the changes produced by the transformation in favour of the return, it *disavows the difference* between Hitchcock's apparatus and his own.

17 Foucault, 'What Is an Author?', p. 237.
18 Martin Jay, 'In the Empire of the Gaze: Foucault and the Denigration of Vision in Twentieth-Century Thought', in David Couzens Hoy (ed.), *Foucault: A Critical Reader* (Oxford, Basil Blackwell, 1986), p.176.
19 Foucault, 'What Is an Author?' p. 243.
20 Bourdieu, 'The Production of Belief', pp. 153–5.
21 Nigella Lawson, 'Now after 125 Novels, I Can Start to Enjoy Reading Again', *The Observer*, 1 November 1998, p. 31.
22 Philip Elliott, 'Intellectuals, the "Information Society" and the Disappearance of the Public Sphere', in Collins et al. (ed.), *Media, Culture and Society*, p. 113.
23 Bourdieu, 'The Production of Belief', p. 132.
24 Roland Barthes, 'Myth Today', in *Mythologies*, trans. and ed. Annette Lavers (New York, Hill and Wang, 1982), pp. 156–9.
25 Elliott, 'Intellectuals', p. 113.
26 Michael Ondaatje in 'The Books Interview', *The Observer*, 1 November 1998.
27 Ondaatje, 'The Books Interview'.
28 Here, I am applying the distinction between 'work' and 'text' developed in Roland Barthes, 'From Work to Text', in *Image, Music, Text*, ed. and trans. Stephen Heath (Glasgow, Fontana/Collins, 1977).
29 T. S. Eliot, 'Tradition and the Individual Talent', in *Selected Prose*, ed. J. Hayward (London, Faber and Faber, 1983).

2

'Where the garment gapes': faithfulness and promiscuity in the 1995 BBC *Pride and Prejudice*

Erica Sheen

Public service broadcasting has pursued a number of characteristically intellectual goals such as the preservation of the national culture by promoting broadcast versions of national classics and maintaining domestic production ... [P]ublic service is no longer viable. Broadcasting has exhausted non-advertising revenue as the licence fee becomes an increasingly unacceptable poll tax. Even without advertising revenue, public service broadcasting has had to compete with commercial systems and become less able to pursue different goals and preserve its own distinct identity.[1]

There is no way out of the game of culture.[2]

Until recently, one might have asserted categorically that the television classic serial reflected a continuing commitment to the essentially literary values associated with the concept of public service broadcasting. The critical standard that monitors the effectiveness of literary adaptation in articulating those values is that of fidelity; 'faithfulness to the text'. Writing in *Screen* in 1982, John Ellis was fully aware of the contradictions sustained by this idea; in particular, of the way those contradictions produce what might be described as the structural promiscuity of the adaptation process:

The adaptation trades upon the memory of the novel, a memory that can derive from actual reading, or, as is more likely with a classic of literature, a generally circulated cultural memory ... The faithfulness of the adaptation is the degree to which it can rework and replace a memory ... Adaptation into another medium becomes a means of prolonging the pleasure of the original representation, and repeating the production of a memory. The process

14

of adaptation should thus be seen as a massive investment (financial and psychic) in the desire to repeat particular acts of consumption within a form of representation that discourages such a repetition.[3]

Later in the same article Ellis criticised Morris Béja for an approach to literary adaptation that 'elides the institutional differences between the novelistic, the cinematic and the televisual',[4] but his own discussion is founded on generalised concepts of 'culture' and 'circulation' that are implicitly those of the public sphere.

Jürgen Habermas's notion of the public sphere has figured significantly in media theory since 1983, when Nicholas Garnham proposed public service broadcasting as its 'embodiment and guarantor'.[5] Reconsidering Garnham's article a decade later, Richard Collins pointed out that, since for Habermas the audio-visual media posed a threat to the public sphere, to use the idea for broadcasting at all was problematic:[6]

> In comparison with the printed communications ... the programs sent by the new media curtail the reactions of their recipients in a peculiar way. They draw the eyes and ears of the public under their spell but at the same time, by taking away its distance, place it under 'tutelage', which is to say, they deprive it of the opportunity to say something and to disagree.[7]

The problem about audio-visual media is 'the problem raised by all forms of mediated communication, namely, how are the material resources necessary for that communication made available and to whom?'[8] Leaving aside the (now clearly) questionable assumption that 'printed communications' are *un*mediated, the point here is that the values generated by these systems of production are *not* in 'general' circulation, but are contained by and directed towards the interests of specific institutions. Since the mid-1980s, when its claim to a licence fee began to be based on its ability to attract a mass audience, the BBC has become subject to the need to produce texts that create value not for 'culture', but for its own system of production. What happens to the notion of textual fidelity in such a situation?

Let me propose at the outset that the important thing about it is *not* the way it functions as a critical concept. Rather, it is the way it *performs* within particular events of reception. A response to an adaptation in terms of whether it is 'faithful' or not is not really an analytical or even evaluative assessment of it. It is an affirmation of the right of a certain kind of literary position to preside over the question. In other words, the concept of faithfulness has *signifiance* within the transmission of an adaptation, not just *significance* within the analysis of it as a text.[9] In this discussion I want to suggest that the measure of the change in the institutional function of the classic serial across the 1980s into the 1990s can be taken by monitoring the way this notion of fidelity continues to *perform* – and I shall want the idea of 'performance' to bring to mind the stock market and music as well as acting.

The BBC's wildly successful 1995 *Pride and Prejudice* provided an excellent opportunity to undertake such a monitoring process. In a highly critical review in the *Times Literary Supplement*, David Nokes used a variant term, 'loyalty': 'Loyal readers of the text', he asserted, 'will more readily forgive omissions than inventions'.[10] If Nokes is right, then writer P. D. James, interviewed in the BBC's *Pride and Prejudice: From Page to Screen*, is *not* a loyal reader: 'I'm only really upset by additional scenes if necessary scenes are cut out to make way for them', she said. The question of the relation between omissions and inventions, and their implications for the spectator of the classic serial, will be my main concern in the discussion that follows. Their contradictions were signalled by actor Alan Cummings, discussing the potential audience of Douglas McGrath's film adaptation of *Emma* with Barry Norman in May 1996. 'We're never going to please everyone ...' he said, '*Especially not those anal Jane Austen types*'. If, for the Lacanian, anal retentiveness is one of the means by which we can possess the Phallus, Signifier of Signifiers – or, rather, defer the recognition that we do *not* possess it – then what is at stake here is nothing less than the question of *ownership*. The 1980s had a very particular ideology of ownership, one that bears significantly on the episodic organisation of the serial text, as those of us for whom the concept of 'instalment' came to mean something more finally demanding than Jane Austen can testify. Accordingly I propose a notion of literary ownership that is regulated by the textual equivalent of something like a '*standard of living*'. This idea, I suggest, can help us towards a theory of adaptation for Thatcherism and beyond: adaptation as *relocation*, a negotiation by which a text goes upmarket, buys into more expensive institutional resources than those of the production system from which it derives. From this perspective, 'omissions and inventions' can be seen as positions of accumulation within a system of textual circulation which offers competitive opportunities for institutional investment. Thus the way scriptwriter Andrew Davies speculated about the fact that Mr Collins's presence in the Bennett household may very well imply that he could have come upon the girls on the upstairs landing with no clothes on, or the way the locations department ransacked the National Trust for the houses it used for Pemberley or Rosings, constitutes the institutional point of entry into the text wherein the material resources of one representational system can offer, as Darcy can offer Lizzy, to support a text in more than the style to which it has been accustomed. From this point of view, we can see the text's very *potential* for meaning as a structural infidelity – a kind of George Wickham, always on the look-out for a semiotic system with a higher disposable income – and the '*loyal* reader' as always an impoverished Miss Bates, sitting alone by the fire in the corner reading, as if for the first time, the same old book; can't afford to go to the opera or the cinema to see, and be seen at, the latest lavish new remake, but pretends fussily she wouldn't want to anyway.[11] This suggestion may seem a little less than serious; but in a significant way it is faithful to Jane Austen herself, who understood long before New Labour that a 'right' to work somehow always concedes historically to the *opportunity*.

All this is not to say that I am approaching my subject biographically. Seeing the literary text as 'always already' under the rubric of adaptation – on the look-out for it, so to speak – makes us realise that attempts to find points of identification within the text for an authorial position of enunciation are fundamentally misguided. Narrative theory may suggest otherwise, but a text is *not* a subject position. It is an *object*, in the full psychoanalytical sense of the word, and it creates value for its author by taking its place in a circulation system that is really just a distinctive cultural version of Freud's *fort–da* game, in which its job, like little Ernst's cotton reel, is to test what signifying systems are available for relocation, and find ways of moving from one to another.[12] From this point of view, we could approach a text's adaptability in terms of the work it does to maintain a *potential* for infidelity within the literary form to which its writer lays claim of ownership, marries into, as it were: the work it does to keep open the possibility of omissions and inventions, always going out for the night and coming back in, looking forward to independence but keeping its foot in the parental door, never quite making its mind up between the two. Which is exactly how Austen's concept of marriage performs within her novels. All her heroines marry, but none ever *really* leave home. What keeps this contradiction working productively *as* a contradiction – rather than blowing its symbolic capital all at once on unredeemable realism – is the fact that Austen doesn't open up the abyss of marital failure in the way the infinitely less adaptable Brontës do. In Austen, infidelity occurs only as a gap within, not a critique of, the social forms her novel presents as 'real'. With the possible exception of Mrs Smith's cloudy past in *Persuasion,* there are no broken marriages, no active wedded promiscuity. In fact, Austen works hard to keep this perspective closed. Mr Bennett, for instance, is actually said to have stopped loving Mrs Bennett, but is described as having refused the 'comforts' to which 'the unfortunate' resort on such occasions. (We imagine him taking just one glass of port too many, rather than ever having been tempted to avail himself of the services of a prostitute, or resorting to serious domestic violence.)[13] Austen's infidelities thus conceal the sheer retentiveness at the heart of her apparent refusal to provide what Colin McCabe has described as a 'hierarchy of discourse'.[14] It is this refusal that makes her work so productive of adaptive imaginings: her omissions and inventions are flirtatious because they elicit, even desire, *another* institutional frame of reference to identify them *as* omissions and inventions, and to provide them, expensively, with local habitations and a name.

Infidelity thus occurs in the switch to a system of representation that helps maintain a competing apparatus. John Ellis's statement, 'the faithfulness of the adaptation is the degree to which it can rework and replace a memory', acknowledges this very possibility. But this act of replacement, one might object, is the recognition that informs cinema rather than TV spectatorship, now sufficiently elaborated on its own institutional terms to allow priority to the imperatives governing a screenplay over those of a novel. Neither critics nor spectators are likely to require a *film* adaptation of a classic novel to be 'faithful'; indeed they will arguably look for, even anticipate, its submission to the consensual ideology of Hollywood. What facilitates the subjection of the TV adaptation to this notion of fidelity is what Paul Kerr has referred to as its 'transparent technology':

The very desire to adapt classic novels for British television stems at least partly from the degree to which television is still seen as a transparent medium and, in Britain, as a transparent technology whose function quite simply is to facilitate the 'transmission' of the writer's work. Indeed, perhaps one explanation for the relative lack of critical work on classic serials is that very assumption of transparency.[15]

As an institution, cinema is predicated on an identification with its apparatus, but broadcasting has effectively naturalised its apparatus within 'the home'. Now, I consider the first part of this last statement to hold true whether you subscribe to a psychoanalytic theory of spectatorship, or not. *Film* spectatorship may or may not be predicated on 'lack' as a psychic mechanism, but *cinema* spectatorship is concerned only with the *material* manifestations of identification with an apparatus. Quite simply, cinema must succeed in making you 'go out'; indeed, in making 'going out' to the cinema regularly more important than whether particular films succeed or fail in making you identify with them. As John Ellis has pointed out, people don't stop going to the cinema because they don't like individual films.[16]

The serial aspect of cinema spectatorship is thus entrusted to elements of its institutional form that differ from those of the TV serial, which are primarily invested into what is referred to as its 'intermittence'. In a discussion which draws on the conceptual configurations of *fort–da*, Philip Drummond has suggested that

> The tenure of the television series ... depends for its effect on its intermittence and its periodicity (weekly and seasonal). Compulsively repetitive, it thus plays a simple game of absence/presence, its invariant features (central characters, plot type, dramatic structure) guaranteeing the success of recognition and identification.[17]

In the 1980s, though, the distinction between TV and cinema spectatorship began to break down, and it did so largely within the domain of those shared areas of output that pertain to serial forms of continuity. Over the last ten years, TV has progressively appropriated those formal and technical resources of film that effectively make its apparatus available for identification in the classical Hollywood way – resources that make you want to be there in front of a screen at the moment a particular programme starts. This has largely been brought about by scheduling American programmes that use cinematic production values to revalorise the home as the space of spectatorship: *Miami Vice*, *LA Law*, *NYPD Blue*, *Twin*

Peaks, Star Trek, ER, Homicide, Murder One. One of the most interesting things about this trend is the way the series began to exhibit
the characteristics of the serial; not simply in what one might
describe as intrinsically hybrid forms like *NYPD Blue* and *ER*, but
in long-running series like *Star Trek* that began to generate modes
of continuity that owe less to televisual 'endless flow' than to the
narrative forms of film genre. At the same time, the reverse seems to
be true of Hollywood. Over the last fifteen years, its production
packages have demonstrated an increasing reliance on serial forms of
continuity, like the sequel, remakes of old TV series – and literary
adaptation.[18] In such an environment, the classic serial has begun to
display signs of the split personality that comes from this attempt to
map the fetishised apparatus on to a transparent technology. In its
handling of the relation between the series and the video, released
before the programme had finished its run, *Pride and Prejudice* drew
on the peculiarly intense effect of identification that resulted from
this. You might have expected the release of the video to produce a
slump in viewing figures. Quite the contrary. The video produced
a pressure within the desire to see the next episode that had an
extremely complex relation to that 'memory spectacle' of
absence/presence observed by Philip Drummond.[19] Supplies of the
video ran out almost as soon as they were in the shop, so you actually had to *watch* each episode because you couldn't get hold of the
thing (that Freudian *object* again) you needed to compensate for the
possibility that you might miss the next episode. Clearly, as a dialec-
tic of spectatorship, 'fidelity to the text' had achieved a quite
extraordinary *Aufhebung*: light years away from the stable literary
text anchored safely in an unmediated public sphere. The domestic
scenario *this* kind of fidelity precipitated was characterised by Mark
Lawson in a description of the scheduling wars that surrounded this
broadcasting event: 'conflict between public service and corporate
performance' which 'is going to lead to more and more cursing over
the channel changer for those at home on the sofa'. Lawson was
identifying very accurately what I described as 'the *material manifestations* of identification with an apparatus'. He went on, 'In addition
to internal imperatives [mass audience versus enough non-commer-
cial public service broadcasting] all four terrestrial channels now face
the pressure of competition from four rival visual forms: satellite and
cable broadcasters, and video shops.[20]

In the circumstances, the way this production rose to the challenge of creating an institutional economy that internalised these pressures into the space of television spectatorship and out of the space of cultural memory was nothing less than breathtaking. Raymond Williams criticised Colin MacCabe's analysis of classic realism as an 'extraordinary flattening' that 'succeeded in hiding the actual and effective [historical] process' (meaning that he thought MacCabe's theory did a disservice to the realist agenda of the nineteenth-century novel).[21] But on the evidence of this production of *Pride and Prejudice*, it could be argued that 'success in hiding the actual and effective process' is now the actual and effective process.

Williams's phrase, 'success in hiding', is very revealing. In this hybridised classic realism – as the Dionysian frenzy that pursued actor Colin Firth out of this production and beyond testifies – the functional intermittence of serial programming began to take on the implications of that mode of semiotic intermittence which Roland Barthes describes in *The Pleasure of the Text*:

> Is not the most erotic portion of the body *where the garment gapes?* In perversion (which is the realm of textual pleasure) there are no 'erogenous zones' (a foolish expression, besides); it is intermittence ... which is erotic: the intermittence of skin flashing between two articles of clothing (trousers and sweater), between two edges (the open-neck shirt, the glove and the sleeve); it is this flash itself which seduces, or rather: the staging of an appearance as disappearance.[22]

The notion of 'gaping' seductively combines the act of looking with the *absence* of a visual object. Thus, Barthes's notion of *tmesis* –

> We do not read everything with same intensity of reading; a rhythm is established, casual, unconcerned with the integrity of the text ... Tmesis, source or figure of pleasure ... confronts two prosaic edges with one another; it sets what is useful to a knowledge of the secret against what is useless to such a knowledge; tmesis is a seam or a flaw resulting from a simple principle of functionality; it does not occur at the level of the structure of languages but only at the moment of their consumption; the author cannot choose to write what will not be read.[23]

– is an appropriate term for the acts of exposure that upset some viewers of this production. As David Nokes said, 'loyal readers of the texts will more readily forgive omissions than inventions', and he was referring to what he saw as an unforgivable invention: the moment when Darcy dived into the pond on his way back to Pemberley from London. There had been two other moments of a similar kind: when Darcy got out of the bath at Netherfield and looked down out of the window at Elizabeth playing with a dog in the garden below, and when he splashed himself with water after spending the night writing to her after she has refused him. Nokes's own idea of adaptation is to find appropriate contemporary registers for a novel's moral force, and this kind of thing, apparently, just doesn't fit the bill. But Nokes misreads the kind of gap he thinks these moments occupy:

> In the book Mr. Darcy does not strip down to his frilly shirt, plunge into a green sun-dappled pool, to emerge spiritually reborn on the other side, like an Adonis from an after-shave advert.[24]

In commercial television, the gaps between programmes are indeed occupied by after-shave adverts; so one might say that Nokes was responding to the function of intermittence, at least on a structural level. But he misrecognised the kind of presence Darcy's body had within it as a visual object. The BBC, of course, doesn't have commercial breaks. Darcy did not suture us into those spaces *inside* a programme where the representational system of commercial broadcasting achieves symbolic form via the *fort–da* of advertising. Rather, he sutured us into the institutional space constituted by the *time between* instalments; the time that turns intermittence into the habit of spectatorship required by the series or the serial.[25] From this point of view it is significant to the question of textual fidelity that these episodes of exposure all occur at a point where there *isn't* any text; more specifically, they occupy positions where the *fort–da* of literary form allows us to stop attending, either for its characters' relief, or for our own (we tend not to follow characters to bed, or to the toilet, nor they us). They all happen at the turn-around of chapters, or where the text itself is somewhere else, attending to completely different character altogether.[26] The bath episode, for instance, is located exactly between chapters nine and ten; the letter-writing takes place between chapters thirty-four and thirty-five, since the chapter closes as Lizzy goes to bed after her rejection of Darcy, and the next chapter opens with her waking. In fact, the way we watch these interpolated moments, and the way they interpellate us,[27] reproduces the curious episode of reversed spectatorship that occurs before the portrait of Darcy at Pemberley, where Elizabeth 'fixed his eyes upon herself ... thought of his regard with a deeper sentiment of gratitude ... and softened its impropriety of expression'.[28] Note the forceful way Elizabeth takes Darcy's look, *and* its improprieties. Adequate grounds, I think, for suggesting that making Darcy take his clothes off and dive into the pond at *exactly the same moment* is faithful, passionately so, to the text's concealed pleasure in its own promiscuity.

So these are not omissions and inventions within the literary discourse; only enterprising productions within available adaptive gaps. In this capacity, Andrew Davies's sense of opportunity was easily matched by that of composer Carl Davis. Outdone, in fact: as we shall see, Carl Davis's work on this production was distinguished by a climax of aquatic impropriety that puts his colleague's pond scene in the shade.

Adaptation from page to screen turns a novel into a soundtrack. In that respect it hands the text over to the composer as much as to the scriptwriter. And it offers that composer temptations that have been at the heart of a theoretical dilemma since the earliest days of sound. The question of faithfulness to the text reproduces the concerns of those critics and filmmakers of the 1920s and 1930s, including Eisenstein, who saw synchronous sound as a limitation of film's artistic potential. What they resisted was the way a text changed when the meanings its music could carry began to be located *within* the film. What was at stake was the subordination of an 'authorial' position of enunciation outside the frame to voices inside it. Thinking about this from a contemporary perspective – something like, say, the Musicians' Union campaign in the 1970s and 1980s to 'Keep Music Live' – Eisenstein's resistance might seem to be part of a process that endows film accompaniment with the status of a relative artistic autonomy. But it was not seen this way at the time. Writing in 1932, Roman Jakobson records the extent to which such music did not count as an 'auditory object'. In support of his case he quotes Bela Balázs – 'we instantly notice the absence of music, but we pay no attention to its presence, so that any music whatsoever is appropriate for virtually any scene'; Paul Ramain – 'music in the cinema is destined not to be listened to'; and Frank Martin – 'its only aim is that one's ears be occupied while complete attention is concentrated on seeing'.[29] From such a historical position, the relocation of music from outside the frame to inside would count as *adaptation* on precisely the terms I have been setting up.

One might say that Carl Davis's working practices are founded on such a strategy of relocation. In an interview on BBC Radio 3, broadcast shortly after *Pride and Prejudice*, he drew attention to the way composers like Bach and Mozart, like him, had to 'work fast', and specifies 'adapting' as one of the activities on 'the practical side of getting things to work.' The music he writes really *is* an object: he describes it as 'on the same level as props, wigs and dialogue'. The *fort–da* aspect of this is significant here: according to him, this means 'you can't have an ego'. His score for this production could be said to enunciate from the space of that disavowal: the relocation of the musician from outside to inside the text is his most consistent adaptive move in this score. In particular, he realises this position of enunciation in Lizzy herself; and it is interesting that no one has seen this as either an omission or an invention, even though it is the biggest infidelity of all. Lizzy, who is said to play 'a little', has turned into a good(ish) piano player; more significantly, she *thinks* and *acts* musically – witness her impromptu recitative with Darcy at Rosings. From this point of view, to put this score 'on the same level as props, wigs and dialogue' is a little disingenuous. Several of the most important episodes are reconceived within entirely musical frames of reference: the invitation to supper at Pemberley with Mr and Mrs Gardiner, for instance, when Lizzy plays and sings a transcription of Mozart's 'Voi che sapete', Cherubino's aria from *The Marriage of Figaro* Act II scene 4 (there is no music at all in the novel at this point).[30] After she has finished her performance, she turns pages for Georgiana – and here for the first time her eyes meet Darcy's. This realisation of the shared glance – the conventional operatic and filmic image of mutual recognition – as the raising of a page-turner's eyes from the page across the instrument towards a listener is a brilliant transformation of literary anagnorisis into a climax of the adaptive transaction. We have already seen that Lizzy herself figures the very distinctive mode of spectatorship this production elicited. Her ability to read across a linguistic text to a musical one, and to facilitate its transmission from performer to audience, articulates expressively her function as the textual source of that attention, not merely its object.

I describe such a reconceptualisation as 'the biggest infidelity of all' because Jane Austen herself doesn't actually seem to like musical performers. Certainly, she doesn't allow them any real agency within the development of her plots. All the characters that play well are gullible (Marianne in *Sense and Sensibility*), stupid (Mary in *Pride and Prejudice*) or deceptive (Jane Fairfax in *Emma*).[31] It's easy to see why she should choose to represent them this way. Musical discourse is both too obvious, and too transparent. On the one hand, the musician cannot equivocate about being the position of enunciation; on the other, music is not a language system that signifies. Another (*Austinian*) way of putting this would be to say that a musician can't play an instrument as if he or she doesn't mean it, but doesn't actually mean anything by playing;[32] whereas the language-user, particularly the *Austenian* language-user, habitually means by not meaning. It is this latter that constitutes the basis of what I have described as Austen's 'apparent refusal to provide a hierarchy of discourse'. What I am saying here is not intended as a negative criticism of Carl Davis's work. Quite the opposite: on the terms of my own analysis, his work is exemplary. If Austen works very hard to keep the textual gap of infidelity closed, Davis invests an enormous amount of credit into it. This is apparent within the subtexts that jostle around beneath the performance of 'Voi che sapete'. *The Marriage of Figaro* is an opera completely preoccupied with the rendering visible of concealed infidelities. The young page Cherubino is in love with Countess Almaviva, but has been dismissed by her husband the Count for flirting with the gardener's daughter. He comes to Susanna's apartment to ask her to help him, but hides behind a chair when Almaviva enters and himself begins to court Susanna. He too hides (behind the same chair) when music master Don Basilio comes in and announces Cherubino's infatuation with the Countess. Almaviva reveals himself, discovers Cherubino, threatens to expose him – but then realises that in doing so he will only expose himself. At Susanna's encouragement, he pardons the page, but only on condition that he sets off immediately for military service in the count's regiment.

Clearly, this aria, and indeed Mozart's opera as a whole, is replete with resonances for Austen's story. Immediately after she finishes singing it, Lizzy concedes the pianist's stool to Darcy's sister, but soon has to run to her aid when Caroline Bingley makes her indiscreet jibe about Georgiana's seducer, George Wickham, whom Darcy helped to establish in the militia after he had squandered a generous inheritance from Darcy's own father. The frames of reference for this little incident are thus entirely anticipated by Lizzy's song. It also anticipates what Lizzy finds out only the very next day, and that is that her *own* sister Lydia has become Wickham's next victim.

These complexly intertextual moments of narrative recognition impose an equally complex historical perspective on the process of adaptation itself, and I finish by drawing attention to what was probably the most ambitious of such moments in the whole series. It is one that seems to strive to relocate *our* recognition of the process of adaptation as one with a primarily musical rather than literary position of enunciation. And in doing so, it fails, because, like Wickham, it aims too high, and thus draws our attention to the absence of those 'more expensive institutional resources' that this adaptation had hitherto pretended so brilliantly to be able to supply. The moment I am thinking of is that elusive little episode, after Lydia's elopement, when Lizzy confides to her sister Jane how badly she feels about Darcy in the aftermath of the Lydia incident.[33] *She* does not yet know that this means she loves him; but if *we* were in any doubt, Carl Davis's score resolves us, because the motif he uses to cut from Lizzy sitting on her bed to a close-up of Darcy returning her glance brings together material from Wagner's *Der Ring des Nibelungen* and *Tristan und Isolde*:[34] from the former, the motifs that Robert Donington has described as 'relinquishment' and 'destiny as the power to which all men must in the end surrender', from the latter, the 'Liebestod' motif, itself the musical realisation of a supercharged romantic glance.[35] Obviously such operatic grandeur is an extremely ambitious thing to attempt; and in the light of the preceding analysis I would dearly like to be able to suggest – with an ambition that may similarly fail – that it invests the adaptation with a dynamic that is nothing less than an *Aufhebung*: an *Aufhebung* of the Adaptive Idea. If Austen's text encourages us to read its closures retentively, then the channel Davis opens up through Mozart to late Wagner situates the production within what might truly be described as the 'grand narrative' of adaptation: the history of the *Gesamtkunstwerk*.

But it *does* fail. And it failed largely because it was *too* ambitious about the kind of resources it could draw into itself. Davis cut the rhythm of the chord sequence into the rhythm of the visual cuts. The rising figure matches the sequence marked out by Lizzy's glance switching to the right, and the cut to Darcy returning her look to the left. Thus the movement within the Wagnerian motif is matched minutely to the spatial articulations of a sequence of point-of-view shots.[36] This foregrounds the syntagmatic structure of the sequence in a way that television conventionally does not. Of course, television *does* use the shot-reverse-shot technique to present dialogue, and it is not even unknown for some kinds of programme-making to use this technique to attempt something like an effect of suture.[37] But here the effect was of just *too* much meaning: too much for Austen; too much for television; too much for us. Coming as it did just before the end of episode five, it climaxed too much and too soon, threatening an immersion, like that at the end of *Der Ring,* that is nothing less than unrepeatable. What saved the day was the fact that, coming as it did at the end of an episode, you could simply go away and take a cold shower.

The final word goes to the BBC itself, which obviously knew how crucially this production articulated the contradictory relationship between cinematic production values and public service broadcasting. Three years on, in the summer of 1998, the BBC released a corporate trail in which the moment where Darcy stands before Lizzy in his wet shirt in the gardens of Pemberley was transformed into publicity for licence fee payment methods. With the help of morphing techniques, Darcy explains to Lizzy that he has come back that crucial day early in order to set up a direct debit to pay his licence fee. Lizzy looks discomfited, and replies, 'we pay by stamps ... my mother you know'. Darcy is mortified, and walks on. In its acute insight into a cultural difference that would surely be fatal to any prospect of union between such devastatingly incompatible families, this constituted an extraordinarily precise perception as to what this adaptation was really all about. If in 1813, Darcy's attraction to his social inferiors lay in his income of £10,000 a year, in the 1990s his value to the classic serial was far greater than that. It was his capacity to offer it the kind of future that is the distinctive achievement of an instalment-plan economy.

NOTES

1 Philip Elliot, 'Intellectuals, the "Information Society" and the Disappearance of the Public sphere', in Richard Collins et al. (eds), *Media Culture and Society: A Critical Reader* (London, Sage Publications, 1986), pp. 112–13.
2 Pierre Bourdieu, *Distinction,* trans. Richard Nice (London, RKP, 1984), p. 11.
3 John Ellis, 'The Literary Adaptation – An Introduction', *Screen*, 23: 1 (1982), p. 4.

4 Ellis, 'The Literary Adaptation', p. 5.

5 Nicholas Garnham, 'Public Service versus the Market', *Screen* 5: 1 (1983).

6 Richard Collins, 'Public Service versus the Market Ten Years On: Reflections of Critical Theory and the Debate on Broadcasting Policy in the UK' in *Screen*, 34: 3 (1993), p. 248.

7 Jürgen Habermas, *The Structural Transformation of the Public Sphere* (Cambridge, Polity), pp. 170–1, quoted in Collins, 'Public Service', p. 248.

8 N. Garnham, 'The Media and the Public Sphere', in C. Calhoun (ed.), *Habermas and the Public Sphere* (Cambridge, MA, MIT Press, 1992), p. 120, quoted in Collins, 'Public Service', p. 249.

9 For the distinction between *signifiance* and *signification*, see Roland Barthes, 'Theory of the Text', in Robert Young (ed.), *Untying the Text: A Poststructuralist Reader* (London, Routledge and Kegan Paul, 1981), pp. 37–9: 'Signification appears as embalmed in the work-as-product. But once the text is conceived as production (and no longer as product), signification is no longer an adequate concept ... It becomes necessary to distinguish carefully between signification, which belongs to the level of the product ... and the signifying work, which belongs to the level of production, enunciation, symbolisation: it is this work that we call the "signifiance".'

10 *Times Literary Supplement,* 26 April 1996.

11 Miss Bates is a character in Austen's *Emma.*

12 The point about the *fort–da* game is that it sets up a temporary but functional equivalence between subject and object that facilitates the process of language acquisition. My suggestion here is that activities like novel-writing should be approached as continuing, higher-level negotiations of that process rather than expressions of the result of its conclusion. For the *fort–da* see Sigmund Freud, 'Beyond the Pleasure Principle', in *On Metapsychology: The Theory of Psychoanalysis* (1920), pp. 269–338 (vol. 18 of the *Standard Edition* trans. and ed. James Strachey).

13 Mr Bennett's marital situation is described at the beginning of chapter 42, in alarmingly unequivocal terms. He is described as having married a woman 'whose weak understanding and illiberal mind had very early in their marriage put an end to all real affection for her. Respect, esteem and confidence had vanished for ever ... But Mr. Bennett was not of a disposition to seek comfort ... in any of those pleasures which too often console the unfortunate for their folly or vice' (Jane Austen, *Pride and Prejudice* [London, Dent, 1963], p. 205; all quotations are taken from this edition).

14 Colin MacCabe, 'Realism and the Cinema: Notes on Some Brechtian Theses', *Screen* 15: 2 (1974), pp. 7–27.

15 Paul Kerr, 'Classic Serials – To Be Continued', *Screen* 23: 1 (1982), p. 12.

16 'People are disappointed with this or that film, but rarely with the cinema as a whole' (John Ellis, 'The Institution of Cinema', *Edinburgh '76 Magazine* [Edinburgh Film Festival, 1976], p. 60).

17 Phillip Drummond, 'Structural and Narrative Constraints in *The Sweeney*', *Screen Education*, 20 (1976), p. 16. Also quoted in Kerr, 'Classic Serials', p. 8.

18 In the cinema, literary adaptation is implicitly serial, in that it refers to and helps maintain an ongoing 'discourse of literature'. See also the Introduction to the present volume.

19 This was an extremely interesting phenomenon, one that merits more of a discussion than I can give it here. The decision to release the video in this way mimicked the 'literary' values associated with the classic serial: it was as if the producers were prepared to gamble that the relation of the video to the serial would be complementary – as in the relation between a book and a film – rather than competitive, which is the assumption that underlies most video releases. One might compare this with the way producers like Stephen Spielberg will delay the release of videos past the standard six month 'window of release' if there is a good enough marketing reason to do so. See my 'How Hollywood Takes the Waiting out of Wanting', in S. Vice, T. Armstrong and M. Campbell (eds), *Beyond the Pleasure Dome: Writing and Addiction from the Romantics* (Sheffield, Sheffield Academic Press, 1994), pp. 159–68.

20 Mark Lawson, *The Guardian*, 15 November 1995.

21 Raymond Williams, 'Forms of English Fiction', in *1848: Proceedings of the Essex conference on the Sociology of Literature* (1978), p. 278.

22 Roland Barthes, *The Pleasure of the Text*, trans. Richard Miller (London, Jonathan Cape, 1976), pp. 9–10.

23 Barthes, *The Pleasure of the Text*, pp. 10–11, Barthes's emphases.

24 *TLS*, 26 April, 1996.

25 'Habit' is of course 'garment' as well as 'pattern of behaviour'.

26 It is of some relevance to my comments here that the 'trailers' that now signal the beginning and end of commercial breaks during the transmission of sponsored film screenings are themselves a hybridisation of the advertising *fort–da* and the literary *fort–da*. Although they are themselves adverts, they figure themselves as *diversionary* within the structure of attention, *not* as times when we are riveted to the screen. The little dramas they present show people *going away* to fetch ice cream, or beer, or to mess around with the pizza delivery man on the sofa, and then *coming back* when the commercials finish.

27 I am using 'interpellate' in the sense associated with Louis Althusser, in 'Ideology and Ideological State Apparatuses', *Essays on Ideology* (London, Verso, 1984).

28 Austen, *Pride and Prejudice*, p. 215.

29 Roman Jakobson, 'Is the film in Decline?', in Stephen Rudy (ed.), *Selected Writings*, vol. 3 (The Hague, Mouton, 1981), pp. 735–6.

30 Transcriptions are, of course, adaptations. Carl Davis's choice of this song was extremely acute. *The Marriage of Figaro* was written and first produced in 1786, with a first London performance, in Italian, in 1812. According to the British Library Catalogue of Printed Books, the first piano and voice transcription of 'Voi che sapete' available in London came out in 1810. Jane Austen started writing her novel in 1797 and finished it in 1813. So it's a very up-to-date piece of music both for Lizzy to know, and for Darcy to have in the house. For us as *their* audience, it's the conjunction of the two – Lizzy knowing it, Darcy owning it – that makes it meaningful.

31 Implicit within Austen's analysis are two related distinctions between amateur and professional, female and male. Since she only ever shows us amateur women, generalisations about how she is aligning these values would be risky.

32 My reference here is to J. L. Austin's contrast between abstract or 'constative' meaning and the 'performative', or speech act, by which one means something by or in saying it (such as promising, threatening, warning, etc.). See *How to Do Things with Words* (Oxford, Oxford University Press, 1976).

33 This episode is not in the novel, at least not as a conversation with Jane. Its material is drawn from a third-person account of Lizzy's thoughts about the situation in chapter 50.

34 A *very* watery opera.

35 These motifs are in any case closely related to each other; so Davis is not only adapting the music, but the terms on which they were available to their own composer for adaption. For the quotations from from *Der Ring,* see Robert Donington, *Wagner's Ring and its Symbols: The Music and the Myth* (London, Faber and Faber, 1963), p. 303.

36 For a full analysis of the POV shot see Edward Branigan, *Point of View in the Cinema: A Theory of Narration and Subjectivity in Classical Film* (New York and Berlin, Mouton, 1984).

37 See for instance John Caughie on 'Rhetoric, Pleasure and "Art Television": "Dreams of Leaving"', *Screen*, 22: 4 (1981), p. 26.

3

Pickwick Papers: beyond that place and time

Robert Giddings

In 'The Pickwick Papers' Dickens sprang suddenly from a comparatively low level to a very high one. To the level of 'Sketches by
Boz' he never afterwards descended. To the level of 'The Pickwick
Papers' it is doubtful if he ever afterwards rose. 'Pickwick' indeed,
is not a good novel; but it is not a bad novel, for it is not a novel
at all ... it is something nobler than a novel, for no novel with a
plot and a proper termination could emit that sense of everlasting
youth – a sense as of the gods gone wandering in England.

G. K. Chesterton[1]

Chesterton certainly puts his finger on it in this famous passage.
Pickwick Papers is unique among Dickens's works. He never wrote
anything like this again. We may forever attempt to locate and identify its particular qualities, but we all recognise its extraordinariness.
Noel Langley's *Pickwick Papers* was released in 1952. It is also a fact
that this film, though not a masterpiece, certainly occupies a significant position in that bunch of British-made black and white
Dickens films – David Lean's *Great Expectations* (1946) and *Oliver
Twist* (1948), Cavalcanti's *Nicholas Nickleby* (1947), Brian Desmond
Hurst's *Scrooge* (1951) and Ralph Thomas's *A Tale of Two Cities*
(1958) – which seem to justify the oft-made claim that Dickens films
well.

It is indeed a fallacy, universally acknowledged, that Dickens
and moving pictures were made for each other.[2] David Paroissien
believes the hypothesis demonstrated by the fact that there are so
many films based on Dickens's fiction. As if to reinforce his case, he
talks about the novels in the metalanguage of film studies.[3]

31

Arithmetic is not frequently called in aid of aesthetics,[4] but he clearly feels the strength of his hand lies in the fact that more than eighty film versions of the novels and stories have been made. Jeffrey Richards is ready to accept this traditional assumption about Dickens and film, influenced, possibly, by the fact that he became a reader of Dickens only after having seen the novels serialised on television.[5] Filmmakers pose themselves a huge task bringing Dickens to the screen, but with *Pickwick* the undertaking is immeasurable. Noel Langley's *The Pickwick Papers* may not be altogether successful; it has qualities which make it an important Dickens film, with a significant place in our cultural history. Inevitably film versions of classic novels have much to tell us about the historic moment of their making. David Lean's impressive *Great Expectations* (1946), with its emphasis on leaving a world of squalor and thwarted opportunity, carries the marks of the post-war settlement and the promise of better things to come – one thinks of the scene at the end of the film (not in the book) of Pip tearing down the curtains at Miss Havisham's and letting in the blazing sunshine.[6] As Britain's dismal economic performance and James Callaghan's 'great Debate' about the need for a more pronounced vocational emphasis in British education became the stuff of headlines, Granada's *Hard Times* (1977) seemed much in tune with the times. As Raphael Samuel so vigorously argued, Christine Edzard's *Little Dorrit* (1987) spoke so eloquently of Heritage Culture in post-Thatcherite Britain.[7]

Although I am unable to accept the all-embracing assertion as to Dickens's filmability[8] I think it is well worth considering each attempt on its own merits.[9] Each time a Dickens novel is filmed, it poses its own challenges and opportunities, and must be considered as a separate case. And *Pickwick Papers* is a particularly interesting example.

On the face of it, dramatising a novel for the screen is a simple matter. All that is required is the translation of what the novelist imagined and wrote in words, into moving pictures and sound. Few would expect exact translation – the precise and literal rendering of the original narrative prose. The art lies in finding the appropriate equivalent, the right style or tone, into which to recast the original. A translation does not replace the original. Discussing this problem with reference to translations of Horace, D. S. Carne-Ross makes the useful point that translation is never a substitute for the original but rather a parallel text that brings to the fore new aspects while playing down others: 'Judging how far a translator's enlargements, his liberties with and additions to his author's poem, are a wanton intrusion of his own substance, and how far (in Dryden's words) they are "secretly in the poet, or may be fairly deduced from him" is a delicate business best decided case by case.'[10]

Few novelists better illustrate this problem than Dickens. Dickens is unmistakable. Dickens's words, syntax, idiosyncrasy of dialogue, picturesque and masterly descriptions of scenes, recreations of moments in life, haunting observations of experience – these qualities are characteristic. Yet, it is equally true that each of his major works is uniquely itself. *Dombey and Son* is unlike *Martin Chuzzlewit*. *Bleak House* is not mistakably like *David Copperfield*. Yet each is characteristic of Dickens.

There is a general claim to be made about the essentially literary nature of Dickens's art, and there is a special case which I believe is particularly relevant in the case of *Pickwick Papers*. This novel was such a bombshell in publishing history that, in terms of proportion and impact, any film version of *Pickwick Papers* must be judged insofar as it measures up to the proportions and power of the novel. An adaptation must give weight to the proportion and scale of its original. We would no more accept media processing of *Pride and Prejudice* which reduces its fibre and sinew to the sentimental flim-flam of J. M. Barrie's *Quality Street*, than we should swallow a version of *Pickwick* which somehow muffles and reduces its breadth and dynamism.

The novel's beginnings are straightforward. Dickens was twenty-three and was working as a parliamentary reporter. He had achieved some literary popularity by publishing short pieces of fiction which had appeared in the *Monthly Magazine*, *Morning Chronicle* and *Bell's Life in London*. They were subsequently published in volume form by Macrone as *The Sketches by 'Boz'*. The newly formed publishing firm of Chapman and Hall was seeking to commission an illustrated novel they intended to publish in monthly serial parts. They had followed Dickens's growing success with interest. These enterprising publishers were impressed by the popular success of the hearty, rip-roaring adventures of the sporting grocer, John Jorrocks, the creation of Robert Surtees, editor of *New Sporting Magazine*, in whose pages these stories regularly appeared. (They were published in book form as *Jorrock's Jaunts and Jollities* in

1838.) Frankly, they intended to cash in on the apparent craze for comic sporting stories. Their initial plan was for the adventures and proceedings of the Nimrod Club, a group of travelling Cockney sportsmen. John Seymour, a leading comic artist of the day, was already contracted to illustrate the episodes. (In the event, he only provided illustrations for the first number, as he committed suicide between the first and second numbers. His place was taken by Hablot Brown, 'Phiz' who was to be Dickens's subsequent illustrator until *A Tale of Two Cities*.)[11] The publishers were keen. Serial publication was booming, and they considered the moment propitious for such a publication.[12] There was no written contract, but a verbal agreement that Chapman and Hall were to pay Dickens fifteen guineas for each number. He required the first two payments immediately – he needed the money to get married. It was agreed that payments would increase if the work sold, and all in all he was paid £2,500.

The serialisation of *Pickwick Papers*, over eighteen months from March 1836, was a triumph previously unknown in literature, with sales of 40,000 an issue at its height. Serialisation, with advertisements in the parts, was rapidly to become standard. *Pickwick Papers* showed what could be done. Advertising as an element of the mass media was well on the way.[13] Chapman and Hall decided to publish the book cloth-bound in volume form after its serial run in 1837. As Graham Smith writes, this conferred the status of literature on *Pickwick Papers* 'as distinct from the transience of miscellaneous periodical journalism'.[14] This was a landmark in the history of attractive, quality book publishing. As Dickens himself ironically commented 'My friends told me it was a low, cheap form of publication, by which I should ruin all my rising hopes, and how right my friends turned out to be, everybody knows.'[15] *Pickwick* struck a deep chord in readers, a chord which resounded in the country's popular culture, and which might well have been recaptured in some equivalent form in a film made in 1952.

Chapman and Hall made him an offer on 10 February 1836. Dickens began writing it on 18 February. The work was planned by Chapman and Hall to be issued in monthly parts (with advertising) over eighteen months and then to appear in volume form.[16] The first number was on sale by 31 March 1836 – with a printing of 1,000 copies. The initial impression of Part 2 was reduced to 500 on a sale or return basis with provincial booksellers. Sales began to rise after Sam Weller appeared. By Part 12 sales reached 14,000. (By this time he was also publishing *Oliver Twist* in *Bentley's Miscellany* each month.) Part 14 reached 20,000. Part 17 reached 26,000. Part 18 reached 29,000. By the end of the run sales reached 40,000.[17] Such phenomenal success was previously unknown in literature.[18] Its international reception was equally impressive – by 1838 it was published in Philadelphia, New York, Paris, Leipzig, Calcutta, Australia. Its domestic sales continued steadily year by year – 1847 first Cheap Edition sold 31,000 in the first year; by 1863 140,000 copies had been sold. And by 1878 1,600,000 had been sold in the UK and USA.[19] Between 1872 and 1892 Chapman and Hall printed eleven separate editions and sold 521,750 copies.[20]

Dickens himself was fully aware that in *Pickwick* he had somehow created a unique and unrepeatable success, and confessed as much to his publishers: 'If I were to live a hundred years and write three novels in each,' he told Chapman and Hall, 'I should never be so proud of any of them as I am of "Pickwick", feeling as I do, that it has made its own way, and hoping, as I must own I do hope, that long after my hand is as withered as the pens it held, "Pickwick" will be found on many a dusty shelf with many a better work.'[21]

Further than this it seemed to speak to the 'heart of the nation' and went vigorously on throughout the succeeding years of the century. It enjoyed an alternative life on the stage, which began even before its publication was complete and lasted well into the twentieth century.[22] *Pickwick Papers* meant more than the sum of its serial parts.

The novel appeared at a portentous moment in our history, when it was felt that particularly fundamental changes were afoot. The country was living through the aftermath of the agitation for the great Reform Bill and its enactment by Parliament, which seemed to presage all manner of possible changes in society. It is a fact that Dickens was writing *Pickwick* at the same time as he was engaged in *Oliver Twist*. This gives an interesting double take on nostalgia for Old England and anxiety about modern times.

The country was at a turning point in its history, changing from a mainly agricultural economy to a commercial and industrial economy. The passing of the Reform Bill seemed to mark a signif-icant moment of change. The country had so long been governed by its landed interests that the changes demanded in reform agitation

– universal suffrage, the secret ballot, annual parliaments – seemed nothing short of revolutionary. The Reform Act was significant not so much for what it achieved (which now seems modest enough) but for what it implied – that change was possible. The sluice gates had been opened. What might now be released?[23] These issues are implicit in the Condition of England Question (which becomes a major theme in the nineteenth-century English novel and notably informs George Eliot's *Middlemarch*). Ambitions for reform had been building in the country for several generations. John Morley characterises these years in his biography of Richard Cobden. The Bill may not have delivered as much reform as had been hoped, but the spirit of reform was now released: 'A great wave of humanity, of benevolence, of desire for improvement – a great wave of social sentiment in short – poured itself among all who had the faculty of large and disinterested thinking. The political spirit was abroad in its most comprehensive form'.[24]

The London Working Men's Association, from which Chartism originated, was founded in the same year that *Pickwick Papers* began its serialisation. Although we tend to associate the aims of this mass movement mainly with parliamentary reform, it should be remembered that ultimately the Chartists' aims were economic, to ensure the happiness of humanity. These social aims were declared in G. J. Harnay's *London Democrat:* 'that all shall have a good house to live in with a garden back or front, just as the occupier likes; good clothing to keep him warm and make him look respectable, and plenty of good food and drink to make him look and feel happy'.[25] This is almost a Dickensian prescription.

To associate Dickens with these ideas is by no means fanciful historicism. As a parliamentary reporter he witnessed this spirit in the making, and following election campaigns he travelled over England, where he heard the reforming speeches of – among others – Lord John Russell.[26] In all his writing Dickens was pulled back by the strength of his patriotic affection for the old rural order and forward by the intense excitement of the modern city and its multitudinous busyness. In much of *Pickwick* Dickens looks back to the Old England from which reform Britain was emerging, and in *Oliver Twist* he was to anticipate a much harsher dog-eat-dog society. The intention to portray the English countryside, coaches, inns, waterways, country fairs, etc. was made clear in the advertisement which appeared in *The Athenaeum*, 26 March 1836, which promised an account of journeys 'to Birmingham in the depth of winter' which would show the beauties of nature and penetrate 'to the very borders of Wales in the height of summer'.

This tone was certainly recognised by contemporaries. Writing in *The Graphic* a few weeks after Dickens's death, Arthur Locker, editor of *The Graphic* commented:

> 'Pickwick' must be to the young almost an antiquarian book, containing descriptions of bygone manners and customs ... Young people know nothing about the Fleet Prison; they never saw ... a genuine stage coachman; they do not associate a commercial traveller with a gig, but rather regard him as a gentleman who passes his days and nights in railway trains ... But to us oldsters 'Pickwick' ... recalls the England and the London of our youth ... As for Mr Weller the elder, I have sat by his side many a time a-top of the old Rocket or Regulator coach bound for Portsmouth ... All that jolly, old fashioned simple sort of life ... has gone by for ever. We have Crystal Palaces and Volunteering, and Athletic Sports, and mammoth hotels, and all kinds of improvements, but somehow England is not such a nice place as it seemed in the thirties ...[27]

It could be said Dickens was writing in the tradition of the *De Coverley Papers*, Oliver Goldsmith,[28] Laurence Sterne,[29] of Washington Irving, even possibly of Jean-Paul Richter.[30] This spirit is particularly strong in the Dingley Dell idyll of the perfect Christmas, which foreshadows so much of the Dickens Christmas mythology. This should not be seen simply as so much Victorian Christmas writing, but recognised for what it is – echoing the eighteenth-century De Coverley ideal and what it represented. And behind the sentimental writing the strongly held belief that such generosity and goodwill to all men were not exclusively the result of Christian conditioning, but were the natural inclination of humanity uncorrupted by the teachings of the modern world's mammonism and vanity. This points not only to Scrooge (who has to be tortured by ghosts and memories before he reverts to human goodness), but also to the simple virtues of the circus clowns in *Hard Times* who have as part of their very nature that good humanity which it takes Mr Gradgrind so much hard experience to learn. This human kindness Samuel Pickwick displays when he sees fellow sufferers in the Fleet. This is the goodness revealed in those Dickens characters labelled idiots by rest of the world – Mr Dick, Newman Noggs, Joe Gargery.[31] This nostalgia is an essential ingredient of

Dickensianism (*Barnaby Rudge*, *The Old Curiosity Shop*, *A Christmas Carol* are full of it). On the other hand, in *Oliver Twist*, which Dickens was concurrently writing, he foreshadows the thrusting, materialistic, tenebrous modern city life which he was later to satirise in the tortured symbolism of Chancery, Circumlocution, Coketown and Dustheaps. We need only contrast Dingley Dell and Bath, with the squalor of Fagin's lair and the evils of London.

It seems that the post-war British cinema's undeniable interest in filming Dickens – *Great Expectations*, 1946 (David Lean); *Nicholas Nickleby*, 1947 (Alberto Cavalcanti); *Oliver Twist*, 1948 (David Lean); *Scrooge*, 1951 (Brian Desmond Hurst); *Pickwick Papers*, 1952 (Noel Langley) and *A Tale of Two Cities*, 1958 (Ralph Thomas) – forms the not wholly stable foundations of that received opinion as to Dickens's suitability for moving pictures. It is, however, precisely because *Pickwick Papers* as a novel is such an electrifyingly pyrotechnic display, and made such an impact when it appeared in 1836–37, that the 1952 film seems such a damp squib.

Noel Langley was a South African screenwriter and director with Hollywood experience, notably on MGM's *The Wizard of Oz* (1939), who wrote the screenplay for Gordon Parry's *Tom Brown's Schooldays*[32] and Brian Desmond Hurst's version of *A Christmas Carol* released the year before *Pickwick Papers*.[33] In praising David Lean's *Oliver Twist* Dilys Powell wrote that the film had been careful in its preservation of the book's skeleton 'since skeleton is all a film has time for'.[34] In Noel Langley's *Pickwick* the bone and muscle has yielded place to flab and cosmetics. *Pickwick* impresses in its stills, but fails to convince on screen. It is clearly naive to expect fiction such as *Pickwick* to translate directly on to screen, but there must be an anatomical resemblance. We cannot expect the sheer size of the original, but we have the right to expect to recognise that same relationship as between the skeleton of a mouse and that of an elephant – we must see the bone structure.

Anyone who has really absorbed that transcending, outward-going, visionary sense which animates Dickens's *Pickwick Papers* would be struck by the curiously stuffy, fussy and confining experience of Noel Langley's film. This is very much studio-bound, with a minimum of exterior, location work. But it is not only that. There is an overriding 'realism' of quaint detail and of self-conscious mannerism which resembles not so much a great classic brought to life, as a pageant by a flourishing branch of some historical or literary re-enactment society.

The film has severely filleted the bones. *Pickwick Papers* is a novel about travelling across the countryside. Noel Langley's film feels confined indoors. Dickens takes us on the open road by coach and horses in jolly company. Samuel Pickwick is a plump, naive, retired businessman. His companions in the Pickwick Club are Nathaniel Winkle, a sportsman who is less skilled than he thinks; Augustus Snodgrass, a fashionably pretentious Byronic poet and Tracy Tupman, a rotund middle-aged amorist. The sound of snorting horses, clattering hooves on cobbles, resounding post horns, the bustle and comforts of warm inn parlours with plentiful food and drink and fireside company – this is the atmosphere which emerges from its pages as the Club goes about its declared intention of observing cultural and scientific matters.

It is a novel about travelling about England in the dim but unforgotten past when life was simpler and humanity more innocent. For all its contribution to that mythical vision of Old England, with its root going way back through *Tom Jones*, *Joseph Andrews*, Smollett, that tradition was long in the making, and the novel draws much of its strength from that tradition. The Pickwickians did in fact travel across considerable areas of recognisable England. The narrative is closely associated with the various visited locations.

Their first tour takes them from London to Rochester (adventures with Jingle and Winkle's duel) and then on to the military field day at Chatham which in turn leads to the idyllic rural Manor House at Dingley Dell.[35] Tupman falls in love with Wardle's spinster sister, Rachael, and Winkle falls in love with Arabella Allen. The famous shooting party takes place. Pickwick hires Sam Weller. The incident takes place with Mrs Bardell, which forms the basis of the breach of promise case brought against Pickwick.[36] A second tour takes them to observe the election at Eatanswill.[37] They attend a party organised by the poetess and seeker of the famous, Mrs Leo Hunter. The third tour takes them to Ipswich, where Pickwick again foils Jingle's amorous intrigues. There is an idyllic Christmas with the Wardles at Dingley Dell and then the notorious trial sequence.

Before going to the Fleet prison, the fourth tour is to the West Country where they visit Bath,[38] Bristol and Clifton which include several fine set pieces. Pickwick then goes to prison. Sam Weller contrives to accompany him. When Pickwick leaves the Fleet he journeys to the Midlands to reconcile Winkle with his father, who opposed his son's marriage to Arabella. This fifth tour has the travellers returning to Bob Sawyer at Bristol and thence to Gloucester, Tewkesbury, Worcester, Droitwich, Bromsgrove, Birmingham, Coventry, Dunchurch, Daventry, Towcester and finally back to London.

The *Daily Mirror* declared the film was 'As welcome as the sun in the morning and as British as cup of tea'.[39] C. A. Lejeune in *The Observer* found much to praise – benevolence personified – and she loved its 'jolly music, genial acting, the comradeship and adventures of the road and a roaring fire and mug of mulled ale at the end of the journey'.[40] But such comments merely appraise its surface quality. The film lacks a sense of time and space and sequence. It fatally loses the rhythm of this novel. The main anatomical failure is a sense of shape and direction, for, despite its reputation, *Pickwick Papers* does have an overriding coherence, of which even readers of its original publication in serial form would have been aware.

Bearing in mind that *Pickwick Papers* was serialised in monthly parts from April 1836 to November 1837, it seems that Dickens composed the unfolding narrative with an awareness of his readers' sense of the passing of the days, weeks and months of the seasons. In much the same way as radio and television today calendarise our experience, he imagines the action as the period between March 1822 and October 1828. The main sequences would reinforce the shape of the year. The writer seems to think himself into his readers' recent experience of time passed. Thus the cricket match is played in June. The shooting sequence is in October. The Pickwickians skate on the ice in February. The idyll of Christmas at Dingley Dell appeared in the January issue. The glorious colours of August were invoked in the September number. Sam Weller sent his Valentine in the March issue. Samuel Pickwick sets forth at Grays Inn on a fine October morning – in the November issue. The sense of the shape of passing time is firmed up by the author's strict adherence to the law seasons. Although allowance must be made in considering translation from the slow and gradual unfolding of serialised narrative prose fiction into a film lasting just under an hour and a half, ignoring the sense of time reduces the impact of the film. A strong sense of the passing seasons of the year would have contributed not only to the charm and picturesque effect, but have strengthened the film's coherence.[41] Apart from the obvious snow and ice effects, there is very little sense of the seasons in Noel Langley's film.

The film is not so much an epitome of Dickens's novel, as a selection of narrative moments. Restrictions of location shooting caused the filmmakers to rely mainly on interior sequences. This not only reduces that vital outdoors, fresh air, galloping across England quality so characteristic of *Pickwick Papers*, but results in the loss of several major sequences. There is nothing to suggest the scenery of Kent and little sense of that England of coaching days, so significant an ingredient of the genre in which this novel was created and which meant so much to Dickens – and which is so vital a part of our very construction of the Dickensian.[42]

We are not lamenting the loss of something quaint and Dickensian here. The opposition of stage-coach and railway was fundamental in the thinking of so many of Dickens's contemporaries, who felt they were living in a time of very rapid change, symbolised in the decay of horse transport and triumph of steam. The majority of Victorians who could recall an age before the railroad felt they had lived in two separate worlds. The railway is a recurring image in Victorian writing as a metaphor of the great, far-reaching and rapid changes which were happening and which finally cut modern times off from the Good Old Days.[43] Thomas Hughes invited readers of his vastly popular novel, *Tom Brown's School Days* (1857),[44] to look out of the railway carriage window and see for themselves how matters stood. Thackeray drew a line in the sands of time, dividing those days before the railways, from the rapidly changing endlessly modern and modernising days he found himself living in:

> It was only yesterday, but what a gulf between now and then! Then was the old world. Stage-coaches ... riding horses, pack-horses, highwaymen, knights in armour, Norman invaders, Roman legions, Druids, Ancient Britons painted blue ... All these belong to the old period ... But your railroad starts the new era, and we of a certain age belong to the new time and the old one ... We are of the age of steam.[45]

Dr Thomas Arnold, observing the Birmingham Railway make its progress through the countryside, connecting the Midlands with London, recorded in his journal for 4 August 1839 that he thought 'Feudality is gone forever'. In his reappearance in *Master Humphrey's*

Clock (1841) Tony Weller had strong words to say about the railways: 'I consider ... that the rail is unconstitootional and an
inwasion o' priweleges'.[46] In Elizabeth Gaskell's *Cranford* (1853)
Captain Brown is killed by a railway train while actually reading
Pickwick Papers.[47]

The significant point is that those living at the time realised that
the changes they observed going on around them were not minor,
isolated, peripheral changes, but that the whole fabric and structure
of their culture and society were changing. The railways, the
mechanical means of industrial production, new methods of
communication, these were the outward and visible signs of truly
radical change. With this important element in the film version so
dramatically reduced, *The Pickwick Papers* stands little chance of full
and proper life. Writing as one who has tried adapting novels to
screenplays, Harold Pinter argued that you can't simply transfer a
book to screen: 'It doesn't work, for reasons which should be
obvious. In a film you have to go for the essence of the story, to give
the film its focus, with the other elements contributing to that
focus'.[48]

The casting is a mixture of the superb and the unfortunate. It is
also taunting, as it makes one think what might have been done.
James Hayter, who had established his Dickensian credentials as the
Cheeryble twins in *Nicholas Nickleby* (1947), managed to be inno-
cently childlike rather than irritatingly childish, and resisted any
tendency towards slapstick. He beams benevolently through his
round spectacles. He was ably supported by his Sam Weller, Harry
Fowler. Winkle was played by James Donald. This might seem a
curious piece of casting, as he was best known for a series of steady
performances in British stiff-upper-lip war films;[49] nevertheless he
assumes a wild-eyed half-crazed remoteness which brought
Dickens's would-be sporting cove plausibly to life. Snodgrass was
rather blankly played by Lionel Murton (the fault was not entirely
his, as the script gave him little to work on). This was a pity, as
Murton had so much that he could have worked up into the role.
His lean face, elevating eyebrows and permanent air of bemused
surprise gave him tons of comic potential in a role such as the self-
consciously wannabee Byron vainly struggling to foster that
requisite air of dark, romantic mystery. His comic credentials were
well established in *Meet the Navy* (1946) and *I was a Male War Bride*
(1949).[50] Tupman was essayed by Alexander Gauge, who barely

sketched in the role, though physically well suited (he was later to be a notable television Friar Tuck). Nigel Patrick combined the right amount of slimy guile and dotty pathos as Jingle (though his clothes might convincingly have been tattier). Hermione Baddeley certainly delivered the goods as Mrs Bardell, in which her considerable stage and revue experience paid vast dividends. One of her earliest stage triumphs was at the age of twenty-one as Ninetta, the Infant Phenomenon in Nigel Playfair's *When Crummles Played*. She also starred in comedy roles in Zoe Akins's *The Greeks Had a Word for It*, in 1934, and in Wycherley's *The Country Wife* in 1940. She showed an enormous gift for revue, and starred in several shows for Noel Coward, including *Fumed Oak* and *Fallen Angels*, 1949. But her range was considerable, as those who saw her in the stage version of Graham Greene's *Brighton Rock* (1943) would testify. She created in Mrs Bardell a cunning, devious, slightly blowsy but nevertheless somehow sympathetic character. Even though she readily and cold-bloodedly duped Pickwick, and would screw him for every penny she could, there was pathos in this betrayal, too. This Mrs Bardell convincingly suggested the world had always short changed her and had much to answer for.

Donald Wolfit turned out a masterly realisation of Buzfuz, which is grotesque but stylistically wholly appropriate. He is obviously a professional advocate, acting up for the sake of client, and his fee. The comedy is irresistible. The Wardle group was a sad disappointment and is hardly given time or space to establish itself and fails to serve the purpose Dickens probably intended – as an example of a loving, extended patriarchal family, all living amiably under one roof. Old Wardle, so called, is a widower of about fifty. He clearly loves his daughters (and tries to exert his care without influencing them too dearly) and has his old mother as well as spinster sister living with him. When the daughters marry, they live nearby. In Langley's film, this set of characters barely has the chance to come warmly to life. Walter Fitzgerald, a sturdy British character actor (who had just previously worked hard in Disney's *Treasure Island*, 1950), resourcefully projects the reliable good nature of Mr Wardle, but fails to suggest the warmth, generosity and round-the-year Christmas bonhomie which, you must feel, might almost turn him into a mythical, fairy-tale character. Dingley Dell is Paradise with a drinking licence, no closing hours and a divinity as landlord. Fitzgerald manages to suggest glowing jollity, but little of the magical.

Kathleen Harrison, fondly remembered for performances as chirpy Cockney chars, scatterbrained nannies, domestics and Mrs Hugget was badly miscast as Rachael Wardle ('There was a dignity in the air, a touch-me-not-ishness in the walk, a majesty in the eye of the spinster aunt'). Placed as they are in the Christmas context, the Wardles are obviously intended to body forth some important Dickensian family virtues. Little of that survives. What we get is a perfunctory Dickensian Christmas – snow, tree, tinsel, the lot.

For the rest, a capable job lot of British character actors was bought in to do their stuff – George Robey, Sam Costa, Hermione Gingold, Joyce Grenfell, Raymond Huntley, Max Adrian. It is in these star turns that the flimsiness of dramatisation really reveals itself. Joyce Grenfell plays Mrs Leo Hunter, who is a formidable creation. She is a caricature of the renowned blue-stocking and hunter of celebrities, Mary Monkton, Countess of Cork and Orrery, who had known Joshua Reynolds, Samuel Johnson, Edmund Burke, Horace Walpole and many others.[51] In *Pickwick Papers* her husband assures Mr Pickwick that she dotes on poetry: 'She adores it; I may that her whole soul and mind are wound up, and entwined with it'. But she is given little to do here. One need only recall Joyce Grenfell's vast experience as a stage monologist, her fruity toff tones and air of deranged sincerity to realise what she could have done with this role. Mrs Leo Hunter's celebrated breakfast – one of the comic gems of the book[52] – is brutally butchered. Joyce Grenfell is wheeled on to do a turn, to recite the immortal 'Ode to an Expiring Frog' costumed (one is led to assume) as Britannia (she should be Minerva, according to the book). Doubtless in tone with 1950s austerity, Mrs Leo Hunter's *Fancy Dress Dejeune* is here presented as a rather utility affair.

Some of the other reductions and omissions in the film are serious. Some characters make only token appearances – Tony Weller, for example, is only introduced to facilitate the necessary narrative support needed to get Sam Weller into the Fleet to support Mr Pickwick. We have lost the superb saga of Tony Weller's marital complexities and the humbling of the Revd Stiggins. Other characters make no appearance. Benjamin Allen and Bob Sawyer might have contributed much to a convivial tone and the loss of the scenes of the Bachelor Party at the house of the Raddles family is seriously felt.[53]

As well as the reduction of Mrs Leo Hunter's jamboree, several memorable sequences which contribute considerably to the impact of Dickens's novel are missing altogether. We have no military field day at Chatham. No Eatanswill election (which Dickens was uniquely qualified to portray, of course). No cricket match. Village cricket is an important part of English mythological memory – we need only to think of the contribution cricket made to the sense of Englishness in such a variety of films as *Goodbye Mr Chips, Happy is the Bride, Tom Brown's Schooldays, The Browning Version, The Go Between*. The significance of cricket as an emerging characteristically English game is demonstrated by the appearance at this time of John Nyren's *The Young Cricketer's Tutor* and *Cricketers of my Time* – both published in 1833.[54] The complete loss of Bath and Bristol sequences is damaging, containing, as they do, some of the finest pages in *Pickwick Papers*. Dickens knew Bath well and here gives us a splendid portrait of the spa in genteel decline.[55]

There are fundamental questions to be raised about the nature of comedy. *Pickwick* is rightly regarded as a comic masterpiece. This was recognised when it was first published, and its reputation has endured. You would not think so if your only evidence was this film. A very considerable element in the comic effect of *The Pickwick Papers* is not so much what happens, as how Dickens portrays what happens. It lies in the narrative voice and the use of indirect speech. The novel is packed with examples.

Recall what Pickwick learns about horse transport. He is told by the driver he interrogates that the horse is forty-two; is kept out for two or three weeks at a time on account of his weakness for falling down when taken out of harness; that when he is harnessed he is strapped in very tight so as to support him and that the carriage has very large wheels so the horse has to run to keep up. Dickens then adds: 'Mr Pickwick entered every word of this statement in his note-book, with a view of communicating it to the club, as a singular instance of the tenacity of life in horses, under trying circumstances' (chapter 2).

How could film do justice to the comic writing in presenting the Pickwickians under the influence of wine? (chapter 2). Or the account of Pickwick's pursuit of his hat (chapter 4). Or Pickwick in casual conversation when Benjamin Allen asks: '"I say, old boy, where do you hang out?" Mr Pickwick replied that he was at present suspended at the George and Vulture' (chapter 30).

These random examples show the supreme comic novelist delivering the goods. This is the condition to which all comic narrative prose aspires. It seems to me Dickens's native language (but Jerome K. Jerome and P. G. Wodehouse run him a very close second). This does not mean that filming *The Pickwick Papers* is impossible, but it does suggest that considerable effort is required to achieve something equivalent to that comic spirit – slapstick, funny walks, pratfalls and falling over furniture will not serve the purpose. This film lacked a coherent style to hold its view of the world together. It alternated awkwardly between fairly standard British historical costume drama (in which it owed much to often mocked but highly influential Gainsborough Films) and knockabout farce (which clearly anticipates Carry On Films). Tony Weller, Dodson and Fogg and Buzfuz seem to have strolled in from another production. The mixture of costume drama and grotesque comedy is an uneasy one. The decor is picturesque rather than romantic or enchanting. That essentially divine or fairy-like quality identified by Chesterton is wholly lacking. What we get is a poor mixture of pantomine and ineffective historical realism. Whatever misgivings one might have about David Lean's representation of Dickens's fiction, his *Great Expectations* and *Oliver Twist* certainly have a convincing stylistic coherence. *Great Expectations* works well because David Lean either omits or considerably tones down the comic and the grotesque elements – Orlick, Trabbs's boy, Wemmick, the Aged Parent – and concentrates on telling the dramatic story. The Miss Havisham element works as she is played as someone genuinely deranged. We see her very much as she is, not as Pip sees her. Coherence in *Oliver Twist* (1948) was very much achieved as a result of the impressive design inspired largely by Gustav Doré's drawings of London.[56] Here we have an evocation of early nineteenth-century London which is geographically coherent and utterly convincing. You could almost smell it.

This film of *Pickwick Papers*'s other major weakness is in its sense of proportion. It is simply that this film lacks the breadth and stature of Dickens's novel. You may be expecting to partake of a hearty banquet, but are offered a buffet of scarcely nourishing snacks. While it may be true to say that every picture tells a story, not all stories can be told in pictures.

Langley's *Pickwick Papers* was released at a moment in modern history which now seems to be at the turning of the tide. The optimistic mood of the post-war settlement and consensus politics began quite rapidly to decline following the closure of the Festival of Britain. It is often argued that David Lean's two classic Dickens films, *Great Expectations* and *Oliver Twist*, significantly mirrored the mood of the period, showing as they did the social horrors of the old world which were to be for ever wiped away in the creation of the New Jerusalem to be achieved in the Peoples' Peace following the People's War.[57] As the 1945 Labour Party manifesto had it: 'The people will have won both struggles (in Europe and against Japan) ... They deserve and must be assured a happier future than faced so many of them after the last war'. The promise was explicit. There was to be no going back to the 1930s. The foundations seemed to be laid and work on the edifice modestly but determinedly undertaken in the five or so years following the end of the Second World War.[58]

The results of the election called by Clement Attlee on 23 February 1950 reduced the Labour government's majority to five, but the administration struggled on.[59] Optimism had been seriously blown off course by the economic crisis of 1947. Britain endured the worst winter of the century and a sterling crisis which it was feared might brankrupt the country. Austerity became the word of the moment. It was in this atmosphere that the Festival of Britain 1951 endeavoured to represent and to celebrate the vigour of modern Britain. With mini festivals and parties all over the land, the nation was supposed to be celebrating its survival in good shape, like a happy family which had survived a crisis. The documentary film-maker Humphrey Jennings was commissioned to make a film to herald the Festival, *Family Portrait*. Jennings, chosen by John Grierson, was the ideal director for such a project as this. During the war he had a series of morale-boosting but deeply poetic films about the nation's endurance under stress – *London Can Take It* (1940), *Listen to Britain* (1941), *Fires Were Started* (1943) and *A Diary for Timothy* (1945). The opening commentary declared:

> Perhaps because we in Britain live in a group of small islands, we like to think of ourselves as a family. And of course with the unspoken affection and outspoken words that families have. And so the Festival of Britain is a kind of family reunion. So let us take a look at ourselves, to let the young and the old, the past and the future, meet and discuss. To pat ourselves on the back, to give thanks that we are still a family, to voice our hopes and fears, our faith for our children.[60]

Although the Festival of Britain was supposed to point the way to the future, the qualities called up in Jennings's film stress our continuity with the past – the landscape, agriculture, traditional heavy industries (coal, iron, steel), cobbled streets, brass bands, pageantry, tradition. In *Culture and Consensus: England, Art and Politics Since 1940*, Robert Hewison discusses the very interesting attack made on Jennings's film by fellow film director, Lindsay Anderson.[61] The family of Britain, Anderson argued, was no more than a sentimental fiction. He took considerable exception to Jennings's sentimentalising of the nation's past, which he suspected was symptomatic of apprehension for the present, and fear of the future: 'The Past is no longer an inspiration: it is a refuge'.[62]

It is in this one respect that Noel Langley's *Pickwick Papers* (1952) parallels Dickens's novel published in 1836–37. Just as Dickens's novel fingered the nation's nerve ends at a time which was perceived as moving into far-reaching, fundamental and irreversible change, so this film used fiction picturesquely to cast one longing, lingering look back to those mythical days of the nation's innocence and childhood, when simple goodness could come out on top. The film prefigured a way of doing Dickens with which we are now all too familiar, brought about by the needs of the heritage industry – quaint, Little Old England Dickens, mass-media *Dickensianism*, conveniently pre-packed and oven ready for the global market.[63] And ultimately questions of fidelity to the original text do not really apply.[64] As Foucault and his numerous disciples are ever ready to assure us, a culture is certainly conceivable where discourse would circulate wholly freed from the restrictions of 'authorship' and all which the term implies. Once committed to paper, printed and published, it may well – in Erica Sheen's telling phrase – become 'subsumed into the general circulation of mass communication'.[65] *Pickwick Papers*, once in popular circulation, rapidly took on other lives, metamorphosing into numerous forms, ranging from imitation, parody, stage plays, musical shows and, in our century, film, radio and television. Noel Langley's version of *Pickwick Papers*, just as much as the original novel on which it was based, is part of the discourse of its historical moment. Dickens's novel appeared in the aftermath of the Reform Bill crisis – a period of remarkable social, political and economic changes which seemed to contemporaries as threatening as much as beneficial. Readers of the monthly serial parts in 1836 were invited to look back at the old world fast retreat-

ing from them. *Noblesse oblige*, individual charity, an economy and
social order closely connected with the land was being replaced with
a growing state, institutionalised welfare, commerce and manufac-
turing industries. Samuel Pickwick, moved to pity by his fellow
creatures personally dispensing charity, was being replaced by the
Union Workhouse. Noel Langley's 1952 film likewise appeared at a
moment of crisis, as the seemingly solid foundations of the post-war
settlement shook under the first waves of insecurity. The first Attlee
government had been elected on the promise of national control of
the commanding heights of the economy, full employment, the
National Health Service and opportunities for all. David Lean's
Dickens films had caused us to look back at the Victorian past; dark,
threatening, cruel, unjust, without the promise of hope. Pip tears
down Miss Havisham's curtains and lets the sunlight in from modern
Britain. These films were made by a man who must have known his
'Dover Beach', who viewed the recent past not as a land of dreams,
but as a world which had no joy, or love, or light, or certitude, or
peace, or help for pain; and felt that the experience of life in
Victorian England must have been:

> as on a darkling plain
> Swept with confused alarms of struggle and flight
> Where ignorant armies clash by night.

Lean showed us a past we should be glad to leave behind. Langley
gave us an illusion to hide behind.

NOTES

1 G. K. Chesterton, *Charles Dickens* (1906), quoted in George H. Ford and
Lauriat Lane, Jr. (eds), *The Dickens Critics* (Ithaca, NY, Cornell University
Press, 1963), p. 109.
2 Cf Brian McFarlane, *Novel to Film: An Introduction to the Theory of
Adaptation* (Oxford, Oxford University Press, 1996), pp. 105 ff.
3 David Parossien: 'Dickens and the Cinema' in Robert B. Partlow, Jr (ed.),
Dickens Studies Annual, vol. 7 (Carbondale and Edwardsville, Feffer and
Simons and Southern Illinois University Press, 1978), pp. 68–9.
4 The same argument would certainly imply that Haydn was a greater
symphonist than Beethoven, or Dick Francis a greater novelist than
George Eliot.
5 Jeffrey Richards, *Films and British National Identity: From Dickens to 'Dad's
Army'* (Manchester, Manchester University Press, 1997), p. 346.
6 A case well argued in *Not as Good as the Book*, a programme about the

adaptation of *Great Expectations*, made by Tetra Films for Channel Four television, 1997.

7 Raphael Samuel, *Theatres of Memory* (London, Verso, 1994), pp. 402 ff.

8 See Robert Giddings, 'Great Misrepresentations: Dickens and Film', in *Critical Survey*, 3: 3 (1991), pp. 305–12.

9 See Robert Giddings, 'Dickens: From Page to Screen', *Canadian Notes and Queries*, 54 (1998), pp. 13–19.

10 D. S. Carne-Ross, Preface, *Horace in English* (Harmondsworth, Penguin, 1996), p. xiv.

11 Dickens was not happy to be subordinate to his illustrator, and further protested that he was 'no great sportsman, except in regard of all kinds of locomotion' and that he should be allowed to come up with his own ideas, as 'it would be better for the plates to arise naturally out of the text'.

12 Pierce Egan's *Life in London*, a series about sporting men and sporting events in London, which starred Tom and Jerry, illustrated by Robert, Isaac and George Cruikshank, had been extremely successful between October 1820 and July 1821. *A Cockney's Rural Sports* by John Poole had recently been given serial publication and Harriet Martineau's *Illustrations of Political Economy* had sold well in serial form – 10,000 a month during 1832. In 1836 Henry Colburn was publishing Bulwer Lytton's *Pelham* and *The Disowned* (whose copyright he had purchased) in six-shilling weekly parts, at the same time that Frederick Marryatt's *Frank Mildmay* was appearing in monthly parts.

13 See Raymond Williams, 'Advertising: The Magic System', in *Problems in Materialism and Culture* (London, Verso, 1980), pp. 170–95, and Bernard Darwin, *The Dickens Advertiser* (London, Elkin Mathews and Marrot, 1930), pp. 26 ff.

14 Graham Smith, *Dickens: A Literary Life* (Basingstoke, Macmillan, 1996), p. 27. See also John Sutherland, *Victorian Novelists and Publishers*, (Chicago, IL, Chicago University Press, 1976), pp. 21 ff, and *Victorian Fiction: Writers, Publishers, Readers* (Basingstoke, Macmillan, 1995), pp. 88–91.

15 Dickens's Preface to the first cheap edition of *Pickwick Papers*, 1847, reprinted in Robert L. Patten (ed.), *The Posthumous Papers of the Pickwick Club* (Harmondsworth, Penguin, 1972), p. 45. All subsequent references are to the Penguin edition.

16 See *The Letters of Charles Dickens*, ed. Madeline House and Graham Storey (Oxford, Clarendon Press, 1965), vol. 1, Appendix C, p. 648, and Robert L. Patten, *Charles Dickens and his Publishers* (Oxford, Clarendon Press, 1978), pp. 64 ff.

17 Robert L. Patten, 'The Sales of Dickens's Works', in Philip Collins, *Dickens: The Critical Heritage* (London, Routledge, 1971), p. 617.

18 See J. Don Vann, 'The Early Success of "Pickwick"', in *Publishing History*, 5 (1977), pp. 51 ff.

19 *Publishers Circular*, 2 July 1892, p. 6.

20 *Publishers Circular*, 13 August 1892, p. 161. See also George H. Ford, *Dickens and His Readers: Aspects of Novel Criticism Since 1836* (New York,

Norton, 1965), p. 6; Richard D. Altick, *The English Common Reader: A Social History of the Mass Reading Public 1860–1900* (Chicago, University of Chicago Press, 1957), pp. 383–6.

21 Charles Dickens, *The Letters of Charles Dickens*, ed. Madeline House and Graham Storey, *Pilgrim Edition*, vol. 1 (Oxford, Clarendon Press, 1965), p. 189.

22 See F. Dubrez Fawcett, *Dickens the Dramatist: On Stage, Screen and Radio* (London, W. H. Allen, 1952), pp. 233–4.

23 See E. J. Hobsbawm and George Rudé, *Captain Swing* (London, Lawrence and Wishart, 1969), pp. 97 ff; Elizabeth Longford, *Wellington: Pillar of State* (London, Weidenfeld and Nicolson, 1972), pp. 226–8; Jasper Ridley, *Lord Palmerston* (London, Hutchinson, 1970), p. 148.

24 John Morley, *The Life of Richard Cobden* (London, 1881), pp. 90–1.

25 *London Democrat*, 27 April 1839.

26 See Frederick Kitton, *The Dickens Country* (London, Adam and Charles Black, 1911), pp. 83 ff.

27 Arthur Locker, 'Charles Dickens', in *Graphic*, 18 June 1870, in Collins, (ed.), *Dickens: The Critical Heritage*, p. 41.

28 It is an interesting coincidence that the Revd Primrose is thrown into prison for debt.

29 There are distinct echoes in *Pickwick Papers*, chapter 51, when Pickwick sees the Dutch clock and the bird-cage on his arrival at the Fleet. It is Sam Weller who explains 'Veels within Veels, a prison in a prison' – an echo of *A Sentimental Journey*. It recalls the poignant episode when Yorick weeps to see the starling in the cage because it reminded him of the prisoner in the Bastille. See John Killham, 'Pickwick: Dickens and the Art of Fiction', in Gabriel Pearson (ed.), *Dickens and the 20th Century* (London, Routledge, 1962), p. 38.

30 Jean-Paul Richter (known as 'Jean Paul') 1763–1825, the chronicler of the quaint, cosy unchanging charm of harmless provincialism, a master of the wayward discursive and whimsically charming observations, his works were very widely read in the early nineteenth century and his influence endured (very strong in *The Old Curiosity Shop*) *Leben des vernügten Schulmeisterleins Wuz* 1793 and *Hesperus, oder 45 Hundesposttage, eine Biographie* 1795 (much imitated passages of landscape description, self-consciously detailed and beautiful) and the unfinished *Flegeljahre* 1805, full of wit, irony and arabesques of humour. I do not claim that Dickens consciously aped Jean-Paul, or was personally acquainted with his work, but I do believe it was part of the intellectual furniture available to Dickens.

31 The motif is repeated in the saviour, Boo Radley, in Harper Lee's *To Kill a Mocking Bird* (1960).

32 *Tom Brown's Schooldays* (George Minter, 1951). Written by Noel Langley, directed by Gordon Parry, with John Howard Davies, who had played Oliver in David Lean's *Oliver Twist*, as Tom Brown and Robert Newton, who had been Lean's Bill Sikes, as Dr Thomas Arnold. James Hayter, who was Noel Langley's Samuel Pickwick, played Tom the porter.

33 *Scrooge* (Renown, 1951). Written by Noel Langley and directed by Brian

Desmond Hurst. It starred Alastair Sim as Ebenezer Scrooge, Mervyn Johns as Bob Cratchit and Michael Hordern as Jacob Marley.

34 Dilys Powell, *The Golden Screen: Fifty Years of Films*, ed. George Perry (London, Michael Joseph, 1989), p. 74.

35 The original of Dingley Dell is to be found at Sandling, in the Sevenoaks District of Kent, three and a half miles north-west of Maidstone. The megalithic tombs – three upright stones and a capstone, known as Kit's Coty House – are probably the original site of Mr Pickwick's discovery of the stone inscribed 'Bill Stumps'. The area was beloved of Dickens, who considered the seven-mile walk between Maidstone and Rochester one of the most beautiful walks in England. See Frederick Kitton, *The Dickens Country* (London, Adam and Charles Black, 1911), p. 201.

36 Dickens reported the Melbourne–Norton divorce case on 22 June the same year.

37 Ipswich was a tempestuous borough, scene of several heartily fought elections immediately prior to the publication of *Pickwick Papers*. The Tory candidate, Fitzroy Kelly, contested the seat several times. In 1832 he lost the seat, but in January 1835 he was successful. But he was unseated on appeal. This campaign Dickens certainly reported for the press. Fitzroy Kelly was Tory MP for Ipswich 1837–41, Cambridge 1843–47 and East Suffolk 1852–66. A successful lawyer, he became Lord Chief Baron and Privy Councillor in 1866.

38 See Percy Fitzgerald, *Pickwickian Studies* (London, New Century Press, 1899), pp. 24 ff, and T. J. Bradley: 'How Dickens Wrote his Description of Bath', *The Dickensian*, 23 (1927).

39 Quoted in John Walker, (ed.) *Halliwell's Film and Video Guide* (London, Harper Collins, 1998), p. 603.

40 Anthony Lejeune (ed.) *C. A. Lejeune Film Reader* (Manchester, Manchester University Press, 1991), pp. 273–4.

41 See Robert Giddings, 'St Louis: Doughnut City', *New Society*, 9 September 1976, p. 541.

42 See Arthur Hayward, *The Days of Dickens* (London, Routledge, 1935), pp. 74 ff.

43 See R. Athill, 'Dickens and the Railway', *English*, 13 (1961).

44 See Ernie Trory, *Truth Against the World: The Life and Times of Thomas Hughes, Author of 'Tom Brown's Schooldays'* (Hove, East Sussex, Crabtree Press, 1993), pp. 117 ff.

45 William Makepeace Thackeray, 'De Juventute' (1860), in *Roundabout Papers*. See David Newsome, *The Victorian World Picture* (London, John Murray, 1997), pp. 27–32.

46 Charles Dickens, *Master Humphrey's Clock* (1841), chapter 3.

47 Elizabeth Gaskell, *Cranford*, chapter 2.

48 Harold Pinter, quoted in Edith De Rham, *Joseph Losey* (London, André Deutsch, 1991), p. 212. Cf. Marshall MacLuhan, *Understanding Media* (London, Routledge and Kegan Paul, 1964), pp. 305ff.

49 *In Which We Serve* (1941), *The Way Ahead* (1944), *Broken Journey* (1947). He turned in as fine performances in *The Bridge of the River Kwai* and *The Great Escape* (1963).

50 Starring Cary Grant and Ann Sheridan, directed by Howard Hawks.
51 Her mother's house in London (she was the daughter of Viscount Galway) was the Mecca of artistic society.
52 *Pickwick Papers*, chapter 15.
53 Emlyn Williams had recently featured these scenes in his celebrated Dickens readings at Drury Lane and the Lyric Theatre.
54 Matches were played on Broadhalfpenny Down, Hambledon, near Winchester as early as 1750. Sevenoaks Vine, Hambledon and Lord's are the oldest Cricket Clubs in the country. See W. S. Shears, *The Face of England* (London, Spring Books, nd.), pp. 161 and 221.
55 See Percy Fitzgerald, *Pickwickian Studies* (London, The New Century Press, 1899), pp. 24–38, and T. J. Bradley: 'How Dickens Wrote his Description of Bath', *The Dickensian*, 23 (1927).
56 Gustave Doré 1832–83, his drawings of London 1869–71 appeared in Blanchard Jerrold's *London*, published by Grant and Company, 1872. He shows the metropolis in a variety of moods – the crowded streets, London at work, at play, night scenes, parks, race courses, the docks – but probably the most striking (and certainly the most influential in the way we picture Victorian London) are his drawings of the east of London. This work has often been a valued source book for stage and film design.
57 See Correlli Barnett *The Lost Victory: British Dreams, British Realities 1945–1950* (London, Macmillan, 1995), pp. 123 ff.
58 Patrick Cosgrove, *The Strange Death of Socialist Britain: Post War British Politics* (London, Constable, 1992), pp. 41–78. See also Arthur Marwick, *British Society Since 1945* (Harmondsworth, Penguin, 1996), pp. 60–73 and 98–107.
59 See Peter Hennessy, *Never Again: Britain 1945–1951* (London, Vintage, 1993), pp. 388–90, and Martin Francis, *Ideas and Politics Under Labour 1945–1951: Building a New Britain* (Manchester, Manchester University Press, 1997), pp. 34–5.
60 *Family Portrait* (1950), written and directed by Humphrey Jennings, for the Festival of Britain Committee. The commentary, written by Jennings, was spoken by Michael Goodliffe.
61 Robert Hewison, *Culture and Consensus: England, Art and Politics Since 1940* (London, Methuen, 1995), pp. 64–5.
62 Lindsay Anderson, in M. L. Jennings (ed.), *Humphrey Jennings: Film Maker* (London, British Film Institute, 1982), p. 59.
63 Samuel, *Theatres of Memory*, pp. 401 ff.
64 McFarlane, *Novel to Film*, p. 164.
65 See Erica Sheen, Introduction, this volume, p. 7.

4

Sentimentality, sex and sadism: the 1935 version of Dickens's *The Old Curiosity Shop*

Jenny Dennett

The decade immediately following the introduction of sound at the end of the 1920s brought with it an epidemic of Dickens adaptations. There were films of *A Christmas Carol* (two), *David Copperfield*, *Dombey and Son*, *Great Expectations*, *The Mystery of Edwin Drood*, *The Old Curiosity Shop*, *Oliver Twist* and *A Tale of Two Cities*. To put this into perspective, there were three adaptations in the 1940s, and five in the 1950s. What was it about Dickens that attracted filmmakers of this period?

Sergei Eisenstein's views on the subject are well known. He praised what he saw as the shared attributes of Dickens's writing and popular film. He had little patience with those who failed to see the connection between film and earlier modes of artistic expression or entertainment – 'It is only very thoughtless and presumptuous people who can erect laws and an esthetic for cinema proceeding from premises of some incredible virgin-birth of this art'[1] – and asserted that Dickens's novels

> bore the same relation to ... [his readers] that the film bears to the same strata in our time. They compelled the reader to live with the same passions. They appealed to the same good and sentimental elements as does the film.[2]

It was Eisenstein who gave wide currency to the connection between Dickens and D. W. Griffith. In 'Dickens, Griffith and the Film Today', Eisenstein picks up Griffith's observation that his approach to parallel action was influenced by the novelist's use of changing viewpoints, and he goes back to the written text (specifically *The Cricket on the Hearth*) to prove that early film montage learned its art from Dickens.

However, other intellectuals of the period saw Dickens's filmic quality quite differently. Alastair Cooke, for instance, acknowledged a link between Griffith and Dickens, but not the one praised by Eisenstein:

> Griffith might explain that he got the idea of the 'flash-back' and much of his lighting from Dickens, but most people would be content to believe he got them from a mawkish imagination (which might be, of course, in that instance, the same thing).[3]

As I shall show in this chapter, this view is representative of the low esteem in which Dickens was widely held at this time. In a critical biography of 1934, Hugh Kingsmill criticised the novelist's sentimentality as an aspect of Victorian hypocrisy: 'By embodying virtue in such unreal figures as Nell ... [they] substituted the pleasure of contemplating virtue for the task of practising it.'[4]

In fact, the decade had opened with a blistering attack by Aldous Huxley. In a discussion of *The Old Curiosity Shop*, Huxley suggested that it is 'distressing indeed, but not as Dickens presumably meant it to be distressing; it is distressing in its ineptitude and vulgar sentimentality.'[5] He judged Dickens guilty, in all his books, and particularly in *The Old Curiosity Shop*, of 'really monstrous emotional vulgarity'.[6] The choice of the word 'vulgar' reveals the class bias behind such a view. Significantly, critics who deemed Dickens vulgar often spoke of the cinema in the same terms. David Cecil assures his readers that Dickens's

> conventional melodrama and [his] sentiment are the conventional melodrama and sentiment of the Cockney, no better and no worse than those which burgeon in flamboyant lusciousness from sixpenny novelettes and super-cinemas to-day; and indeed very like them.[7]

This class-bound attitude to both Dickens and the cinema is revealed most strongly by Q. D. Leavis in *Fiction and the Reading Public*, first published in 1932. She opposes Dickens, Reade and Wilkie Collins, 'idols of the man in the street', to George Eliot and Trollope as writers who were revered by 'the educated'.[8] Serial publication allowed subscribers of a lower class to read Dickens's novels:

Dickens is one with his readers; they enjoyed exercising their emotional responses, he laughed and cried aloud as he wrote. We [the educated elite] miss ... the adult and critical sensibility of the older [eighteenth-century] novelists, who wrote for the best, because it was the only, public.[9]

Leavis saw Dickens as uneducated and immature emotionally, and equated his readership with the audience of cinema:

Dickens ... discovered ... the formula 'laughter and tears' that has been the foundation of practically every popular success ever since (Hollywood's as well as the best seller's). Far from requiring an intellectual stimulus, these are the tears that rise in the heart and gather in the eyes, involuntarily ... though an alert critical mind may cut them off at the source in a revulsion of disgust.[10]

A link between Dickens and Hollywood is also made by Cecil: 'He overstates. He tries to wring an extra tear from the situation ... No Hollywood film-director, expert in sob-stuff, could more thoroughly vulgarise the simple and the tender.'[11]

Hugh Kingsmill suggested that Dickens's 'comic genius' offered 'a brief escape from the hot-house of ... sentimentality'.[12] If Dickens was regarded at all in the 1930s, it was for his comic characters. Silent filmmakers may have been attracted by the plots and general mood of his novels, but sound offered the chance to recreate his idiosyncratically verbal characters. Campbell Nairne, writing a joint review of adaptations of *David Copperfield*, *Great Expectations*, *Edwin Drood* and *The Old Curiosity Shop* in *Cinema Quarterly* in spring 1935, exhibited the typically reductive view of Dickens held by intellectuals in the 1930s:

It is interesting to speculate on the motives which induced the movie-makers of Hollywood and Elstree to embark almost simultaneously on screen versions of Dickens' novels. Dickens would appear to exercise a fatal fascination over the minds of production executives. Perhaps it is that they share with him the delusion that he could write strong stories.

He continued, in what George J. Worth would describe as a 'hard-boiled, tight-lipped' vein:[13]

When one examines the Dickensian philosophy ... it is not really surprising that producers should so often have gone back to Dickens for their screen material ... Virtue is rewarded and vice punished – which is exactly the comfortable code that has informed picture-making since the earliest days of the movies. Whether it squares with the facts or not is no matter; it suits the vested interests of filmdom that the public which lines up at the box office should be put to sleep with that opiate and persuaded to accept a false standard of values.[14]

Notwithstanding, Nairne praised the film of *David Copperfield* because it made characterisation its strong point. He believed that it was comic characterisation, not 'long, rambling stories' that could be successfully transcribed into film form. He was clearly won over by this: at the end of his review, rigour gives way and he welcomes the fact that 'a good warm feeling of happiness, such as pervades *Copperfield*' could be a box-office winner.

The *Daily Telegraph* had little time even for Dickens's characters.[15] Its review of *The Old Curiosity Shop* opened with this rhetorical question: 'Did Dickens ever draw a human being, or are his creatures all just caricatures – types or "humours" (in the Jonsonian sense), distorted to suit the Victorian passion for heroic virtue, blackest villainy and obvious farce?'

His conclusion was that none of the characters 'ring true'. The *Sunday Times* appeared more favourably inclined, but even this reviewer's compliments were double-edged. His review of *The Old Curiosity Shop* began with the suggestion that 'the plots and characters invented by Charles Dickens must seem to many people ideal for the purposes of the screen'. (By contrast, the *Daily Telegraph* admitted to being unconvinced that 'Dickens ever wrote a story suitable for stage or screen, with the exception of *A Tale of Two Cities*'.) He continued that he considered Dickens's work suitable for adaptation into film because, there, sentiment could be restrained and verbal efflorescence curtailed:

> The flourishes and trimmings possible in a novel cannot be introduced into a picture, and with Dickens his ornamentation is not only part of his charm, but frequently the sole excuse. Stripped of this method the work of Dickens stands convicted as thinly disguised and unconvincing melodrama.[16]

In a review of the film of *A Christmas Carol* the *Sunday Times*'s reviewer held himself aloof from such criticism:

> Dickens is, however, not the literary fashion of the day. He is too often the subject of scornful cliches, the despised of pseudo-

intellectuals who accuse him of prolixity, extravagant characterisation, theatricality, cheap emotionalism, adjectival mania and
sentimentality ... Yet remain his works imperishable, yet survives
the magic of his stories, intense with human appeal.[17]

Dickens himself would be hard-pressed to improve on such an
insufferable piece of humbug.

If sentimentality, both in Dickens's writing and in cinema, was the
stumbling-block for critics of the 1930s, its equivalent today is the
representation of women. The following quotation could well be
taken as an accurate description of the roles available to women in
mainstream cinema over the last hundred years:

> Household ornament, guardian angel, playful kitten, Good Sister,
> Good Provider – ... a young girl or a woman may ... represent any
> of these types, or a blend of more than one of them, for the benefit,
> comfort or pleasure of the men in her domestic grouping. Any
> assertion of herself as a person, however, with her own needs,
> demands and desires is invariably presented ... as something
> grotesque.

In fact, it comes from Michael Slater's study, *Dickens and Women*.[18]
Kate Flint similarly writes of Dickens denying women their sexuality or treating it entirely from a male angle 'with a malodorous relish
which vacillated between the lascivious and the coy'.[19] Again, this
analysis could well be used to describe the representation of women
in Hollywood cinema. Interestingly enough – and despite the fact
that there is a significant connection between sentiment and the
Victorian representation of women – writers of the 1930s seemed
unconcerned either by Dickens's or by the cinema's female characterisations. As a case study, I propose to examine contemporary
critical response to the 1935 adaptation of *The Old Curiosity Shop*.[20]
   The Dickensian, the journal of the Dickens Fellowship, had a
strong stake in *The Old Curiosity Shop*. The editor, Walter Dexter,
was a consultant on the film and the film's director, Thomas
Bentley, was a member of the Fellowship. Thomas Bentley had
made two silent versions of the novel (1914 and 1921) and had also
directed silent versions of *Oliver Twist*, *David Copperfield* and *Barnaby
Rudge*. Since he had a proven record of interest in Dickensian
subjects, the film version of *The Old Curiosity Shop* could be
expected to be faithful to the novel. And indeed, when it was

released *The Dickensian* described it as 'undoubtedly a faithful and complete representation of the story and of the well-known and almost immortal characters'. Other reviews noted the film's fidelity to the text, but were less than positive about this. *The Times* called it:

> a piece of pure reconstruction, and for the most part fantastically, almost unkindly, like Dickens ... So obviously authentic, indeed, is the guttering sentimentality of the three old men round her death-bed that it is not in the least painful and can be accepted simply as a curiosity of the past. For by this time there is no question of entering into the story or sympathising with the characters; precisely because the film is so Dickensian it seems like a mere commentary or criticism – a very interesting criticism – of his mind. To bring Quilp alive ... is only to expose the more clearly the exuberant morbidity of his creator's imagination.[21]

Behind this view, as we have seen, lay that 1930s fear of Dickensian sentimentality. Other reviewers criticised the film's fidelity to its novel for more cinematic reasons. *Picturegoer* noted that 'it could have done with rather more imaginative treatment, and further rejection in the matter of characters and scenes, in order to speed up the action a little, but it nevertheless, provides a picture of particular interest to Dickens' admirers'.

The Observer took a very superior attitude to the whole production:

> Nobody need be afraid of finding a frivolous treatment of Dickens in the present work. Miss Kennedy's adaptation sticks grimly and loyally to the author's pages. Thomas Bentley, too, the director, is a reverent person ... [he] would not presume to take liberties with a work that is noted on the programme – 'The Greatest of all Charles Dickens' Classics'. Nor would such eminent players as Mr. Ben Webster and Mr. Hay Petrie ... It is safe to say that practically everyone associated with the making of 'The Old Curiosity Shop' has followed the descriptions, the characters, and the incidents of the book with meticulous care. The result is a sedulous, reputable, and entirely loyal translation of nineteenth-century English narrative, but one of the dullest films it has ever been my lot to see.[22]

I am not going to try to judge whether the film is dull or loyal. I am now going to concentrate on Little Nell, her relationships to the male characters, and on the presentation of the Marchioness, in both the film and the novel.

The Dickensian commented on the performances of all the main actors and actresses, with the exception of the role of the Marchioness – a significant omission to which I will return later. Elaine Benson (Little Nell) was praised for her 'wistfulness and naturalness of expression', 'her diffidence and sweetness' but the reviewer believed she would have been more convincing if she had been a little less educated.[23] *Film Weekly* devoted a two page spread to Benson, complete with photographs.[24] The article tells us that she is fourteen, the daughter of a bank manager and that she got the part because her mother sent a photograph to Bentley. Her real name was Smorthwaite, but it was changed (by Bentley?) to Benson. In a portrait of her in costume, one can plainly see the band that depresses her burgeoning breasts. As a representative young woman of the 1930s, Elaine Benson was thus deprived of her name, her sexuality and criticised for her education. The reviewer in the *Monthly Film Bulletin* described Elaine Benson as 'a sweet and gentle Little Nell, but she is neither demonstrative or convincing'. By contrast, Quilp is considered very convincing: 'The outstanding character is Quilp, his personality dominates all the others and Hay Petrie gives a very finished performance ... the personification of malevolence.'[25]

The reviewer in *Picturegoer* called Petrie's performance 'very good' but believed it 'a little too grotesque in make-up'. Elaine Benson is said to make 'a pathetic figure of Little Nell'.[26] The *Sunday Times* described Hay Petrie's performance as: 'a triumph. Even in the most repulsive moments of the part he retains our interest and fascinates us. He plays a foul little person with a diabolic sincerity and quaintness. His reading of this character ought to satisfy the most hypercritical Dickensian.' Elaine Benson was praised as 'a sweetly simple and effective Little Nell'.

The *Daily Telegraph* was equally enthusiastic about Petrie: 'The Quilp Mr. Petrie gives us is no whit more fantastic than the Quilp of the novelist, with his bared fangs and air of a panting dog, and he is certainly entertaining. You await his every move with eager curiosity, uncertain whether he is about to take a bite out of Nell's arm or produce a rabbit from a hat.'

This reviewer made no comment about the role of Nell, apart from naming the actress, but even then he got her name wrong. Significantly, the two reviewers most dismissive of Dickens are the two most captivated by Petrie and least interested in Benson. They had more in common with Dickens than they may have wished to acknowledge.

Much has been written about Dickens's relationships with young women, specifically with his sisters-in-law and Ellen Ternan. Little Nell is usually seen as Dickens's maudlin tribute to Mary Hogarth, who died young. John Carey typifies this when he writes that 'the gruesome union of girl and aged man, which so appealed to Dickens, intimated in the closeness of Nell to her grandfather ... plainly relates to this erotic paternalism' [Dickens's relationship to Mary].[27] Michael Slater suggests that, rather than being a portrait of Mary, there is actually much of the child Dickens in Little Nell. Adriane LaPointe claims that Dickens's choice of a little girl to represent himself reflects his

> sense of himself as maimed, as characterized by absence – specifically, the feeling that in his warehouse experience in being deprived of an education, in being deprived ... of his chance to rise in the world, he had suffered a sort of 'castration' at the hands of his father.[28]

Both Slater and Carey agree on Dickens's interest in 'the bright pure child in the mouldering house'[29] who struggles to support unworthy relatives and, as Slater writes, 'making the child invariably female increased both the heroism and the pathos'.[30] This assumes that the female has the capacity to be more heroic and more pathetic than the male. (It's not clear whether Slater believes this himself or whether he merely believes it to be the view of Dickens's readers.) In common with 1930s film reviewers, Dickens himself stresses the pathetic side of woman rather than the heroic. Dickens's friend Forster welcomed the fact that *The Old Curiosity Shop* brought Dickens's powers as a pathetic writer to the attention of the public. George J. Worth shows the contrast between the highly verbal vicious characters and the figures of pathos 'who are for all practical purposes speechless as well as helpless'.[31] (The association of Dickensian women and children with pathos raises an interesting possibility regarding the extreme 1930s hostility to Dickens's sentimentality. It suggests an attitude motivated in part by unease with the way in which Dickens pushed his readers – through, as Leavis has it, 'involuntary tears' – into contact with, and acknowledgement of, the neglected, the vulnerable, and the victimised.)

Dickens has heroines but, as Slater writes, they 'find themselves chiefly occupied not with their lovers but in ministering, or seeking to minister, to selfish, querulous or brutally indifferent fathers and brothers'.[32] What Dickens generally omits is woman as desiring subject. Had he wished to describe this aspect of woman, he would have been inhibited by the requirements of the Victorian family audience. But he was also inhibited by personal confusion about his own sexual responsiveness to young women. In *The Old Curiosity Shop* this confusion surfaces in the portrayal of the pure Nell and the sexually rampant Quilp. Aldous Huxley claimed that 'the creator of so many ... gruesome old Peter Pans was obviously a little abnormal in his emotional reactions'.[33]

When examining Dickens's treatment of women we need to look above all at the way Dickens handles the narrative voice. Peter Ackroyd defines *The Old Curiosity Shop* as a novel 'where sexuality is everywhere apparent but nowhere stated'.[34] As we have seen, Kate Flint writes of Quilp hungrily smacking his lips at the female sex. She suggests that male desire is strongly present in Dickens's work, not in the passions that motivate Dickens's heroes and villains, 'but in the implicit creation, in terms of point of view, of a particular bond between narrator and male reader'.[35] The female reader has to find her own way around Dickens's treatment of women in the same way that the female spectator in the mainstream cinema has to find a way to counter her exclusion. As Teresa de Lauretis has put it,

> cinema defines woman as image: as spectacle to be looked at and object to be desired, investigated, pursued, controlled, and ultimately possessed by a subject who is masculine, that is, symbolically male. For the system of the look, the fundamental semiotic structure of cinematic narrative, attributes the power of the gaze to the man, be he the male protagonist, the director (or, more properly, the camera, as the function of enunciation), or the spectator.[36]

Recent film theory has done much to challenge, or at least to elaborate on, the model of the 'gaze' presupposed by this analysis, but it fits the way the Dickensian woman is represented in this early film. Little Nell is a spectacle to be looked at, initially by Master Humphrey. In the film, our first view of Nell is doubly framed. Trent's brother is telling the schoolteacher of his hopes of finding a surviving niece who resembles the woman he and his brother loved.

An iris-out reveals a framed portrait of such a woman (Nell's deceased mother) and the camera then pans to Nell herself. She is shown as the daughter of a portrait and as an object to be viewed herself.

Nell is an object to be pleasurably viewed, and desired, by the idiosyncratic men whose paths she crosses. Specifically, she is desired by Quilp. Interestingly, Quilp's sexual interest in her is revealed sooner in the film than in the novel. In the second scene, he invades the shop stealthily, only his legs initially visible. When fully revealed, he carries a long, dark shadow behind him. He addresses Nell familiarly as Nelly, ogles her and blows kisses after her as she leaves the room. When he has finished his business with Trent, he passes through the room where Nell is giving Kit his writing lesson. He enters as she is telling Kit that a ewe is 'a little girl lamb'. 'Like you, Nelly', he says, and asks for a kiss. To Quilp, this girl is an animal that will soon be ripe for slaughter. This scene is partially invented and partially transposed from chapter six.

Nell is investigated by the single Gentleman, pursued by him and Quilp, controlled by Dickens, the male author – and ultimately possessed by the Daddy-of-them-all, Death. At her burial scene the chief mourners are old men. Even here, Nell is the object of the voyeuristic male gaze.

As Laura Mulvey has pointed out, voyeurism is almost inevitably associated with sadism.[37] Sadism plays a key role in *The Old Curiosity Shop*. Many of Dickens's male – and even a few female – characters are sadists, and most of his women are masochists. The prime example of the sado-masochistic relationship in Dickens's work is the relationship between Mr and Mrs Quilp. Significantly, many writers have linked the character of Quilp with Dickens himself. Kingsmill wrote that 'with his tedious wife and interfering mother-in-law, [Quilp] is not far removed from an incarnation of Dickens himself in his more freakish moments'.[38] Michael Slater agrees (and again, it's not clear whose side he is on):

> There was, one suspects, a definite element of Quilpishness in the bond between Dickens and Catherine [his wife]. Her softness and mildness, especially if accompanied by an air of 'bashful sensuality' must have been deliciously provocative to a man like Dickens.[39]

Carey also comments on the element of fear in Dickens's relations between men and women:

> The male appetite needs to be whetted by the fearfulness of its prey. When the Dickensian maiden does exhibit any consciousness of sex, it's obligatory that it should strike her all of a quiver. Marrying a child is pleasurable; but marrying a frightened child, more so.[40]

Fear is fundamental to the relationship between Quilp and his wife. In both book and film he threatens her constantly, both verbally and physically. The film retains his threat to 'bite her' if he catches her again with her female friends. In the novel, Dickens presents a stereotypical account of gossiping women to amuse his male readers. Quilp sarcastically says of his wife, 'The best of her is that she's so meek, and she's so mild and she never has a will of her own'. Such passivity drives Quilp to excess. This pervasive air of fear and threat has its roots in sexuality. The most famous example of this – and one that has acquired a startling contemporary resonance – is the scene at the end of chapter four where Quilp keeps his wife up all night by him while he smokes a cigar, the end of which becomes 'a deep fiery red'. Gabriel Pearson describes this as 'the closest we get to downright copulation in early Victorian fiction'.[41] In the film, the scene is intercut with scenes of Trent losing money gambling, returning home in anguish and telling Nell that she must go on an urgent message to Quilp. Her response is to drop her eyes and bring her hands in front of her body in a protective gesture. By this means, the young girl is brought into physical proximity with the sexually domineering Quilp. That the scene is supposed to have sexual connotations in the novel is shown by Mrs Jiniwin's 'embarrassment' at finding the couple together in the morning and by Quilp's 'leer of triumph'.

Quilp's sexual interest in Nell becomes explicit in his request to her that she should become his 'number two'. In the novel, chapter six, we are told that, 'the child looked frightened, but seemed not to understand him'; so he spells his meaning out:

> To be Mrs. Quilp the second, when Mrs. Quilp the first is dead, sweet Nell, ... to be my wife, my little cherry-cheeked, red-lipped wife. Say that Mrs. Quilp lives five years, or only four, you'll be just the proper age for me.

In the film, only 'five years' is mentioned: four would presumably have been completely beyond the bounds of propriety. Nell's response is to look at Quilp guardedly and fearfully. The conversation between Mrs Quilp and Nell (overheard by Quilp) is much truncated in the film. In the novel the child cries as she tells her troubles to this seemingly friendly woman. When he re-enters and sees her crying, Quilp pats her on the head. Nell shrinks from his touch. The film omits the tears, making Nell a slightly less pathetic figure; but Quilp kisses her hand as he ushers her out, stressing the physical side of his interest in her. It can thus be seen that the film-makers sometimes heighten the sexuality, sometimes draw back from it.

From this perspective, another interesting comparison is offered by the film's treatment of scenes in chapters eleven and twelve. In chapter eleven, Quilp and Brass have taken up residence in the shop. Nell goes quickly in and out of her room to collect some things. But while she is there, Quilp tells Brass that he is going to take the room for his own, and enters it, 'throwing himself on his back upon the bed with his pipe in his mouth, and then kicking up his legs and smoking violently'. In chapter twelve, when Nell and her grandfather are secretly leaving the shop, Nell has to enter her old room again to get the key. Brass is asleep in the shop but Quilp is sprawled out on Nell's bed. The sight of him, and the sound of his breathing, transfixes her with terror.

In the film, the first of these scenes is conveyed with great impact – and considerable explicitness as to its sexual content. The room is dappled by sunlight, and the image of an angel is prominently on view on Nell's bed-head. This is contrasted with a shot of Quilp looking at her through the doorway. As he enters the room, he takes up position in front of a statue of Pan – a priapic emblem, out of shot until this point. As in the novel, he bounces on the bed, his masculine energy violating her place of refuge. The contrast between Quilp and Nell is stronger in the film than in the novel, and there is stronger emphasis on Quilp being on the bed. However, in the second scene his position has changed: he is sleeping on the floor with Brass as Nell tiptoes by with her grandfather. It was presumably impermissible for a young girl to be seen alone in the same room as a sleeping man. In the 1930s it would seem that the visual medium of film allowed for the heightening of the symbolically erotic, but necessitated the curbing of the sexually explicit.

It is interesting to note that in a film version which necessarily has to dispense with many characters and episodes (for example

Fred, the Garlands, Miss Monflathers and the Edwards sisters, Little Bethel, the barge journey to the industrial town and the night by the furnace) time and space is found for virtually an entire paragraph, verbatim from chapter twenty-eight, describing the sexual atrocities performed by Mr Packlemerton on his fourteen wives. This speech is spoken in the novel by Mrs Jarley as she teaches Nell her lines for presenting the waxwork figures. In the film we see Nell herself describing the crimes to the shocked approval of a mixed audience. Of course the hyperbolic account is meant to be humorous; but it is another example of the extent to which the film is prepared to endorse the way the novel puts its women under threat.

Such threats are conveyed by the use of light and shade. Nell's grandfather is often shown lurking in the shadows. John Kucich has suggested that:

> The image of the parental, sheltering figure as a veiled threat appears throughout the book – not only in the grandfather, who robs Nell, in a nighttime scene that has the emotional impact of rape, but also in her brother Fred, who nearly pimps her to a drunk; in Codlin and Short, who, while protesting their friendship, want to turn Nell in for a reward ... The benefactor-as-threat image works to produce this erotic seam between trust and violation and to create in our conception of Nell a constant, vivid, erotically desired awareness of violation and loss.[42]

An example of this, given stronger emphasis in the film, is Codlin's visit to Nell's room (chapter nineteen). In the novel, Nell opens her door when Codlin taps at it. He stresses the sincerity of his friendship and concern for her, and then leaves. Nell's response is described as 'a state of extreme surprise'. In the film, Codlin staggers drunkenly upstairs, falls against her door and enters uninvited. Nell holds one hand up to her face, and the other protectively across her chest. As Codlin lurches over her with his drunken expressions of devotion, she wrings her hands and cringes away from him. When he leaves, she rushes to lock the door. Although this drunken behaviour is humorous (not least because it is the antithesis of this character's usual misanthropy), the scene might indeed be said to have 'the emotional impact of rape' – an effect which is endorsed by a menacing musical accompaniment.

I want now to look at the film's presentation of the Marchioness. Although Little Nell is an object of sexual desire she exhibits no sexuality herself: she is presented as a child. The same is not true of the Marchioness. In the casting, clothing and make-up of this character the film makes no attempt to be faithful either to Dickens's words or to the illustrations in the novel. It is odd that *The Dickensian* makes no comment on this lapse in a production that had otherwise been praised for its fidelity. The Marchioness's first appearance in the novel is in chapter thirty-four. She is described as 'a small slipshod girl in a dirty coarse apron and bib, which left nothing of her visible but her face and feet'. In the film she appears at an earlier stage and an incident that occurs in chapter fifty-seven is conflated with her first appearance. In the film she has bare, plump arms and big eyes. She twists her hands coyly in her apron and flutters her eye-lids (to 'twee' musical accompaniment). She wears lipstick and eye make-up and her eyebrows are plucked. In the novel Dick brings her bread and beef to eat; in the film he tells her to shut her eyes and then feeds her a sausage – an unmistakably erotic image. When she overhears calumnies against Kit and the details of the plot she makes her eyes and mouth into enticing circles of surprise. When she sees Sally Brass running after Kit crying 'Stop thief!', she holds her hands up on either side of her face, fingers spread in a gesture derived from Lilian Gish or Fay Wray.[43] In her final appearance in the film, when she is heroine of the hour, she is a beautifully groomed, confident figure, in stature equal to Dick. She looks nearer twenty than twelve. For voyeurs without Victorian paedophiliac desires, *The Old Curiosity Shop* lacked a satisfying female figure. The 1935 film version provided such a figure – and it did so with the tacit approval of the Dickensian Fellowship.[44]

The question of the sexuality of the Marchioness is not, however, settled by asserting that the filmmakers moulded her to their needs. Hugh Kingsmill, ever quick to condemn Dickens's perversions, is not troubled by her. He writes that she 'is only eleven or twelve, and no taller than a child of seven. There was therefore no question of introducing the love motive'.[45] But Michael Steig has suggested that Dickens and Phiz both held ambivalent views on her:

> Dickens' frequent care to describe the Marchioness as a child ... might be a sign of his nervousness over the degree to which she threatens to become a woman. And Dickens' original intention to make the Marchioness the illegitimate daughter of the overtly sexual Quilp and the perverse and demonic Sally Brass suggests a strong ambivalence in his attitude toward his character.[46]

A film version of *The Old Curiosity Shop* must grapple with the sentimentality of the story. This was clearly a particularly difficult
challenge in the 1930s. Margaret Kennedy, who was responsible for
the adaptation, felt constrained to suggest in *The Mechanized Muse*
that:

> characters created on a purely sentimental formula have often no
> appeal save for a local and temporary public ... Our grandfathers
> wept over Little Nell. We mock at her.[47]

Certainly many newspaper reviews mocked the story, and the film
made from it.

Despite the absence of the Bachelor and Mr Garland, the final
scene of the film, where Trent cannot accept that Nell is dead, is
recreated faithfully from the novel. Many of the same words are
used. But other sentimental scenes are excised. In the film we are
not offered Nell's walk in the first churchyard and talk with the old
widow, the dying schoolboy incident, the devotion of the Edwards
sisters to each other. The incidents in chapters fifty-two to fifty-five,
where Nell wanders about the churchyard, church and tower medi-
tating on her own or with any other willing person on the subject
of death, are all omitted from the film.

This is perhaps not surprising: the post-First World War generation had less of an appetite for morbidity than the Victorians.
However, contemporary criticism is fully responsive to connection
between death and the erotic. John Kucich claims that:

> It would be inappropriate to claim that our interest in Nell's viola-
> tion is purely sexual and that we are all voyeurs at heart. Certainly
> the violation of purity and innocence is erotic, but sexuality is ulti-
> mately not so important to this novel as the eroticizing of death.
> Fundamentally it is death, not Quilp, that hovers over Nell.[48]

In the extremely sentimental presentation of Little Nell's death
Dickens implies a certain logic in Nell's progress from child victim
to corpse: the latter condition is the most extreme version of her
living status as a desired object, who is without the capacity (or
right) to reciprocate as a desiring subject. Arguably, Dickens was
ahead of his time in his presentation of such disturbing juxtapositions: in many films of the 1980s, woman's role is similarly less of an
object of desire than an object to be annihilated. The sentimentality
of Dickens's narrative voice serves as means of encouraging our

sympathy for his stories' victims, but it also disguises some of the more brutal associations between sex, suffering and death. In the 1930s, Dickens's sentiment seemed distasteful to many, but certain aspects of cinema as a visual medium, notably its representation of women, still required some sugaring of the pill in order that the full implications of the written word should not be made explicit in the novels' translation to the screen.

NOTES

1 Sergei Eisenstein, 'Dickens, Griffith and the Film Today', in G. Mast and M. Cohen (eds), *Film Theory and Criticism* (New York, 1985), pp. 370–80.
2 Eisenstein, 'Dickens, Griffith and the Film Today', p. 371. D. W. Griffith is on record as saying that, 'the root and spring of beauty are in worthy sentiment', quoted by A. L. Zambrano, *Dickens and Film* (New York, Gordon Press, 1977).
3 Alastair Cooke in *Footnotes to the Film*, ed. Charles Davy (London, Lovat Dickson, 1938), p. 240.
4 Hugh Kingsmill, *The Sentimental Journey* (London, Adelphi: Wisehart and Co., 1934), p. 75.
5 Aldous Huxley, *Vulgarity in Literature* (London, Chatto and Windus, 1930), p. 57.
6 Huxley, *Vulgarity in Literature*, p. 54.
7 David Cecil, *Early Victorian Novelists* (London, Constable and Co., 1957, first pub. 1934), p. 51.
8 Q. D. Leavis, *Fiction and the Reading Public* (London, Chatto and Windus, 1965, first pub. 1932), p. 33.
9 Leavis, *Fiction and the Reading Public*, p. 157.
10 Leavis, *Fiction and the Reading Public*, p. 156.
11 Cecil, *Early Victorian Novelists*, p. 30.
12 Kingsmill, *The Sentimental Journey*, p. 73
13 In *Dickensian Melodrama* (Kansas, Lawrence: University of Kansas Press, 1978), p. 1, George J. Worth observes that the 'unbridled ... emotionalism of stage melodrama has tended to cheapen it ... in the minds of many sophisticated, hard-boiled, tight-lipped twentieth-century people'.
14 *Cinema Quarterly*, (Spring 1935), pp. 173–5.
15 *Daily Telegraph* (4 February 1935).
16 *Sunday Times* (3 February 1935).
17 *Sunday Times* (12 January 1936).
18 Michael Slater, *Dickens and Women* (London, J. M. Dent, 1983), p. 363.
19 Kate Flint, *Dickens* (Brighton, Harvester Wheatsheaf, 1986), p. 112.
20 *The Old Curiosity Shop*, dir. Bentley, prod. Wardour 1934 (released 1935).
21 *The Times* (4 February 1935).
22 *The Observer* (3 February 1935).
23 *The Dickensian*, 31: 234 (spring 1935), p. 137.
24 *Film Weekly*, 13: 329 (1 February 1935), pp. 6, 7.

25 *Monthly Film Bulletin*, 1: 12 (January 1935), p. 118.

26 *Picturegoer*, 4: 201 (30 March 1935), p. 24.

27 John Carey, *The Violent Effigy* (London, Faber and Faber, 1973), p. 158.

28 Adriane LaPointe, 'Little Nell Once More', *Dickens Studies Annual*, 18 (1989), p. 22.

29 Carey, *The Violent Effigy*, p. 149.

30 Slater, *Dickens and Women*, p. 338.

31 Worth, *Dickensian Melodrama*, p. 16.

32 Slater, *Dickens and Women*, p. 338.

33 Huxley, *Vulgarity in Literature*, p. 55.

34 Peter Ackroyd, *Dickens* (London, Sinclair Stevenson, 1990), p. 315.

35 Flint, *Dickens*, pp. 57 and 129.

36 Teresa de Lauretis, *Technologies of Gender* (Bloomington, Indiana University Press, 1987), p. 99.

37 Laura Mulvey, 'Visual Pleasure and Narrrative Cinema', *Screen*, 16: 3 (1975), p. 14.

38 Kingsmill, *The Sentimental Journey*, p. 82.

39 Slater, *Dickens and Women*, p. 114.

40 Carey, *The Violent Effigy*, p. 167. As an example Carey gives the relationship between Kit Nubbles and Barbara. This relationship does not appear in the film as the Garlands and Barbara have been cut.

41 See Pearson's chapter on *The Old Curiosity Shop* in Gross and Pearson (eds), *Dickens and the Twentieth Century* (London, Routledge and Kegan Paul, 1962), pp. 77–90.

42 John Kucich, 'Death Worship among the Victorians: *The Old Curiosity Shop*', *PMLA of America*, 95 (1980), pp. 58–72.

43 Molly Haskell claims that such 'agitated gestures and flutteriness can be more erotic that the explicit semaphore of the vamp, since they suggest the energy of pent-up sexuality engaged in its own suppression', *From Reverence to Rape* (Chicago, University of Chicago Press, 1987), p. 56.

44 It is worth noting that the most popular female film star for most of the 1930s was Shirley Temple.

45 Kingsmill, *The Sentimental Journey*, p. 76.

46 Michael Steig, 'Phiz's Marchioness', *Dickens Studies*, 2: 3 (September 1966), pp. 141–6.

47 Margaret Kennedy, *The Mechanized Muse* (London, G. Allen and Unwin, 1942), p. 31.

48 Kucich, 'Death Worship', p. 64.

5

'Beholding in a magic panorama': television and the illustration of *Middlemarch*

Ian MacKillop and Alison Platt

CNTVS and CNFA

If there is the 'classic novel', then there is also the 'classic novel TV serial'. By comparison with the usual term – 'classic serial' – the phrase is clumsy; but we think the words 'novel' and 'serial' must both be included to avoid the implication that the serial and the original are 'classic' in the same way. The 'classic novel TV serial', or CNTVS, as we shall call it henceforth, is a special television mode, and one that has perhaps had less attention than it should.[1] To define it provisionally, and to introduce the 1994 BBC *Middlemarch* as the subject of our discussion, we will begin by comparing the CNTVS with the classic novel film adaptation or CNFA (which can be a 'made-for-TV' film).[2]

There have been two good recent examples of CNFA. The excellence of Douglas McGrath's *Emma* (1996), and Amy Heckerling's *Clueless* (1995), derives from the fact that in each case the work is adapted from something into something: the receiving medium, so to speak, is as strong as the transmitting medium. (The fact that the transmitting medium is Jane Austen perhaps has something to do with this.) Thus McGrath's *Emma* renders a *place* and Heckerling's *Clueless* has a *language*. This may sound odd, considering that one of these Austen adaptations uses Los Angeles High School patois and in the other, Emma's Highbury blooms more gorgeously than we expect of Austen country: it looks more like the State of Georgia than the fields of Hampshire, nearer *Gone with the Wind* than an English county. Emma herself has the bounce of a particularly lively friend of Scarlett O' Hara. But that is fitting, for in the figure of Emma we must have a vital self-sufficiency which has to look foreign in the British 1990s or she would seem, for example, patronising in her jolly demeanour on Highbury high street. Gwyneth Paltrow triumphed in this. This version of *Emma* 'makes it new', and so does Heckerling's *Clueless*, an even more imaginative adaptation of the novel. This film rewrites the novel in terms of shopping mall and High School, following in the line of Heckerling's earlier *Fast Times in Ridgmount High* (1982). High School speech has nourished a genre of American film writing, through Heckerling, Richard Linklater and Hal Hartley. In *Clueless* it matches Austen style for style. It is not that Heckerling's style is 'as good as' Austen's. The point is rather that there is a matching of strong discourses.

This kind of creative adaptation, proper to the best CNFA, is impossible in the CNTVS, for several reasons.

The limitations of TV adaptation have been well rehearsed.[3] CNTVSs are of an impossible length: after first transmission a video may be published, but who will watch it? A five-hour video fits no known type of audience, except specialists. Yet, on first transmission, the CNTVS must have a wide constituency, so its language (both verbal and film) has to be easy to take. The range of possible accessibilities need not be here detailed: it is enough to say that CNTVSs (unlike CNFAs) must not be in *a* language. The CNTVS is committed to a literal respect for the original – correctly so: we do not undervalue respect for an original because we have cited two flighty *Emma*s, but there is respect and respect. The CNTVS is constrained by the *bienséances* of TV, its shifting patterns of prudery. A radio adaptation can conclude with Inspector Morse inviting Sergeant Lewis to accompany him to an afternoon show at a sex cinema, something unthinkable for middlebrow TV. (D.I. Jane Tennison may take a lead here.) Finally, CNTVSs are costume dramas which are difficult for the imaginative designer whose work is forced to lag behind innovation in theatrical costume design.

CNTVSs have, then, restrictions. They must serve their originals. A CNTVS may be replaced by a Mark II version ten years later. As a mode, CNTVS is part of a continuum of reproduction in a way that CNFA is not. The CNFA is anxious to supersede its predecessor by means not wholly dependent on technological advancement. Its need to differ (*pace* Harold Bloom) provides the impetus for risk-taking. CNTVSs do not take risks, but, nonetheless, they have in their expensive, expansive and sadly disposable way the chance to be a site of ideas and interpretation. We are very unwilling to be superior about CNTVS and are enthusiastic about the BBC *Middlemarch*. We do not want our criticisms to mask our admiration. The experience of following the serial set up for us a valuable complex of relationships in which there was interchange between the illuminating and the valuably problematic. We will start with examples of both.

A performance-medium like TV can be said to be simplistic by 'serving up' interpretation, leaving too little to the mind of the viewer, though cinematography can offer nuances of feeling and provoke consideration, for example, in the very, very slow close-up awarded to Dorothea Brooke (e.g. I: 0.16.57–0.18.10) in the BBC *Middlemarch*. At such moments we are given time to work out possibilities within the character's reaction: our mind speaks, as it were, for a narrator. We have to follow visual clues. Although things must happen very quickly, they are still meant for retention. At the beginning of the TV *Middlemarch* there is a shot of a country road on a dull day, with a coach and a flock of sheep being herded and sweeping across the verges. This is, for the sake of the whole work, as suggestive as a painting, but its brevity (31 seconds: I: 0.00.49-0.01.20) does not mean it is only of momentary interest. How long does a metaphor 'last'? This scene is an example of illumination.

An example of the valuably problematic is to be found in the visual presentation of Dorothea. In CNTVS characters may look wrong, but it must be in the right way. For example, people cannot be as pale as they would have been in 1832 because that signifies illness to us. More subtle adjustments have to be made. Some characters are there, so to speak, for inspection. But in the case of Dorothea we must not only look, but also *go along with her*. There must be no risk of our 'taking against her', being irritated by her walk, for example. She must be of our time. And for this Juliet Aubrey is perfectly cast, capturing the warm, still presence of Dorothea and the assured independence so vital in a heroine of our own time. (Is there not also an androgynous quality typical of our period?) Aubrey, as well as conveying Dorothea's 'voice of deep-souled womanhood', a voice that reminds Caleb Garth of bits of Handel's *Messiah*, [4] also believably offers 'that kind of beauty which seems to be thrown into relief by poor dress', as dictated by the novel's opening sentence.[5] Clearly George Eliot meant our initial picturing of Dorothea to be crucial to a reading of the novel. However, the main thing in transfer to TV is that the 'attitude' should be right, to use Eliot's own word when she discussed the picturing of Romola with the painter, Frederic Leighton.[6] Aubrey is not in conflict with how Eliot and her age saw Dorothea (see below), but she is still of our time. And we must have some anachronism: it is our gateway to the work. We can make allowance for a 1994 Dorothea in our reading of the CNTVS. This is valuably problematic.

'Dorothea' by Frederic Dielman from *Scenes of Characters from the Works of George Eliot, a series of illustrations by eminent artists* (London, Alexander Strachan, 1988). By permission of Bodleian Library

Pictures and history

We have introduced a general problem of CNTVs: though serving originals, and being accurate 'costume dramas', they have also to be anachronistic. This becomes a specific problem with *Middlemarch* which, unlike *Ivanhoe*, is an anti-visual novel. When Eliot wrote to Leighton about 'attitude' she meant mental attitude, the embodiment of states of mind. As D. H. Lawrence pointed out, in George Eliot the real action is on the inside. She is concerned not so much with what you see, but what you see the characters seeing. Significant visual detail in Eliot often takes the form of internalised imagery within a character's thought process. 'Language gives a fuller image, which is all the better for being vague', wrote Eliot. 'The true seeing is within; and painting stares at you with an insistent imperfection'.[7]

Only one of Eliot's novels, *Romola*, appeared in an illustrated form on its first publication, but the popular cheap edition of her works was illustrated, to her embarrassment. In 1877 she remarked (agreeing with G. H. Lewes) that the pictures were 'not queerer than those which amuse us in Scott and Miss Austin [sic], with one exception, namely, *that* where Adam is making love to Dinah, which really enrages me with its unctuousness. I would gladly pay something to be rid of it.'[8] Apart from the aesthetic and technical insufficiency of these pictures, Eliot's sense of herself as a writer was in conflict with illustration and its association with popularisation. Her distrust of mass movements, as opposed to individual, 'unhistoric' human agency, was, of course, thematised in *Middlemarch* itself. 'No exquisite book,' she wrote to Harriet Beecher Stowe on 8 May 1869, 'tells properly and directly on a multitude.'[9]

Early editions of *Middlemarch* are notable for their lack of illustration, save for the new edition of 1874 which was published with a title-page engraving of a poorly defined Dorothea (and Monk) before a landscape fringed by an equally ill-defined 'Coventry'. Such illustrations as there were in the Eliot *œuvre* were in the style of the 1860s, that of single characters, or pairs, caught in a dramatic moment, as used to illustrate Gaskell and Trollope. These naturalistic illustrations differ, of course, from the Dickens illustrations which remain familiar, those giving the big event as favoured by 'Phiz'. The 1860s style, now forgotten, well suits the intimacy of Eliot's fiction whose important scenes may involve only one or two characters: Maggie and Philip in the Red Deeps, Hetty Sorrel contemplating suicide beside the pool, Dorothea's night of anguish preceding her early-morning wake-up call to a new condition.

Beginnings

One of the greatest differences between the manner of the BBC *Middlemarch* and that of the novel is that on the screen the intimate style does not dominate. Understandably, perhaps, its illustrative mode tends towards the style of the Dickens illustrations. The reader of the novel might have been surprised to see on the screen a town so vastly populated. The opening scenes show the building of the new railway ('The future', Lydgate ominously remarks). The main street teems with market traders, carriages, and townsfolk milling about. We are on Planet Past where towns are always 'bustling'. This is in stark contrast to the beginning of the novel itself which, like the title-page vignette of the 1874 edition, places 'Miss Brooke' in the foreground. The BBC *Middlemarch* begins with the town and works in the key characters through a process of layering. It prefers to show the total community: each episode has a focus on a big event, whereas in the novel one follows individual characters and sees the events through their eyes.

We do not want to overstate this point: the proportion of big event scenes, public scenes, is relatively small when set against the number of private exchanges in the six hour traffic of this CNTVS. However, we think the trend in meaning is towards 'Society (= History) and Individual'. It looks like an educational 'module' with those words in the title. Eliot, on the other hand, does not separate these entities. The BBC *Middlemarch* does not give the priority implied by Eliot's 'Book I: Miss Brooke', so the 'history–individual' parity is encouraged. It also ignores Eliot's one-and-a-half page 'Prelude' and so accentuates the collectivist bias. This is a serious omission because the 'Prelude' guides our subsequent reading, setting the grave, solemn tone which ensures that we do not feel somehow cheated by the final fate of the leading characters. The sense of wastage at the end of the novel does not take the reader by surprise. Without the 'Prelude' (or any sense of it) in which Dorothea is indirectly positioned as a latter-day St Teresa the notion of the ardent individual unsupported by a 'coherent social faith' is lost and the ending is in danger of seeming an unprepared anti-climax.

The novel's gravity is one element which makes it intellectually satisfying. Meaning is built on the foundation of knowledge: this is what gives the novel its tragic dimension, its 'Greekness'. In the serial, as in many fictions without narrators, knowledge is successively and therefore temptingly revealed to the reader. Gravity is replaced by suspense. In the serial we suspect something will become of Lydgate; in the novel we *know* it, and build on this knowledge.

Endings

Middlemarch is a novel conceived very much in terms of its ending, an ending which, like its 'Prelude', justifies the sad and faintly ironic tone of the book. On the screen one receives a sense of deadlines needing to be met, of a desire to wind the production up as quickly and painlessly as possible, but with a novel in which so many characters are actively seeking keys to life (whether to all mythology or all histology) it is important to take care, and avoid haste, in showing why such grand schemes ultimately fail, so more foundation is necessary. In spite of the final voice-over, in which we learn about the fate of the key characters, we do not get the impression given by the novel (Eliot brings the surviving characters close to her own present) of what it's like thirty or so years later: the viewer is left with the sense that nothing comes out of Middlemarch except a Radical MP and a distinguished farmer. Yet Lydgate leaves behind 'a treatise on Gout' (so far-removed from his search for the primitive tissue), Mary Garth writes a book of children's stories taken from Plutarch. Rosamond flourishes as the wife of an elderly doctor, making 'a very pretty show' wherever she goes. Dorothea disappears within Ladislaw's career, giving 'wifely help' in her husband's struggle for progress. There is a kind of ironic edge to the end of the novel that the screen does not capture. More importantly it does not give the sense that the novel has of admiring the anonymous life, the life that can contribute more to the growing good of the world than any Radical MP can hope to: the life that history cannot record but 'the one bright book of life' can. (Perhaps an inability to sympathise with the anonymous life is another characteristic of the late 1980s and early 1990s.) The penultimate scene in which Ladislaw stalks across the well-kept BBC lawn to embrace Dorothea, significantly dead-heading flowers, offers the kind of satisfaction one derives from seeing the guy get the girl after all, and we are at least thankful, after the BBC *Pride and Prejudice*, that there is no lake in the grounds of Lowick as at Pemberley. We were right, it seems, to imagine that what we were enjoying was primarily 'a love story' though this means parting with the earlier emphasis on the collective.

The novel offers a completely different perspective on the whole scene for it emphasises the accidental nature of their coming together. A storm worthy of Hammer horror rages, so that Ladislaw can do what he does best – fail to leave. When he does finally manage a 'Good-bye' Dorothea bursts into passionate sobs, they embrace again and this time they are not to be parted. The whole scene is a piece of dramatic brilliance. However, the resolution by Andrew Davies is rather slick and sedate. In the novel Ladislaw and Dorothea only just make it. Her release from paralysis, her sobbing admission that she hates her wealth, might have been kept in check until after Ladislaw's departure. The BBC offers a muffled cry where there could have been a roar.

That omniscient author

The 'realist novel' appears to be eminently suitable for adaptation for the screen. But this is an illusion: the material may be suitable, but its prose – its identity – is not. (Poetry is a better survivor.) The most memorable lines in the novel *Middlemarch* come in by means of authorial comment. Andrew Davies, voicing a common criticism, finds such direct address to the reader irritating: 'One thing I've always hated about George Eliot,' he says, 'is the way she'll write a brilliantly dramatic and moving scene and then spend the next few pages pointing out all the subtleties, just in case we missed them.'[10] A committed George Eliot reader would think differently: the authorially discovered subtleties usually come as revelations rather than unnecessary reiterations.[11] But his irritation as a screenwriter is understandable because the options open to him when faced with a novel which is so strenuously narrated are limited. Voice-over inevitably draws attention to the 'literariness' of the material. (Actual quotation of letterpress on the screen belongs to avant-garde TV and travel programmes.) Another possible method is that of giving the narratorial voice to chosen characters. Hence in Davies's CNTVS of *Pride and Prejudice* the famous opening sentence is adjusted and popped into the mouth of Elizabeth Bennet. 'For a single man in possession of a good fortune must be in want of a wife,' she asserts waggishly. Davies knows that if Lizzie lets on that such is a 'truth universally acknowledged', she is at risk of sounding very pompous (rather like Mary, her younger and Johnsonian sister, one of whose functions in the novel is to give the incompetent version of Austen's gift for apophthegm.). There are some sentences, it seems, that only narrators *can* utter. In *Middlemarch* it is down to Dorothea Brooke to explain the 'roar on the other side of silence', arguably the novel's most quotable passage. On the screen, however, Dorothea informs Lydgate:

> I sometimes wake very early, go out alone and imagine I can hear the cries of all the scurrying creatures in the grass. There is so much suffering in the world. I think of it as a kind of muffled cry on the other side of silence – if our senses were sharp enough to apprehend it all I think the pain of it would destroy us. I think we should be glad that we are not too sensitive and work in any small way we can to help our fellow creatures.[12]

This speech, tactfully delayed to the final episode, is a mixture of words Dorothea might say to Ladislaw and George Eliot's own voice. In the novel the lines are phrased quite differently and are situated early on as a meditation upon Dorothea's unhappy honeymoon in Rome:

> If we had a keen vision and feeling of all ordinary human life, it would be like hearing the grass grow and the squirrel's heart beat, and we should die of that roar which lies on the other side of silence. As it is, the quickest of us walk about well wadded with stupidity.[13]

That she is able to imagine hearing this 'roar' (albeit as a 'muffled cry') is what separates Dorothea off from the rest of the town. Yet on the screen it is also what makes her sound slightly portentous. Dorothea, although 'ardent, theoretic, and intellectually consequent' is not an intellectual and in her conversations with Ladislaw she resists the assumption that she might be, saying of her belief-system that '*It is my life.* I have found it out, and cannot part with it'.[14] Yet conversing with Lydgate, offering him what has on the screen the feel of a set speech, Dorothea is made *more articulate* than the reader of the novel might expect. 'She speaks in such plain words, and a voice like music,' says Caleb Garth to his wife.[15]

Introducing the narratorial voice into that of a character inevitably alters that character. The narrator's sophisticated presentation of a character's point of view – often a point of view the character is incapable of articulating at that particular point – must be distinguished from the character's expressed voice. The insertion of narratorial speech can also give a wrong impression of the novel. *Middlemarch* is a novel, on the whole, of rather terse speech. Inserted narration makes it sound unduly bookish. In this exchange the silence of Lydgate and the abruptness with which the scene shifts leaves the speech still hanging in the air – proving that there really can be no response on the part of a character to the words of the 'narrator' and specifically not in a realist text. In fact, there is something even comic in the matter-of-factness with which certain of the more weighty scenes end on the screen, as if the characters cannot quite cope with the moral earnestness of Eliot's words.

This kind of treatment may be endemic to adaptation in which narratorial commentary infiltrates spoken language. On these occasions the dialogue appears embarrassed by itself. (We might call this type of throat-clearing dialogue the 'Ahem Phenomenon'.) When Lydgate, voicing the narrator, mentions the terror that the individual suffers in facing the certainty of his own death, Dorothea responds with a pragmatism which – in spite of her intense, serious facial expression – lies dangerously close to indifference: 'Yes. I'm sure you're right. This is a fine place Dr. Lydgate.'[16] This time it is Lydgate's words which fall flat and one senses that any subsequent response has to be a platitude. The problem is, perhaps, largely a temporal one. On the screen there is little time to move through the necessary phases that belong to 'conversation'. Momentarily Dorothea sounds here like her sister, the cheerful Celia, who knows the value of not dwelling too long on awkward subjects.

Style

So this CNTVS cannot well handle the moral weight of Eliot's words, and it is not only weight from which it shies away. There are other vitalities for which it cannot find a verbal or cinematographic equivalent. One misses many Eliot voices: the eloquence in Rome, the exquisite toughness ('The troublesome ones in a family are usually either the wits or the idiots.') To find equivalence to her style cannot be done without having some style. We suggested that

CNTVS has to be conservative when it comes to cinematic innovation, and is unable to use some techniques that could help to convey the narratorial voice. The BBC *Middlemarch* is not unaware of cinematic style: it alludes to Stanley Kubrick (*Barry Lyndon*) and to Ingmar Bergman (*Fanny and Alexander*). It is, perhaps, from Greenaway's *The Draughtsman's Contract* that this CNTVS borrows a binding motif, that of the 'document'. *Middlemarch* is a world of fallen Titans, like that of Keats's *Hyperion*. Its idealists strive for the real seeing of Moneta, struggling through and against half-a-dozen kinds of document or scribal charters. This *Middlemarch* flickers through Lydgate's anatomical pastels, the calligraphic notebooks of Casaubon, and his will and codicil, the *Pioneer* proof-sheets, even the hustings-effigy, 'Brooke of Tipton'. (Unfortunately, Casaubon's posthumous message is labelled *Instructions to Mrs. Casaubon for 'The Key to all Mythologies'*, not *Synoptical Tabulation for the Use of Mrs. Casaubon*.) We see a dusky portrait of one of Sir James's ancestors, a Crusader, which is in the same category. Interestingly, it is only in a 'document' that we see a rare smiling face, the tiny painting of Casaubon's aunt.[17]

Subtle equivalence to effects in the novel is sometimes achieved. Farebrother's touching farewell to Mary Garth is framed by Eliot with a concluding sentence: 'In three minutes the Vicar was on horseback again, having gone magnanimously through a duty much harder than the renunciation of whist, or even than the writing of penitential meditation.'[18] The BBC *Middlemarch* expresses Eliot's lack of sentiment by a prompt cut to a piano jig at the hands of Rosamond.[19] On the other side of the coin, are moments of clumsiness: Mrs Cadwallader pronounces on madness mostly out of the frame, the same cinematographic track down Middlemarch high street is put to regular service, and a crane appears only to have been rented for the last day's shooting. 'Dutch interiors' are emulated, in lighting, and beautifully, but not set-dressing: there are few *things*, decorative or symbolic. Except for these documents, we do not learn much about what people handled in 1832, though Brooke convincingly wipes his mouth on a table cloth. But the costumes (by Anushka Nieradzik) are stylishly conceived and knowledgeable. The Vincys appear as they do to Mrs Cadwallader, a 'set of jugs'. Lydgate has 'every requisite of perfect dress', of careful colourings, compared to the uniform-like upper-class garb of Sir James and Brooke. There is an extraordinary moment in which we see Mrs Bulstrode in her shift, taking her jewels from her bare shoulders.[20]

There are, therefore, attempts to get to the style of *Middlemarch*, but there is also awkwardness.

Characterisation

We think the BBC missed the point about Ladislaw. He is after all a dilettante, a figure whose point of view is relative to the particular moment of his development. He grows up during the course of the novel. On the screen, however, he dominates: he is fully formed, glowing and glowering.

In the CNTVS Ladislaw loses the playfulness he shows in the novel where he is seen, for instance, as a Pied Piper. He has no troop of 'droll children' to take nutting or for Punch-and-Judy shows, and he never lolls on a sofa. He sings only in Italian and the ditty he improvises walking to church, during which he resembled 'an incarnation of the spring', is omitted. 'You know Ladislaw's look,' remarks Lydgate, 'a sort of Daphnis'. There is no 'sunshiny laughter'.[21] Yet it is in his uninhibitedness that Eliot represents Ladislaw as a force of nature, and as such Dorothea's fascination for him has the greater force and innocence. If there is not much more to Ladislaw than the drop-dead-gorgeousness of his appearance, he becomes a sanctimonious adventurer, so fulfilling the suspicions of Dorothea's friends. Rufus Sewell's Ladislaw has a Chopin look, but there are no smiles at or from him. When he informs Dorothea that 'the best piety is to enjoy [life] – when you can', we see little evidence that he does so himself.[22] The same is true of Dorothea. In the novel she can make fun of herself, of her 'naughtiness' and 'great outbursts', but self-mockery seemed hard to handle in the presentation of women in 1994. There is no problem with her sister, not because Sloanes (such is Celia) are inherently funny, but because they are able to send themselves up.

The BBC has a soft spot for a constitutional rebel (the later Byron), and it is perhaps unfortunate that it is from this point of view that we see Dorothea. It would have been better – is it manageable? – for Ladislaw to have been seen from hers. George Eliot is often accused of favouring Ladislaw, but in the novel the language used of him is often sharply ironic. This does not translate to the screen: in fact, he is vividly endorsed throughout the BBC *Middlemarch*, and so, uncriticised, he is very much at the centre of the production. We see less clearly what Dorothea is able to do *for* him, other than make him less solemn. This reverses the role she has in the novel. Sewell, while displaying excellent curls (signalling the new generation), offers us a Ladislaw caught out by a sudden change of wind at about the time he first encounters Dorothea. Hence the 'pouting air of discontent' becomes his only expression. Eliot's Ladislaw with his 'grey eyes and bushy light brown curls' has a good deal of amiability, which, along with his shiftlessness, makes him in some respects and at some times rather like Brooke, the person he so much despises. On the screen Robert Hardy's nodding, grimacing, 'y' knowing' Brooke provides much of the light relief in an otherwise austere production, but because he seems so idiotic and is so often to be seen with Ladislaw, his 'protégé' (as he calls him), Ladislaw acquires an air of gravity and political acumen by contrast.

It is a pity that the BBC *Middlemarch* gives Ladislaw so much maturity, because it is one of Eliot's ideas that Ladislaw can and should develop, unlike Brooke who remains a late eighteenth-century dilettante with a fear of 'going too far into things' which always lead him nowhere. Ladislaw is too conveniently made into the agent of progress, the young vibrant spirit who has his finger on the pulse of his expanding age, offering words of solace to the disgruntled masses, words not dissimilar, presumably, from those that he will (in the novel's afterlife) speak in the House of Commons:

> Fellow citizens of Middlemarch, you know and I know that a great change is sweeping this country and not before time. [Crowd noise: 'Aye!, Aye!' etc.] Now as never before we have the chance to free ourselves from the crushing yoke of the past, aye, and not by bloody revolution, or by civil war, but peacefully, by humane reform. Is that not good news?[23]

In the novel Ladislaw's interest in politics is cursory; it is on a par with his enjoyment in sketching or composing verses. It is Dorothea who, albeit 'unhistorically', is the real agent of change, who, in the words of the 'Finale', ensures that things 'are not so ill with you and me as they might have been'.[24] Interestingly these are the very words that are omitted from the screen's voice-over. Instead the cosiness of the particular vision is subsumed by the generality of 'the growing good of the world'.

If the structure of the relationship between Dorothea and Ladislaw seems incorrect in the CNTVS, the texture, the play of connection between them, is good. The actors capture the gravity of Ladislaw and Dorothea's conversations. There is no teasing, no flirtation, just a growing mutual respect and desire to pour out the soul. 'My life is very simple,' she tells Ladislaw, 'I have no longings'.[25] She cannot say such things to Casaubon: her consciousness lies outside his parenthetical reasoning. One of the key features of the conversations that Dorothea holds with Ladislaw in the novel is their urgency. Always there is the threat of interruption and so every word has to count. It is a shame, therefore, that these scenes are so short and so abruptly rounded off on the screen. When Ladislaw, brimful of Platonic ideals, says to Dorothea, 'My religion is to love what is good and beautiful when I see it and I'm a rebel. I do not feel bound to submit as you do to what I do not like', Dorothea replies 'How long my uncle is, I must go and look for him'.[26] Then she leaves. The implication, one supposes, is that Dorothea wishes to escape from the notion that his words point to, namely that she is trapped in an unhappy marriage. This places Ladislaw in a dominant position: we see Dorothea through his eyes. The gist of the relationship is altered. Ladislaw does indeed *lurk*, shaman-like, watching, waiting, knowing and frowning.

George Eliot mistrusted herself in writing from the male viewpoint. This is one reason why Ladislaw is so often seen through Dorothea's eyes in the novel. But it is more than this. Dorothea is the character who is able to save situations by explaining failure in human terms, doing in her life what Eliot does in the novel. She explains Casaubon first to herself and then to Ladislaw, she restores to Lydgate some belief in his former self and returns his basil plant, Rosamond, to him. She is the reason why Ladislaw stays still long enough actually to achieve in the end a profession. Seeing Dorothea on the screen through Ladislaw's eyes feels wrong. He is right to criticise her (no one else dares to do this) and to encourage her to 'take more delight in the world', but one cannot help believing that this is simply a part of his desire for there to be less distance between them.

As for Dorothea, we want to stress that Juliet Aubrey is completely excellent in her own handling of the role, and in her collaboration with director and designer. It was a very good cluster of production conceptions that led to her being chosen.[27] She *is* of the early 1990s, but that is necessary, our gateway. That said, there are large discrepancies between the CNTVS Dorothea and Eliot's. In the novel Dorothea is a physical force, with 'powerful, feminine, maternal hands'; yet she has not grown out of being the girl who showered kisses on the pate of her bald doll. In the crucial episode before Casaubon's seizure, the film drains her, whereas in the novel she is energised.[28] On the screen she is seen copying, comforted in her labours by her maid, Tantripp. She goes and quarrels with Casaubon, then retires in exhausted dejection. In the novel a Blake-like vitality is engendered when she returns to her desk: she writes and understands better. 'In her indignation there was a sense of superiority'.[29] Then Casaubon's heart fails: Dorothea rises as he falls. The CNTVS does not allow Dorothea (or Ladislaw) to be *formidable*.

Likewise, Andrew Davies does not choose to inform us about Lydgate's past dalliance with the murdering Laure, so we do not have a knowledge of the 'spots of commonness' that predicate his failure. We see him in softer or more 'victimistic' terms (perhaps typical of the early 1990s) as one brought down by Middlemarch petty-mindedness and an extravagant wife. The BBC Lydgate is simply too likeable. He has none of that aristocratic *hauteur*, that careless grace possessed by Eliot's character. In turn we see a Rosamond not quite so steeped in low cunning, not quite so desperate to leave the provincial life of which she is very much a part. Simon Jenkins in his piece called 'Messing about with George' objects strongly to the proposal scene between Lydgate and Rosamond on the grounds that it reduces the CNTVS to soap opera, and poor soap opera at that. He writes:

> Lydgate speaks the words and then charges across the room at the sight of Rosamond's tears. To swelling background music she sobs, 'I'm so unhappy if you do not care about me.' He seizes her in his arms and they subject each other to instant, jaw-crushing mouth-to-mouth resuscitation. *Middlemarch* gets a sudden dose of *Neighbours*.[30]

Jenkins travesties the scene, which, to the triumph of the actors and director, depicts untold fluctuations in thought and feeling in the space of just over a minute.[31] There is nothing 'instant' about these kisses, and kiss*es* they are. The range of touches and caresses shown is detailed and observant: within a tiny span we learn much about the sexual natures of Lydgate and Rosamond. The rendering shows unusual powers of observation of sexual behaviour. Credit must be given to the director for the quality of this scene: Anthony Page has a distinguished history in the direction of passionate drama, going back to his work (*Inadmissable Evidence, A Patriot for Me*) at the Royal Court Theatre in the 1960s. And the scene's sexuality has a larger dimension: Lydgate *is* a doctor with a compulsive commitment to the relief of pain, in this case Rosamond's. So we think Jenkins is wrong to make fun of the scene. It is packed with material and is right because Lydgate's crime is partly one of passion. But in the whole treatment of him there is a good deal missing. It is the aristocratic disdain in him which demands only the best furniture, the finest silverware and a sweet, docile, graceful wife, that characterises him in the novel. Lydgate, as early critics first thought, was most certainly not based on G. H. Lewes whose admiration and respect for Eliot's intellect is widely known. Altogether, the screen Lydgate is not quite *grand* enough which prevents us from seeing him as anything other than a victim of provincial society rather than as a victim of self.

This 'flattening' in the handling of the central protagonists spreads elsewhere. Eliot does say of Casaubon that 'for my part I am very sorry for him,' an avowal which does not defuse the savagery of her rendering of this lost soul.[32] Patrick Malahide's delicate frame and narrow head rhyme with the physical slenderness of Sewell's Ladislaw. He is the sadder for seeming less old than his years. Davies gives the root of Casaubon's marital loneliness, that is, his equation of Dorothea's view of the *parerga* with that of other scholars. He is seen in a library haunted by her urgings, covertly watching his learned neighbours, physically solid, out of Mantegna.[33] Musically (Christopher Gunning and Stanley Myers), the Casaubon motif on woodwind is admirable.

Blandness damages the CNTVS elsewhere. The Lydgate of Douglas Hodge is never really 'cold'. There is no *tic-douloureux*, though he does attempt the 'excited effort' and 'talking widely for the sake of resisting any personal bearing' of Lydgate, but this is in a concocted scene with Farebrother, in which he speaks the language of the 1980s: 'I feel as if I have been losing control of life' and 'It's only money, after all.'[34]

There is some erosion of distinctiveness in the heights and depths of behaviour. As Featherstone, Michael Hordern's familiar whinneying is a long way from Eliot's 'aged hyena'. Mary Garth (Rachel Power) displays only shock at his deathbed tyranny. She does not say 'I will not let the close of your life soil the beginning

of mine.'[35] Some elevated language has to be omitted, to avoid
tiring a mass audience, but Mary's eloquent resolution at this
moment is indispensable, indeed, *is* Mary. As in the case of
Dorothea, the film prefers the female to be more of a victim than in
the Victorian original. No wonder Farebrother does not recommend directness and honesty to Mary as 'noble'. He only says they
are 'kind'. And more than her 'nobility', Mary's buoyancy ('merri-
ment within') is missing. Throughout the BBC *Middlemarch* there is
a shortage of 'sweet delight'. (Blushing seems finally to have
departed from the visual arts.) But our complaints must be halted by
reference to the Reverend Camden Farebrother who is played with
composed diffidence by Simon Chandler, his neat, controlled
gestures (handling a straw hat or loading Mary's basket) beautifully
delineating the third fount of intelligence in *Middlemarch*.
Farebrother is given a wonderful Orwellianly plain face and precise
animation, fully in keeping with what Lydgate says of him, that he
is 'original, simple, clear'.[36] Chandler also gives Farebrother the
right air of unfulfilled potential. The viewer, like Lydgate, senses
that he 'ought to have done more than he has done.'[37]

The 'sacrifice' of Dorothea?

We began by differentiating the classic novel TV series from the
classic novel film adaptation; a simple distinction, but not, we think,
one without moment. We would like to end by restating the point,
bluntly. The CNFA is *a work*, accomplished under the same conditions as many other works of art. It is an adaptation, but what, we
wonder, isn't? CNTVS is different: each one is complementary to
the work, each a performance, a supplement, an edition. The BBC
Middlemarch is an honourable edition for TV.

We will say at the end of this essay something about how such
an 'edition' can be used, but would like at this stage to comment on
one of the types of pleasurable instruction that adaptations give.
Anyone who teaches literature will have noticed that there is such a
thing as a common experience of a literary work – an all-too-
common experience, it seems. If you take fifty student essays about,
say, *Middlemarch* we guess that in them a high proportion of the
references (quoted material, allusions) to the novel will be the same.
The novel 'becomes' 80 citations out of (let's say) a potential 500
citations. This last figure is, of course, arbitrary: a true number

would depend on how an analyst breaks down the novel into citable units. But the general point seems to us true: a large, complicated fiction ends up as a packet of familiar allusions. Great tracts of prose remain, it seems, dormant, ignored because of the pedagogies and anxieties which drive student readers.[38] An edition like the BBC *Middlemarch* can bring to life some of the beauties that may have been sleeping within the novel. For example, when we saw Brooke on the screen doing his estate business and saw how his tenants reacted to him, we realised how poorly he keeps his charge, something which had not lodged in us when reading the novel. An edition as good, in its way, as the BBC *Middlemarch* can *restore* a work, as a painting can be restored by cleaning.

The BBC *Middlemarch* does, though, have a hairline crack – or a peculiarity that is very much of the early 1990s. Both the novel and the CNTVS obviously end with Dorothea's commitment to private life in the service of her partner-to-be, Ladislaw. This conclusion has caused concern, even from the time of publication and certainly in the early 1990s, among those who want something better for Dorothea. It was a worry for Rosemary Ashton in her Introduction to the 1994 Penguin edition of *Middlemarch*. She finds 'ambivalence'. She notes that Eliot can be scathing about male domination, but that nonetheless the novelist 'allows' her heroine to become merely a help-meet partner, one who will contribute only indirectly to 'the growing good of the world'. It is Ladislaw who will enjoy a *career*, while Dorothea must live 'a hidden life'.[39] Ashton says that to describe Dorothea's future Eliot does at least use 'a positive group of words' ('incalculably diffusive', 'growing good', 'faithfully') which to some degree counteract those 'melancholy' ones used about Dorothea's ultimate fate. But in spite of them Ashton still finds the conclusion of the novel anomalous, coming from a progressive novelist who is, broadly speaking, a melioristic feminist. But, then, Ashton admits, the novel is complex: Eliot is capable of seeing many sides of a question. We do not doubt this, but we do not see anything anomalous in Eliot's account of the destiny of Dorothea. Indeed, we think that to find anomaly is to miss some of the points of the novel whose aim is to evaluate the *un*-historic act and to validate the individual life:

> Full many a flower is born to blush unseen,
> And waste its sweetness on the desert air.

Thomas Gray was, in his 'Elegy written in a Country Church-yard', truly 'melancholy' about those lost to society. The message of *Middlemarch* is different: it is about how society is made by its unhistoric actors. It is a book about contributions to a culture, a whole society not about goodness in politics. There is no betrayal of feminism in Dorothea's destiny. It is not a 'plight'.

The BBC *Middlemarch* seems to have been slightly disappointed by the novel, responding to the same elements in it which Ashton calls 'anomalous'. One imagines that Andrew Davies was restless because he could not find enough politics. Obviously there was no way of altering Eliot's view of Dorothea's future. So the CNTVS turned to Ladislaw whom it politicised and dignified. He became more dominant, as we have suggested, and a political figure of some moment. If we cannot have Dorothea succeed, at least, says the serial, we can put into Parliament the nearest thing in *Middlemarch* to a New Man. Interestingly, this manoeuvre does not make Dorothea less of a feminist success than she is in the novel, which, after all, only gives her the role of help-meet to a skittish young man, and not to the potential parliamentary dynamo of the serial which would put her, one imagines, really in the shade. Because the TV Ladislaw is so attractive, so Byronic, he is almost as good as a woman and therefore his potential political success, in the CNTVS, virtually amounts to a win for feminism. (This adaptation of *Middlemarch* belongs to the period when the word 'sexy' began to mean 'viable': Ladislaw is 1990s 'sexy'.)

We said there is this hairline crack in the BBC *Middlemarch*: the elevation of Ladislaw and the transformation of the book into what is mainly a social drama. Perhaps this is not so bad a flaw. The serial is of its time and it will become increasingly clear how much it is so. This is the fate of CNTVS. The *Zeitgeist* told Andrew Davies – he would scoff at the imputation – that somebody had to succeed politically in this adaptation and Ladislaw was near enough a girl, a rather old-fashioned girl, to suit the occasion. It is possible that Davies was driven by his medium, the genre of CNTVS itself, into making Ladislaw a figure of political moment, the voice of his age (and, unwittingly, *our* age). He becomes the forerunner to the growing good of the world (our world) because 'the growing good', that is, progress, is only seen in political terms. What else, after, all, could it be? CNTVS requires crowds ('bustling'), crowds mean society and society needs social-*ists*. So we have New Ladislaw – even New

Labour? Perhaps that is what was happening at Television Centre when the BBC *Middlemarch* was in preparation in the months leading up to Christmas 1993.

What of the BBC *Middlemarch* in the long term? The effect of CNTVS is like the effect of news: sales of the novel rise and it momentarily enters a place in the national consciousness. Then it becomes like one of yesterday's discoveries in some models of the history of science: it survives only in its absorption into current practice. *Brideshead Revisited*, by its very lavishness and slowness, set standards of attentiveness to the detail of novels that made emulation expensive, well-nigh impossible. By taking so impressively serious a work as *Middlemarch* and *making its difficulties apparent* (at least in part) the BBC has set a new industry standard, making the format available again and restoring the possibility that television may interpret texts more dense, and more complex than *Poldark* and its kind.

NOTES

1 The acronyms CNTVS and CNFA are used throughout this essay in the singular, plural and abstract, depending on whether what is being referred to is an individual instance of the mode, or the mode itself.

2 The BBC *Middlemarch* was screened from 12 January to 16 February 1994, produced by Louis Marks, written by Andrew Davies and directed by Anthony Page. Texts referred to throughout this chapter are George Eliot, *Middlemarch*, 1871–72, ed. Rosemary Ashton (Harmondsworth, Penguin, 1994) and the BBC's two-cassette video *Middlemarch* (London, BBCV 5253, 1994). Our references are to 'volume' (i.e. cassette tape) -hour-minute-second, starting at the BBC logo. Our title is taken from the novel, pp. 782–3: 'It seemed to him [Ladislaw] as if he were beholding in a magic panorama a future where he himself was sliding into that pleasureless yielding to the small solicitations of circumstance, which is a commoner history of perdition than any single momentous bargain.' Part of this essay appeared in a different form in *The George Eliot Review*, 25 (1994) and is used with the Editor's permission. We recommend *Screening Middlemarch: Nineteenth Century Novel to Nineties Television* (London, British Film Institute/BBC Education, 1994). We are appreciative of the comments of Roger Gard and Brian Nellist on earlier drafts of this essay.

3 For example, by Jonathan Miller in *Subsequent Performances* (London, Faber and Faber, 1986), and by Catherine Bennett in 'Hype and Heritage' (*The Guardian*, 22 September 1995).

4 Eliot, *Middlemarch*, p. 593.

5 Eliot, *Middlemarch*, p. 7.

6 'The exigences of your art must forbid perfect correspondence between the text and the illustration; and I came to the conclusion that it was these

exigences which had determined you as to the position of Bardo's head and the fall of Romola's hair. You have given her attitude transcendently well, and the attitude is more important than the mere head-dress.' '?5 June' (sic) 1862, *Selections from George Eliot's Letters*, ed. Gordon S. Haight (New Haven and London, Yale University Press, 1985), p. 274.

7 Eliot, *Middlemarch*, p. 191.

8 Gordon S. Haight (ed.), *The George Eliot Letters*, 9 vols (New Haven and London, Yale University Press, 1954–78), vol. 6, p. 335.

9 J. W. Cross (ed.), *George Eliot's Life as Related in Her Letters and Journals*, 2 vols (Edinburgh, William Blackwood and Sons, 1902), vol. 2, pp. 243–4.

10 *Screening Middlemarch*, p. 40.

11 Eliot herself was wary of the adapter. To W. L. Bicknell, concerning his desire to adapt *Romola* for the stage, she wrote: 'You will no doubt on reflection appreciate as well as imagine the reasons that must prevent a writer who cares much about his writings from willingly allowing them to be modified and in any way "adapted" by another mind than his own. And with regard to *Romola*, the state of our stage would make me shudder at the prospect of its characters being represented there', 9 October 1879, Haight (ed.), *Letters*, vol. 9, p. 275.

12 BBCV, *Middlemarch*, II: 2.28.22.

13 Eliot, *Middlemarch*, p. 194.

14 Eliot, *Middlemarch*, p. 392, our italics.

15 Eliot, *Middlemarch*, p. 552.

16 BBCV, *Middlemarch*, II: 2.00.14.

17 BBCV, *Middlemarch*, I: 0.56.03.

18 Eliot, *Middlemarch*, p. 518.

19 BBCV, *Middlemarch*, II: 1.05.49.

20 BBCV, *Middlemarch*, II: 2.22.59.

21 Eliot, *Middlemarch*, pp. 190, 496.

22 Eliot, *Middlemarch*, p. 219.

23 BBCV, *Middlemarch*, II: 0.29.30.

24 Eliot, *Middlemarch*, p. 838.

25 BBCV, *Middlemarch*, I: 2.45.20.

26 BBCV, *Middlemarch*, II: 2.45.40.

27 Juliet Aubrey must have been cast as Dorothea partly because she was 'an unknown'. The point about an unknown actor is that he or she has no intertextual presence. The corollary of this should be remembered: that with 'knowns' we bring our knowledge of their past roles to the present one. This knowledge is little used in commentary on TV performances as if it somehow vaguely gives unfair advantage to the critic who has seen a lot of TV – surely a nonsense, because it has to be noted, for example, that Patrick Malahide's Casaubon significantly succeeds his fractious police inspector in *Minder* and complements his excellent Kenneth Halliwell (Joe Orton's partner) in Simon Moss's play, *Cock Ups*. We explore this subject in a forthcoming paper, 'Television Drama and the Intertextuality of Performance'.

28 BBCV, *Middlemarch*, I:1.49.46–1.54.00.

29 Eliot, *Middlemarch*, p. 283.

30 Simon Jenkins, *Against the Grain: Writings of a Sceptical Optimist* (London, John Murray, 1994), p. 188.

31 BBCV, *Middlemarch*, I: 2.12.34–2.14.56.

32 Eliot, *Middlemarch*, p. 280.

33 BBCV, *Middlemarch*, I: 1.25.33.

34 BBCV, *Middlemarch*, II:1.24–36.

35 Eliot, *Middlemarch*, p. 316.

36 Eliot, *Middlemarch*, p. 494.

37 Eliot, *Middlemarch*, p. 494.

38 It would be interesting to have a computer-generated breakdown of a novel into units and then analysis of frequency of citations in a sample of student essays. J. F. Burrows's *Computation into Criticism: A Study of Jane Austen's Novels and an Experiment in Method* (Oxford, Oxford University Press, 1987) does electronic analysis of fictional prose, but not of reader's prose.

39 Quoted by Ashton in Eliot, *Middlemarch*, p. xviii.

6

Hardy, history and hokum

Keith Selby

It was David Lodge, in an early article on *The Return of the Native* (1878), who first called Hardy a 'cinematic' novelist – by which he meant not that Hardy was influenced by film (even Hardy's last novel, *Jude the Obscure* (1896), was published well before film had properly evolved as a narrative medium), but rather that he emulated it. Lodge writes:

> Hardy uses verbal description as a film director uses the lens of his camera – to select, highlight, distort, and enhance, creating a visualised world that is both recognisably 'real' and yet more vivid, intense and dramatically charged than our ordinary perception of the real world.[1]

The view that Hardy's art is commonly 'visual' has now become generally accepted.

However, to concentrate on that art at the level of narrative would be to tell only part of the story. Despite the fact that Hardy classified both the novels I will be focusing on here – *Far from the Madding Crowd* (1874), and *Tess of the d'Urbervilles* (1891) – as 'novels of character and environment',[2] the manner in which these two novels present their narratives shows a difference in Hardy's conception of his fictional rural world. This difference is most noticeable in his depiction of the rustics, and illustrates a difference in Hardy's attitude towards his audience and subject-matter. While the depiction of rural characters in the early *Far from the Madding Crowd* has these characters as an innocent chorus to the main action, by the time of *Tess of the d'Urbervilles* these rural characters have taken on a credibility which places them far beyond the smock-frocked Hodges of the earlier novel. When, in *Far from the Madding Crowd*, Bathsheba inherits the farm, things go on in the rural world pretty much as before; but when Tess's father dies and the life-holding on the cottage is lost, the family is homeless. Tess turns to Alec, and the fatal consequences of the straightforwardly social requirement for money and shelter leads to the novel's tragic dénouement. There is thus in *Tess* a far greater particularity about the pressures of the social world, a particularity which reveals much about Hardy's changing attitude to his characters and to his audience. If a tendency for hokum – 'theatrical speech, action, etc., designed to make a sentimental or melodramatic appeal to an audience'[3] – is evident in the rural chorus of *Far from the Madding Crowd*, by the time of *Tess of the d'Urbervilles* it has all but disappeared. The question I will address in this chapter is whether that difference is reflected in the character and work of two filmmakers who adapted these novels: John Schlesinger and Roman Polanski.

Hardy is a novelist who displays not only a magnificent virtuosity in narrative and storytelling and a refined consciousness of the forces of society: he is also a writer working at a moment in the history of the English novel when the tension between the realist and self-conscious modes was, perhaps, most marked. This tension was first noted in Hardy's fiction by John Peck, who pointed out that although there is often much that is direct and evocative in Hardy's descriptions of people and of places, this visual impression is commonly followed by a paragraph of 'polysyllabic awkwardness as Hardy attempts to analyse the character or situation he has just presented in such an uncomplicated way.'[4] This certainly holds true for the first few paragraphs of *Far from the Madding Crowd*. The novel opens:

> When Farmer Oak smiled, the corners of his mouth spread till they were within an unimportant distance of his ears, his eyes were reduced to chinks, and diverging wrinkles appeared round them, extending upon his countenance like the rays in a rudimentary sketch of the rising sun.[5]

This is certainly a highly visual piece of description, verging, almost, upon caricature, but the reader cannot go far wrong: the picture suggests a simple-hearted, good man, so closely in touch with nature that he is manifestly a part of it. It is also a picture which the rest of the novel goes out of its way to stress. In what is probably one of the most famous scenes in the novel, the hay-rick scene (chapter thirty-six) it is Oak who reads the signs of nature warning that a storm is brewing, and Oak who in consequence saves Bathsheba from financial ruin, while Troy and Bathsheba's drunken labourers are sleeping off their overindulgence.

If this opening paragraph is a model of visual description, the second paragraph puts the description firmly back in the hands of language:

> His Christian name was Gabriel, and on working days he was a young man of sound judgement, easy motion, proper dress, and general good character. On Sundays he was a man of misty views, rather given to postponing; and hampered by his best clothes and umbrella: upon the whole, one who felt himself to occupy morally that vast middle space of Laodicean neutrality which lay between the Communion people of the parish and the drunken section – that is, he went to church, but yawned privately by the time the congregation reached the Nicene creed, and thought of what there would be for dinner when he meant to be listening to the sermon. Or, to state his character as it stood in the scale of public opinion, when his friends and critics were in tantrums, he was considered rather a bad man; when they were pleased, he was rather a good man; when they were neither, he was a man whose moral colour was a kind of pepper-and-salt mixture.[6]

There is nothing here to contradict, or even to expand on the impression the reader had already formed: we might probably have predicted that Oak would be uneasy within the formal confines of the church and would be thinking more about dinner than the vicar's sermon. But what is interesting is that, for Hardy, conceptual abstraction is at least as fascinating as physical reality. There are critics, no doubt, who will argue that this is an example of the characteristic pretensions of the self-educated man. Others may allude to Hardy's oft-quoted sentiment that art was 'no mere copying of life' – hence his dismissal of what he called 'photographic writing' as an 'inartistic species of literary produce'.[7] The opening of this novel is not just a particular response to the world at a particular moment in social history. It is also an aesthetic response to the novel form at the tail-end of the nineteenth century. It is out of this amalgam that Hardy emerges as a 'cinematic' novelist: on the one hand, a novelist who gives us direct, visual access to his fictional world; and on the other, a novelist who makes us wonder at its meanings.

Far from the Madding Crowd was the first novel in which Hardy used the setting of 'Wessex', a setting which rapidly asserted itself as a quasi-real place with its own history, places and personages.[8] It is obvious that such a 'reality' would rapidly attract the attention of the filmmaker.[9] For one thing, the fiction world of the novel is a simple one, telling a simple story of simple lives in rural England, with plenty of opportunities for period costume, Barsetshire accents and ritualised ale-swilling. However, the fact that Hardy himself did not conceive of the novel as hokum is evidenced in the title itself – an ironic invocation of Gray's 'Elegy Written in a Country Churchyard' (xix), 1750:

> Far from the madding crowd's ignoble strife
> Their sober wishes never learned to stray;
> Along the cool sequestred vale of life
> They kept the noiseless tenor of their way.

Certainly, this novel is no rural idyll. With its bunch of rustic simpletons and simple rituals, customs and habits, it may be set far from the madding crowd, but it tells a dark and dangerous tale, with characters at the mercy of almost uncontrollable passions and forces, both in themselves and in nature. This is a story in which an innocent and pregnant woman is left by her seducer to die in the workhouse, a story in which one man is financially ruined, another is murdered, and another confined for life as a madman. Paradoxically, there is a very real sense in which Hardy captures something of Gray's philosophical predicament: simple renunciation of the great, wide world is not enough, because 'from the tomb the voice of nature cries' ('Elegy', xxiii). This sentiment is echoed in the novel by Troy, to Bathsheba, standing beside Fanny's open coffin: 'This woman is more to me, dead as she is, than ever you were, or are, or can be ... You are nothing to me – nothing ... A ceremony before a priest doesn't make a marriage. I am not morally yours.'[10]

The question for the filmmaker – whose language and grammar is of the descriptive and the visual – is whether he or she can hold together the presentation of visual content and complexity of artistic form. This was precisely the task undertaken by John Schlesinger in his version of the novel for MGM (UK) in 1967. The cast included Julie Christie as Bathsheba Everdene, Terence Stamp as Sergeant Troy, Alan Bates as Gabriel Oak, with a script by Frederic

Raphael and cinematography by Nicolas Roeg.[11] The location, taken exclusively in Dorset and Wiltshire, has much to do with the magnificence of many of the landscapes, even when page-by-page scripting seems to slow the film almost to a stop. In fact, everything in the film, as in Hardy, is driven by landscape, so that what we see is beautiful even when the characters or situations are not. There is, indeed, plenty of room for hokum: 'In this rather plodding film the insufficiency of the foreground is partly offset by the winsomeness of the backgrounds. The very sheep are so engaging as to entice our gaze into some extremely amiable woolgathering', writes John Simon.[12] But something has happened in the thirty years since the film was released. Alan Bates and Julie Christie remind us of 1960s hippies taking in the sunshine on the south coast. They look as if they have arrived on the set after a shopping-spree in Carnaby Street or the Portobello Road – Christie in an Indian print cotton off-the-shoulder number (but no cow-bell), while Bates, as a struggling sheep-farmer, appears to be sporting a kaftan. What we are seeing, of course, is not a nineteenth-century novel, but a 1960s adaptation of a nineteenth-century novel. There is nothing unusual about this, since as audiences and readers we are almost always aware of our own historical position relative to the text.

But it must be said that Schlesinger made little attempt to do anything very exciting with the novel. There is a good deal about the film that is highly reminiscent of those worthy Sunday tea-time dramatisations which rattled off the Barry Letts assembly-line at the BBC during the late 1960s and into the 1970s: something good, clean and morally uplifting before going to bed (if the audience happened to be young) or before settling down to enjoy the evening (if the audience happened to be adults). This is not surprising: as a student at Oxford University from 1945 to 1950, and later as a producer-director at the BBC from 1956 to 1961, Schlesinger was well-steeped in the notion of the English literary classic and English public service broadcasting. Victorian fiction had always been a rich source for material of this nature, but it had been Dickens, rather than Hardy, who had attracted the programme-makers' eyes. There was a very good reason for this. Dickens's genius in large part lay in being able to mix sentiment and melodrama so brilliantly – the former indulgent but seldom in bad taste, the latter stirring and exciting without toppling into Gothic excess unsuitable for a middle-class Sunday afternoon.[13] Hardy, however, with his tendency for gloomy pessimism and the occasional flighty woman who ends no better than she should have been, was a different matter. If there was bravery in Schlesinger's dramatisation of the novel, it was, perhaps, in the fact that he took it on at all.

In fact, Schlesinger develops Hardy's story with rigorous even-handedness. The opening displays a sensitivity to Hardy's visual dramatisation of his landscape which is quite stunning. It is worth analysing the first few minutes of the film in some detail:

1   The film opens with titles over the sea and sky, with solo flute playing in the background. Tilt and pan-shot to a steep cliff-edge. Low tilt, revealing sheep-tracks on wild landscape, but no signs of any human habitation.

2   Slow pan and tilt, almost as if the camera is looking for some-thing, the landscape changing now to rolling valleys, the music becoming more formal and orchestral. There are the first signs of human habitation, a ploughed field and a small farm building. Diegetic sound: sheep and a dog barking, the dog in the distance running wild, chasing the sheep, ignoring the man's shouted commands.

3   Man, sheep and dogs in mid-shot; one dog out of control, chasing and biting sheep viciously and at random.

4   Cut to horse in distance being ridden by a female. Solo flute, the sea in the background. The woman is riding along the cliff-edge, her hair blown by the wind, then off track on to rough grass.

5   Cut to medium close-up of the woman waving to Oak in the distance, who waves back. Cut again to see her in long-shot. She rides out of the rough and back on to a small sheep-track.

6   Cut to Oak carrying a lamb, walking across neat green fields. Cut to Bathsheba looking out of a window. Oak is accompa-nied by a dog. Bathsheba hides at the back of the house, while Mrs Hurst invites Oak indoors, where he sits awkwardly in the parlour, Mrs Hurst opposite him and the lamb upon his lap. Oak explains that he was intending to ask Bathsheba to marry him, but Mrs Hurst, who is evidently unimpressed, tells him that Bathsheba has many other suitors. He leaves.

7   Cut to Bathsheba chasing after him. He stops and offers her his hand which she, significantly, refuses, explaining, as she does so, that she does not in fact actually have dozens of suitors. He

appears to accept this, and appears to assume also, therefore, that they will be married. Then follows a series of shots inside a barn and gradually moving out during which Oak is telling Bathsheba of the various luxuries she can expect as his wife: a small piano; a £10 gig for market; a frame for cucumbers; to have the marriage announced in the papers, likewise the births of the babies. The final suggestion does not appear to please Bathsheba, who looks coy.

8   Tracking-shot to Oak and Bathsheba outside the barn. Bathsheba explains that she cannot marry him because she doesn't love him. There is the sound of wind rising in the background throughout this interview between the two characters.

9   Cut to aerial long-shot of the dogs, rounding up the sheep, driving them towards a man, presumably Oak. The camera pulls back further, further and further, the details of the scene becoming almost unidentifiable.

I think it is fair to say that this is brilliantly executed, and conveys precisely the overall thematic concerns both of its specific novel and of Hardy as a writer in general. At the broadest critical sweep of Hardy's novels, it can be said that the fundamental pattern of Hardy's novels is that they will contain one or more characters who are in conflict with the world in which they find themselves – characters like Bathsheba, Eustacia and Clym in *The Return of the Native*, Henchard in *The Mayor of Casterbridge* (1886), Tess, Jude and Sue. These characters can generally see the value of conformity, but something in their personality makes it impossible for them to conform. Their instinctive, natural and human response to others and to situations is at odds with the orderliness of society. This is paralleled by nature itself – the landscape, the weather – which appears often indifferent to the plight in which human beings find themselves; sometimes wilfully destructive of all of humanity's attempts to create meaning and pattern in the physical world. This fundamental conflict – between society and order on the one hand, and the instinctive unruliness of human behaviour on the other – is evident through the novel, and brilliantly evoked by the opening few minutes of Schlesinger's film, which serves not only almost as a self-contained piece of drama, but also almost as an opening of a symphony, rehearsing all the tensions, motifs, tropes and structures which are to be found in the novel as a whole.

The sea and sky in the opening shot establish the overriding impression and role of nature in the novel: it is huge, pure existence, simply, apparently, looking on. The movement of the camera in these opening sequences reinforces this sense of distance: many of the shots, for example, are in long-shot, with people being either absent from the land entirely, or barely distinguishable upon it. This is a technique we recognise from many of Hardy's novels, one of the most memorable being, perhaps, that marvellous description of Tess, insignificant against the temporal and spatial scale of the earth and the universe at large, 'like a fly upon a billiard table'.[14] Both in Hardy's novels, and in this opening sequence, everywhere we look, we find this fundamental conflict. As we see the ploughed field, the first sign of human habitation, so the solo flute (the instrument played by Oak in the novel), gives way to formal orchestral music. The dog, out of Oak's control, is obeying its own, instinctive and unruly desires to attack the sheep, despite Oak's attempts to train it. The horse – long a symbol of this same conflict between the passions and the need to control them – is being ridden by Bathsheba close to the cliff-edge, and she is obviously and significantly well off the beaten track. Oak, carrying a lamb, offers it to Bathsheba for a pet – yet another reference to the conflict between the natural and the social. This opening perfectly summarises the novel's thematic concerns and interests. It grasps the novel as a whole and translates it into a visual representation of its patterns, concerns and interests. This world of both novel and film is fundamentally a thematic one in which characters play out their lives against a much broader backdrop.

But the historical reality of 'Wessex' at that time was wildly at odds with the kind of picture presented by both Schlesinger and Hardy. Throughout the last half of the nineteenth century, and even into the first decade of the twentieth, Dorset was experiencing that social phenomenon now euphemistically referred to as the 'depopulation of the English village'. During the fifty years of the period 1860–1910, about 350,000 agricultural workers simply disappeared from the land. The historical, social, and economic reasons for this depopulation have been well documented:[15] the development of the American wheat prairies hit cereal-farming severely, just as the importation of cheap wool from Australia and of refrigerated meat from the Argentine undercut the wool and meat markets. The consequence of this was one of the greatest agricultural depressions ever known. Only a hundred years previously, at the end of the eighteenth century, many of the small villages about which Hardy writes were thriving, agricultural communities. Winfrith Newburgh, about eight miles east of Dorchester and about two miles from Wellbridge Manor (the Woolbridge manor in which Tess and Angel spend the first night of their ill-fated honeymoon), is just one such parish. John Hutchins records in his monumental *History of Dorset* (1774), that Winfrith Newburgh then contained: 'about 100 houses, three hundred and fifty inhabitants, ten teams, seven freeholders, and twelve copyholders'.[16] And farming, too, was good: 'there is fertile corn land, and good sheep downs, about 2000 sheep being kept in the parish'. Not that these material benefits necessarily filtered through to the agricultural workers; labourers' wages were then 'about 1/- a day, mechanics' 1/6d; and provisions in general very dear; the price of butchers' meat 4d a pound'.[17] Even so, Winfrith thrived economically in the first half of the nineteenth century, reaching its peak about 1850, when – as the 1851 Census records – over 1,100 people were living in the parish. A century later, in 1951, this number had fallen to 587.

The ending of the Napoleonic Wars in 1815 had brought with it an immediate recession in agriculture, and a consequent increase in the price of basic foodstuffs. Further, the agricultural labourer, largely denied his rights over common lands by the active enclosures of the period, found it impossible to subsidise his family's food supply as he had in the past. A piece of folk-rhyme of the period accurately details the effects of enclosure, and the local hatred of the landed classes that was to follow:

> The law arrests the man or woman
> Who steals the goose from off the common,
> But leaves the greater rascal loose,
> Who steals the common from the goose.

It was this widespread enclosure of common land, low wages and poor living conditions which gave rise to several decades of agricultural unrest in Dorset, the most famous being the notorious 'Captain Swing' riots – taking their name from the mythical signatory of the threatening letters sent to landowners, and commonly tied to a stone thrown through their windows. The widespread rioting, machine-breaking, and rick-burning of the Captain Swing period – which led in large part to the eventual and over-zealous transportation of the

Tolpuddle Martyrs – was recorded by Mary Frampton, sister to one of the most active and unpopular magistrates of the time, James Frampton of Moreton:

> November 28th [1830] – Notice was received of an intended rising of the people in the adjacent villages of Winfrith, Wool, and Lulworth ... [the rising at Winfrith] ... took place on the 30th. My brother, Mr. Frampton, was joined very early that morning by a large body of farmers ... all special constables, amounting to upwards of 150, armed only with a short staff ... The mob ... would not listen to the request that they should disperse. The Riot Act was read. They still surged forward and came quite close to Mr. Frampton's horse; he collared one man, but in giving him charge, he slipped from his captors by leaving his smock-frock in their hands.[18]

The degradation and misery that lies behind these stories are hidden by the images Hardy was himself feeding to his London-based publishers and reading public: images of the pastoral and the smock-frocked Hodge. At the time he was writing *Far from the Madding Crowd*, one of the most vociferous commentators of the period, the aristocratic rector of Durweston from 1848 to 1875, Lord Sidney Godolphin Osborne, was trying to raise public awareness of the destitution and grinding poverty found amongst the Dorset poor.[19] Osborne, or 'S.G.O', as he signed himself in his numerous letters to *The Times*, soon became involved in bitter personal controversy with George Bankes, Conservative MP for Dorset (1841–56). Bankes upheld the Corn Laws, whilst Osborne argued that Peel was right to repeal them. Osborne, along with other commentators, such as Joseph Arch, accused Bankes of painting a misleading rosy picture of labourers' conditions to Parliament, whilst Bankes scoffed at what he called 'the popularity-hunting parson' for grossly exaggerating the hardships of the poor.[20] Admirers interpreted the initials S.G.O as 'sincere, good, and outspoken', and outspoken he certainly was. He spoke of Yetminster, a typical Dorset village of the time, as:

> the cesspool of everything in which anything human can be recognised ... whole families wallowing together at night on filthy rags, in rooms in which they are so packed, and yet so little sheltered, that one's wonder is that physical existence can survive as it does the necessary speedy destruction of all existing moral principle.[21]

That other great agitator of the period, Joseph Arch, commented, when he was attempting to organise the General National Consolidated Trades Union movement in Dorset in 1872, that 'the condition of the labourer in that County was as bad as it very well could be ... and worse than that commonly found in the negro plantations of the American south'.[22] Little indeed was being actively done to improve things. Given, for example, that in Hutchins's day Winfrith Newburgh had consisted of 'about 100 houses' with a population of 350–400, by the time of the 1851 Census, and with the population in Winfrith having virtually trebled – to over 1,100 – the number of households had risen to only 161. The Parliamentary Report on the Employment of Women and Children in Agriculture comments, in 1843, that 'such villages as Bere Regis, Fordington, and Winfrith ... (in which there is an average of seven persons to a house) ... are a disgrace to the owners of the land and contain many cottages unfit for human habitation'. There is in this that always rather shady distinction between the 'house' and the 'household': the Reverend Eldon S. Bankes, rector of Corfe Castle, records in 1867 (only seven years before the publication of Hardy's novel) that in one cottage on Corfe Heath, divided into three 'households', there were thirty-three people living. And in Winfrith, in common with many other Dorset villages, landlords – willing rather to pull down cottages than to build and maintain new ones – found it more economically practical to have single 'houses' partitioned into several 'households'. Living conditions for that de-smocked Hodge at the hands of Mr James Frampton must have been as cramped, squalid and unhealthy as they possibly could be.

This puts the chorus of rustics in *Far from the Madding Crowd* in a rather different light. For them, the news that Dicky Hill's wooden cider-house has been pulled down, and that Tompkin's old cider-apple tree has died and been rooted up is proof enough of the 'stirring times' in which they lived. The luxury of smoky evenings spent in the cosiness of Warren's malthouse belonged to an earlier age altogether – if they ever existed at all. To complain about this would be rather like complaining that Austen did not mention the slave trade or the Napoleonic Wars, or that Dickens was not a feminist. But it does mean that when we watch Schlesinger's adaptation of the novel, it's not him we have to accuse of hokum.

By the time of *Tess of the d'Urbervilles* Hardy's history had changed considerably. Unlike the earlier novel, which was begun and finished in a relatively short time and which – notwithstanding a certain cautiousness over the Fanny Robin story – had a relatively easy relationship with its editor, *Tess* was much longer in the writing, and had a much more troubled passage into print. It was written, Hardy claimed, to shield 'those who have yet to be born' from misfortunes like those of Tess, and plans for the novel were begun as early as the autumn of 1888.[23] Just over half the novel was accepted by the newspaper syndicate of Tillotson & Son for publication under the title of 'Too Late Beloved' (or 'Too Late, Beloved'), but when the first sixteen chapters reached proof stage in September 1889, serious objections were raised by the editors and the agreement was finally cancelled at Hardy's request.[24] The story was then declined by the editors of *Murray's Magazine* and also by *Macmillan's Magazine*.[25] By about the end of 1890, the novel was ready for serial publication in *The Graphic and Harper's Bazaar*, but it was not until March the following year that Hardy finished the novel. Of the various changes Hardy made to make the novel suitable for serial publication (this included the loss of the baptism scene)[26] the most notorious is probably that involving Angel's use of a wheelbarrow to carry the three dairymaids in turn over the flooded road – close physical proximity obviously proving too much for the editors of the day.

Tess of the d'Urbervilles tells an age-old story: that of a woman's sufferings in a society whose attitudes towards sex and women have condemned her. Again, what is at the heart of the novel is a conflict between instinctive behaviour and the social dictates which restrict behaviour. What is interesting, however, is the extent to which this novel, written almost twenty years after *Far from the Madding Crowd*, places the depopulation of the Dorset villages at centre-stage – 'the process, humorously designated by statisticians as "the tendency of the rural population towards the large towns", being really the tendency of water to flow uphill when forced by machinery'.[27] Indeed, in *Tess,* the consequences of depopulation take a front seat: John Durbeyfield is a poor, struggling farmer, a man dispossessed of his once-great family, and of almost any means of sustenance: when the horse, Prince, is killed, the single remaining means of maintaining his family dies with it, and it is this 'spilling of blood', which leads Tess to agree to go to the d'Urberville house, which in turn leads to the loss of her virginity, social condemnation and the final, symbolic spilling of Alec's blood when he is stabbed by Tess: 'The oblong white ceiling, with this scarlet blot in the midst, had the appearance of a gigantic ace of hearts.'[28] Quite unlike the situation in *Far from the Madding Crowd*, it is the reality of that great agricultural depression which acts like the spring on the trap which is finally to net Tess. When Angel's mother advises him not to be 'so anxious about a mere child of the soil',[29] the same tension is implicit in Tess's character as we find throughout, not least in her use of language: Tess, 'who might have been a teacher, but the fates had decided otherwise', had passed the Sixth Standard at the National School, where she had learned to speak 'correct' English. On the one hand, 'she spoke dialect at home'; on the other, 'ordinary English abroad and to persons of quality'. Tess thus quite literally 'spoke two languages',[30] and this is symbolic of how awkwardly she is poised between the worlds of the old, rural, agricultural community, and the new, social world, which is draining the life out of the old:

> Between the mother, with her fast-perishing lumber of superstitions ... and the daughter, with her trained National Teachings ... there was a gap of two hundred years as ordinarily understood. When they were together, the Jacobean and the Victorian ages were juxtaposed.[31]

When Tess is herself sent off to make her fortune in this new Victorian age with the family of incomers, the Stokes, who have bought the family name of d'Urberville, the tragedy of the past confronting the present must inevitably follow.

Clearly, a story of this kind demands a very different kind of filmmaking to *Far from the Madding Crowd*. On the face of it, Roman Polanski would seem to fit the bill. If Schlesinger's background in Oxford and the BBC equipped him to provide us with a classic adaptation for an audience weaned on public service broadcasting, Polanski's backgound qualified him to understand the darker values of the later novel. His own life seems to mirror many of its most tragic events. Born in Paris in 1933, Polanski's life includes his internment as a child in a German concentration camp, the early death of his mother at Auschwitz and the horrifying murder of the actress Sharon Tate, his second wife, to whom the film *Tess* (Columbia, 1979) is dedicated. Polanski was charged with the seduction of a fourteen-year-old girl in 1977 and fled America to avoid the remainder of a gaol sentence. There he had made some of his greatest films − *Rosemary's Baby*, *Chinatown*, with its flawless handling of plot and characterisation − bringing to Hollywood the technical innovation he had learnt in film school in Poland. At the moment of writing, Polanski is still attempting to arrange an out-of-court settlement with his alleged victim, which would enable him to return to America, and to mainstream filmmaking once again. *Tess* was in some ways a return to his much earlier work, most notably *Noz w Wodzie* (*Knife in the Water*, 1962), which was co-written with Jerzy Skolimowski and the last he made in Poland.

It is easy to see why Polanski should find the novel so perfectly suited to his own interests and concerns, preoccupied as they often are with alienation, individual isolation and the understanding of evil. It is the fate of an individual in an alienating society which fascinates Polanski, and he uses Hardy's novel as a framework within which to couch this idea. Throughout the film, we are struck by the result of Tess's non-conformity in a conformist society. Tess craves the security which conformity would give her, and yet there is something both in her character, and in her past − both ancestral and individual − which makes that conformity and security unattainable.

But where the novel takes in the broad span of a disappearing rural community, Polanski's adaptation focuses much more locally on the simple domestic reality of Tess and her relationship with Angel and Alec. The film opens with music strongly reminiscent of Percy Grainger, part of the English country-garden movement with which we associate cosy Edwardian high-teas on tidy Edwardian lawns, ladies in long cotton dresses and the sound of tennis. There are even strains of Greensleeves in the opening music, which serve only further to reinforce our sense of a secure, reliable and pretty past. And pretty *Tess* certainly is. The opening few shots of the film fill the screen with gorgeous distant landscape bathed in a golden light, but then, as the camera pulls back, more of this landscape is revealed. There is a scrubby track in the bottom left corner of the screen, which seems only accidentally to be a part of what we see. This is one of the characteristics of this opening: we are constantly given the impression that all this is happening quite coincidentally, that the camera may just as easily be filming another story elsewhere, and that it is simply recording whatever is happening. Coincidence is important in Hardy's novels, and in *Tess* particularly; if Angel had found the letter Tess had pushed under his door, perhaps he would have been able to see her past in a different light. Coincidence is also central to the camera work in the opening to Polanski's film. It is consistently unobtrusive, so that we receive paradoxically a strong sense both of verisimilitude and of the fact that the film is artlessly conceived and executed. Of course, quite the reverse is the case, with the film hiding its own processes of structuration so carefully that we are almost totally unaware of how our responses are being managed and manipulated. While the camera appears merely to sit, unobtrusively watching, we see, along this revealed track, in the bottom left-hand corner of the screen, a group of people dancing or walking along towards us to the tune of a highly stylised folksy tune. Everything is slow-moving at this point of the film and occurs in real-time, in stark contrast to the careful pacing and editing towards the end of the film, when Tess and Angel are attempting to escape the police after the murder of Alec.

Throughout this opening, the impression is that things cannot be hurried: actions, events, simply happen, and the camera is simply watching. This not only serves to increase that strong sense of verisimilitude, but also ties in precisely with the effect of fate upon an individual's existence, a theme common to Polanski, and to Hardy: 'As Tess's own people down in those retreats are never tired of saying among each other in their fatalistic way: "It was to be". There lay the pity of it.'[32] There is clearly much in the overall impression of the opening to the film which we find in Hardy also. But it is in how this overall impression is developed through the details of the piece that we find the most noticeable differences.

In the opening to the film, the procession of young girls, all dressed in white, all heavily decorated and garlanded in the floral mode, and all gaily waving switches presumably pulled from the local hedgerows, are preceded by four musicians – elderly men making music of a delivery and scale which seems quite beyond both them, and beyond their simple instruments. This is the first of many visual contrasts in this opening between youth and old age, between the past and the present. Characters seem to be drawn almost coincidentally to this spot somewhere in an ill-defined rural setting, and somewhere in an ill-defined rural past. As the procession passes, the camera merely follows abstractedly, refusing to focus on any particular person or thing. The procession of young girls crosses another track, and, as they move out of shot, so we see another character, a straggling old man coming towards us. This is John Durbeyfield, the haggler, and is the first precise shot of many in the film where we see characters moving first towards us and then away from us, along their own roads. Characters in this film are fundamentally alone, each following his or her own track. Camera movement reinforces this point immediately. First, the camera follows Durbeyfield, then tracks to give us his point-of-view of the procession now moving away from him. These are people whose paths quite literally cross, but who are fundamentally and symbolically following their own, isolated little tracks. Further, the past and the present (represented by the young girls, the four elderly musicians who precede them and John Durbeyfield, respectively) see each other differently, and from different perspectives. The focus at this opening of the film is very much upon such issues, and serves to foreshadow the idea of individual isolation and alienation from others and from society.

It is at this point that we return, as it were, to Hardy's novel: Durbeyfield is greeted by Parson Tringham, riding on a horse, who relays to him the story of the past grandeur of the d'Urberville family and recognises in him the final relict in the male line: 'Yes – that's the d'Urberville nose and chin – a little debased.'[33] Parson Tringham is the first representative of the Established Church; here, he is sitting on a horse, talking down to Durbeyfield, in much the same way that the Established Church later, both in Angel Clare's family, and in Tess's attempts to have her baby baptised, talks down to her also. Tess is at a transitional point in history, the past has decayed, and the established present which is replacing it is a world in which people like Tess and her kind have no place. We then cut to Parson Tringham riding away from us, again from Durbeyfield's point-of-view, another shot of people retreating along their own track. There is then a cut to the club-dancing scene and the girls dancing merrily together, followed by another cut to three young men approaching along the road towards us, dressed in Sunday-best. One of the young men, who turns out later to be Angel Clare, intends to join in, but the other two (his brothers, both in training for the Church), decide against the idea, concerned that somebody may see them mixing with common country-folk, again foreshadowing the idea of correct social behaviour. Angel grabs the nearest pretty young girl (we do not know at this stage of the film whether this is Tess), and dances. Again, the role of the camera here is simply to watch, simply to see, and we are not aware how carefully our responses are being managed. We note in this scene, for example (and again, this is done almost in passing), one of the local lads trying to take the hand of Tess in dancing. We do not know at this stage in the film that this young girl is Tess. But we do see her rebuff the local youth's attempt to make her join in with the dancing. This is clearly significant, and illustrates a good deal of Polanski's intention and attitude to Tess here: the fact that we don't yet know this is Tess, and the fact that we see her decline the youth's offer to dance, tells us that, at least so far as Polanski is concerned, this young woman believes she is rather better than the rural community. This may or may not be Hardy's attitude to Tess in the novel; certainly, we are told that Tess 'had hoped to be a teacher, but the fates had seemed to decide otherwise'.[34] But in the film the simple fact that Polanski has his Tess behave in a way which tells so much of her character without revealing her identity reveals in its turn a great deal about Polanski's interpretation and presentation of that character.

This, then, is *Tess*; but it is Polanski's *Tess*, not Hardy's. In the novel, there is a diffidence in her character which does not square with the defiance we see in her character at this point in the film, a point which is underscored by the cinematic use of sound and image: as Clare leaves the club-dancing, so the music and the sunlight fade also, and we cut to Angel walking past the defiant Tess. Throughout the novel, Angel's social prejudices are stronger than his natural feelings. Here, and later, he has to leave Tess behind, simply because she threatens his deeply-rooted sense of correct moral behaviour. As he moves away from her, into a retreating distant point, so the darkness of the scene is rapidly increasing, and with it goes the whole sense of security and stability of the club-dancing scene. Things take on an almost absurdist sense of threatening inconsistency. Out of the increasing darkness lurches Durbeyfield, drunk, and in the back of an open cart; silhouetted against a darkening and brooding red sunset; we cut to the girls dancing, but the camera-angle is now low, the girls now looming above us, weird shapes in the darkening light. Polanski pushes imagery as far as he can take it without destroying the mastery with which he has constructed the whole illusion of verisimilitude in these opening scenes. The next cut is to Tess approaching her parents' cottage, and the lighting is actually brighter although it is supposedly contiguous in time. Polanski is quite willing to sacrifice a mere detail of continuity editing in order to reinforce or to estab-lish a meaning – here, the threatening and brooding potentiality of the scene that he wants to capture, the sense of potential alienation and loneliness. But these meanings are Polanski's, not Hardy's. If Schlesinger is true to Hardy's hokum rather than Dorset's history, Polanski is true to his own history rather than Hardy's, so that in the end he, too, is guilty of a kind of hokum.

And this is the difference. An excellent film though it undoubtedly is, the sensation when watching *Tess* is akin to what we feel when we read a travel book by a writer who has passed through a place in which we live. The places sound the same in the telling: but they don't feel it. In his *Notes from a Small Island* (1995), Bill Bryson gives us his impression, as an American living in England, of drinking beer in an English pub:

> So I sat and drank beer, and watched, as I often do in these circumstances, the interesting process by which customers, upon finishing a pint, would present the barman with a glass of clinging suds and golden dribble, and that this would be carefully filled to slightly overflowing, so that the excess froth, charged with an invisible load of bacteria, spittle and micro-fragments of loosened food, would run down the side of the glass and into a slop tray, where it would be carefully – I might almost say scientifically – conveyed by means of a clear plastic tube back to a barrel in the cellar. There these tiny impurities would drift and float and mingle, like flaky pooh in a goldfish bowl, awaiting summons back to someone else's glass. If I am to drink dilute dribble and mouth rinsings, then I do rather wish I could do it in a situation of comfort and cheer, seated in a Windsor chair by a blazing fire, but this appears to be an increasingly elusive dream.[35]

All very interesting stuff: knowledgeable, detailed, and delivered with considerable panache. Total nonsense, of course, but stylish nonsense. We know the place, we may even share Bryson's particular hokum for the Windsor chair, the real ale, the blazing fire, the bygone and more secure age – but it's not quite right, this picture of the English pub as a place where the English go merely to exchange saliva.

We could, of course, take it on at the physical, practical level: turn to the Licensed Victuallers' Association to check out the accuracy of Bryson's observations. Or we may consider instead how it is that we do actually know the hokum of which Bryson is talking, since we share his notion of an England and of a time that never was. And similarly, of course, we must also remember that Hardy often simply wrote to his own audience's hokish expectations, temporarily and variously having them seated, as it were, in Warren's malthouse, or The Pure Drop, or Rollivers, the inevitable chorus of rollicking rustics rattling and burbling around them. For in a sense it really is this simple, even if difficult to quantify absolutely; like a shadow passing briefly across a window, this hokum is something we glimpse, a palimpsest of a recreated past that never could and never has existed.

Or could it? On 11 September 1997, the *Poole and Dorset Advertiser* carried the following note:

> Local people of all ages have the rare chance to appear in the latest TV production of a Thomas Hardy classic about to begin filming. London Weekend Television is appealing for those who would like to appear in its new £1m-plus version of *Tess of the D'Urbervilles* to attend a casting session for extras.
>
> It takes place at the arts centre in School Lane near the Grove in Dorchester – where Hardy's statue stands – tomorrow, Friday, September 12, between 9am and 5pm.
>
> Everyone is welcome but anyone interested should make sure they bring a recent photograph with them. The producers say they are particularly looking for character.
>
> Seven weeks of filming for *Tess* takes place in Devon and Dorset between September 26 and November 3.
>
> The three-hour TV film is due to be shown on the ITV network in February.
>
> Locations include Swanage Pier as well as Cerne Abbas, Minterne Magna, Turnerspuddle and Burton Bradstock.

History will be well catered for in this new offering: Swanage Pier doubling as Hardy's Bournemouth (Sandbourne); Cerne Abbas (with symbolic glimpses of the well-endowed Giant) as Tess's Marlott. And we may be assured that there will be room, too, for something in the way of hokum: 'The producers' – prospective applicants, be warned – 'are particularly looking for character'.

NOTES

1 David Lodge, 'Thomas Hardy and Cinematographic Form', *Novel*, 7 (1974), pp. 254–64.
2 See, Thomas Hardy, 'General Preface to the Novels and Poems', 1912 edition of his works.
3 This is the definition of hokum offered by the *OED*.

4 John Peck, 'Hardy and Joyce: A Basis for Comparison', *Ariel*, 12: 2, pp. 71–86 (p. 83).

5 Thomas Hardy, *Far from the Madding Crowd* (London, Macmillan, 1965 [first published 1874]), p. 1. Subsequent references are to this edition.

6 Hardy, *Far from the Madding Crowd*, p. 1.

7 Florence Emily Hardy, *The Life of Thomas Hardy 1840–1928* (London, Macmillan, 1962), p. 351.

8 See, F. B. Pinion, *A Hardy Companion: A Guide to the Works of Thomas Hardy and their Background* (London, Macmillan, 1968), p. 28.

9 The filmography of *Far from the Madding Crowd* and of *Tess of the d'Urbervilles* is remarkably similar. *Far from the Madding Crowd* was first dramatised for film in 1915, directed by Larry Trimble, who also wrote the screenplay. It was not then remade until 1967, when it was directed by John Schlesinger (see note 11, below). *Tess of the d'Urbervilles* was first filmed in 1924, directed by Marshall Neilan, screenplay by Dorothy Farnum and cinematography by Dave Kesson. It was then not remade as a film until Roman Polanski's *Tess*, 1979.

10 Hardy, *Far from the Madding Crowd*, pp. 352–3.

11 *Far from the Madding Crowd*, 1967, MGM, 165 minutes, colour.

12 John Walker (ed.), *Halliwell's Film Guide* (London, HarperCollins, 1993).

13 Robert Giddings, 'Hooked on Classics', *New Socialist*, December 1985, pp. 40–1.

14 Thomas Hardy, *Tess of the d'Urbervilles: A Pure Woman* (London, Macmillan, 1974 [first published 1891]), p. 159. Subsequent references are to this edition.

15 See Merryn Williams, *Thomas Hardy and Rural England* (London, Macmillan, 1972), p. 111: 'In the eighteen-seventies, after the Agricultural Workers' Union had given a further strong impetus to migration, Dorset was one of only nine counties in England which recorded an absolute population decline. The so-called golden age of agriculture had brought real benefits only to the farmers and landowners.'

16 John Hutchins, *The History and Antiquities of Dorset*, 1774 (1st edn); 4 vols, 1973, vol. 4, p. 279.

17 Hutchins, *History and Antiquities*, p. 282.

18 *The Journal of Mary Frampton of Wool*, 1885.

19 See Cecil N. Cullingford, *A History of Dorset* (London, Phillimore, 1980), pp. 109–12.

20 Cullingford, *History of Dorset*, p. 110.

21 Cullingford, *History of Dorset*, p. 111.

22 Williams, *Thomas Hardy*, p. 194.

23 Pinion, *A Hardy Companion*, pp. 46–7.

24 R. L. Purdy, *Thomas Hardy, A Bibliographical Study* (London, Oxford University Press, 1954), pp. 71–2.

25 This time, Hardy knew the 'fearful price' he had to pay 'for the privilege of writing in the English language'. See 'Candour in English Fiction', in Harold Orel, *Thomas Hardy's Personal Writings* (London, University of Kansas Press, 1966; Macmillan, 1967), pp. 150–1.

26 This was published in *The Fortnightly Review* in May 1891 as 'The

Midnight Baptism: A Study in Christianity'.
27 Hardy, *Far from the Madding Crowd*, p. 436.
28 Hardy, *Tess*, p. 471.
29 Hardy, *Tess*, p. 455.
30 Hardy, *Tess*, p. 58.
31 Hardy, *Tess*, p. 61.
32 Hardy, *Tess*, p. 108.
33 Hardy, *Tess*, p. 35.
34 Hardy, *Tess*, p. 88.
35 Bill Bryson, *Notes from a Small Island* (London, Corgi, 1995), p. 252.

7

A taste of the Gothic: film and television versions of *Dracula*

Jonathan Bignell

The genre of Gothic literature is difficult to define. I shall give a brief explanation of what is meant by the Gothic in literature, then narrow my focus to *Dracula* and adaptations of the novel in TV and especially film. I shall attempt briefly to describe the extent of *Dracula*'s penetration into the film and TV media, but also to account for the fascination of this character and story. Victor Sage has characterised a diverse group of historical romance novels of the eighteenth century, including for example Lewis's *The Monk* (1796) and Mrs Radcliffe's *Mysteries of Udolpho* (1794), as offering to their contemporary readers an experience of terror and sublime feeling.[1] This group of novels Sage calls 'the Gothick', a first surge of cultish popular fiction which was then followed by nineteenth-century re-elaborations of supernatural and macabre themes in Mary Shelley's *Frankenstein* (1818) and novels by authors such as Wilkie Collins, Edgar Allen Poe and Bram Stoker. It is this later nineteenth-century phase of popular writing which is now normally termed the Gothic (without the 'k'), and it includes works like *The Woman in White* (1860), *Dracula* (1897) and *The Turn of the Screw* (1898).

Stoker's *Dracula* was thus far from an isolated example of fiction about the eruption of unnatural creatures into the comfort of English society and the apparently secure world of the middle-class home. By the end of the nineteenth century, the literary tradition of the Englishman confronting savage beasts at home and abroad was firmly established. Around the same time that *Dracula* was published, the security of the private sphere (home and family) and of the public sphere (nation and Empire) was violated in fiction by, for

instance, the Beast People in H. G. Wells's *The Island of Dr Moreau*
(1896, filmed in 1996), and by the under-evolved and uncivilised Dr
Jekyll in Robert Louis Stevenson's *The Strange Case of Dr Jekyll and
Mr Hyde* (1886, most recently filmed in 1996 as *Mary Reilly*).

We should recall that the England of the late nineteenth century
was regarded as the highest point of human civilisation, when industrial technology and the power of science appeared to offer a
thoroughgoing conquest of nature. But such assurance brought with
it a fear of relapse into a savage past, and an anxiety about other
forces (especially those within the psyche) which had yet to be
explained. Victorians were afraid of degeneration back to a pre-
civilised state, known as atavism. Dracula's origins in the 'backward'
east of Europe, his unrestrained 'primitive' appetite and sexuality are
among the characteristics which made him alien and fearful to
Britons. But he is also at home in modern London, strolling the
streets like a cosmopolitan urbanite. Similarly, the central characters
in the novel use modern technology in their attempts to catch
Dracula, primarily by recording information and producing writing,
but also by travelling on the new pan-European rail networks and
using modern medical science. What succeeds, however, are the
weapons of pre-urbanised culture; the garlic and wooden stakes of
superstition and myth. What we find in the Gothic are attempts to
reconcile contradictions between civilisation and primitivism, ratio-
nality and superstition. Victor Sage's description of this fiction as an
'equivocal explanation of irrational phenomena' might not be sufficient in itself to distinguish a whole genre of writing, but it points
economically to some of the issues I want to discuss here in relation
to the Gothic in general, and versions of Bram Stoker's *Dracula* in
particular.[2]

Both cinema and the novel are narrative media, and it is hardly
surprising that film and television have adapted novels for the
screen. Starting from Sage's phrase – 'the equivocal explanation of
irrational phenomena' – we can begin to see how the Gothic novel
is suited for film and TV adaptation. Ghosts, vampires, telepathic
communication, transformations of the body, and unexplained
appearance and disappearance are 'irrational phenomena' which are
routinely found in Gothic fiction and which the technical properties of the film and television media can render as if real. The iconic
quality of the visual sign in film and TV, whereby the two-dimensional image appears to render three-dimensional objects faithfully,

gives the stamp of authenticity to what is seen on the screen, while electronic recording technologies also simulate sounds in a realistic way. 'Phenomena' are things which are perceived to exist, yet these existent things are not susceptible to 'rational' investigation; they remain real, but in a particular and limited sense. Gothic fiction and film and television fictions, since they are narrative forms, are occupied with 'explanation' of these phenomena, in the sense that they portray them and account for them in a way which allows the reader or viewer to accept them in the context of a narrative. But at the same time these narratives convey their shocking and uncanny characteristics through equivocation – by failing to provide enough information for a rational explanation to do away entirely with their emotional and psychological effects.

Gothic then, in its literary and its more recent media forms, is constituted by two sets of features which are themselves composed of radically different elements. Irrational phenomena lead us both to the realism of what seems phenomenologically true, but also to the uncertainty of the fantastic. Equivocal explanation offers us the linearity and closure of a narrative account, but an account which will not deliver a quotidian solution to the enigmas which are presented to us. This rich mixture of the believable and the unbelievable, the coherent account and the accumulation of startling moments of intense experience, is perhaps the source of the power of the Gothic for its readers and for the audiences of adaptations in film and TV. But this internal mixing in the genre has also been the reason for the devaluation of Stoker's novel and other examples of the Gothic, which in their day were regarded not as 'literary', but as entertaining thrillers. The highbrow literary magazine *The Athenaeum* reviewed *Dracula* in 1897, concluding that the novel

> is highly sensational, but it is wanting in the constructive art as well as in the higher literary sense. It reads at times like a mere series of grotesquely incredible events ... Still, Mr Stoker has got together a number of 'horrid details', and his object, assuming it to be ghastliness, is fairly well fulfilled. Isolated scenes and touches are probably quite uncanny enough to please those for whom they are designed.[3]

There is a definite implication here that readers of the novel are people likely to be seduced by the 'ghastliness' of the tale, and not sufficiently discerning to notice its apparent failings in literariness.

Despite the striking sensations which are produced by the writing, and yet because of their presence, the novel is said to be incoherent, disjointed: an accumulation of moments rather than a flowing narrative.

The problem with *Dracula,* it seems, is that it can suspend the reader's critical faculties and draw her or him into the role of duped consumer. We might even argue that the effect of the novel on its readers is parallel to the effect of Dracula on his victims: just as Dracula enslaves women to an appetite for excessive consumption of blood and frees them from civilised inhibitions, so *Dracula* turns readers into indiscriminate consumers of fiction and deprives them of educated judgement.[4] But the pleasure of this absorption in the narrative was described much more positively by another reviewer, in the *Daily Mail* newspaper in the same year:

> By ten o'clock the story had so fastened itself upon our attention that we could not even pause to light our pipe. At midnight the narrative had fairly got on our nerves; a creepy terror had seized upon us, and when, at length, in the early hours of the morning, we went upstairs to bed it was with the anticipation of nightmare.[5]

Here there is a relish in the pleasures of being seduced and made to forget the everyday (like lighting one's pipe). The ambiguity of the phrase 'got on our nerves' tells both of the potentially unsettling loss of control which reading produces, while also testifying to the unnerving thrill of the emotions generated in response to the text. The effects of the text, which has insinuated itself enough to produce nightmares after finishing the book, are both pleasurable and threatening to the reader's sense of self.

This kind of reaction to fiction, in both written and visual forms, can still be seen today in responses to paperback horror fiction, slasher films, 'body horror' and other 'video nasties', and some graphic novels. While Stoker's novel played on the anxieties of its time, contemporary film and TV Draculas recast the story in order to address the fears of our own time. One of the criticisms of a recent *Dracula,* Coppola's 1992 film version, was that the film is loaded both with the subtexts of Stoker's novel and also with an excess of contemporary subtexts (for example AIDS and drug addiction).[6] Because *Dracula* is so familiar, its story can be written-over and filled with new allusions and themes. *Dracula,* then, was the pulp fiction of its day, both castigated and enjoyed for its ability to fascinate and absorb its readers, and the fact that the novel has been in print continuously since first publication shows both the endurance of its appeal and its openness to contemporary reinterpretations.[7]

If we turn to more recent published versions of Stoker's *Dracula*, and examine the publicity blurb on the back of the recent Oxford World's Classics edition, the terms of evaluation have changed. It points out that to read Stoker is to return to the source of the Dracula story, and that the text is now considered a 'classic' novel. It promises the reader a fascinating and seductive experience, repeating the focus on 'irrational phenomena' and their attractions.

> The Dracula mythology has inspired a vast subculture, but the story has never been better told than by Stoker. He succeeds entirely in his aim to terrify. His myth is powerful because it allows evil to remain mysterious. Virtuous action has no more impact than Jonathan Harker's shovel. The high virtue of Lucy can simply be drained away, as her blood is drained away, until she too joins the vampire brood. Van Helsing's high-thinking and scientific skill cannot resist the dreadful potency of the undead. Only the old magic – a crucifix, garlic, a wooden stake – can provide effective weapons against the Count's appalling power.[8]

Stoker is now offered as a writer of consummate skill, rather than the peddler of sensation. His 'aim to terrify' is now a legitimate goal, and his creation of Dracula acquires status as an origin for a 'vast subculture' of popular fiction. The blurb contrasts the elite values of Victorian culture, 'virtuous action', 'high-thinking and scientific skill' with the fascination of the irrational, 'the dreadful power of the undead' and 'the Count's appalling power'. Just as the effectiveness of 'the old magic' of pre-rational belief overcomes Dracula, so the century-old original text authored and authorised by Stoker is claimed to exceed its more contemporary popularisations. So while the ingredients of the Gothic remain basically 'the equivocal explanation of irrational phenomena', the evaluation of these components has changed in the new context of twentieth-century culture and the shifting hierarchy of rational and irrational, popular cultural fascination and high-cultural literariness.[9]

It would be incorrect to suggest that the visual media have entirely supplanted the popularity of written versions of the story. While film and TV adaptations could be called parasitic on the literary text, they have nevertheless breathed new life into the literary version, so that in 1992 when Coppola's film *Bram Stoker's Dracula* was released in the USA, the novel appeared in the American best-seller lists. The film also gave rise to a book of the film by James Hart (the film's scriptwriter) and Fred Saberhagen (an American writer of vampire fiction). Hart contributed a preface to this novelisation, in which he recommends that his readers should also read Stoker. Hart's and Saberhagen's text is an assemblage of various other kinds of text, including an afterword by Coppola, stills from the film and photographs showing the making of the film, and extensive reuse of extracts from Stoker's *Dracula*.

Stoker's novel, too, in common with many Gothic fictions, is composed of a range of different discursive forms. The story takes shape from the journals kept by various characters, newspaper reports, letters, and transcriptions of phonograph recordings. As the character Jonathan Harker notes at the end of the novel, 'in all the mass of material of which the record is composed, there is hardly one authentic document; nothing but a mass of typewriting'.[10] In the Gothic, readers (and the protagonists) are presented with ambiguous and partial information, which it is their task to decode. This extends from the construction of texts from corrupt and partial sources (like the pages of journals, newspapers or legal documents), to the scattering through the novels of portraits, dreams and other kinds of image.[11] Each of these sources of information appears to offer the reader or protagonist access to knowledge, but each plays a teasing game of veiling its true significance. The decipherment of what can be seen on the surface hints at, but does not give access to, a depth beneath it. This technique makes the 'irrational phenomena' of the story subject to 'equivocal explanation', since the story is disjointed and multiply narrated from different points of view. But it also thematises the fact that what we read is always a later meditation on the action, a constructed record made up of layers of subsequent commentary.

This method of deferring presentation by multiplying the layers of intervening commentary is set against the immediacy and believability of what is described. These two forces in 'equivocal explanation', of veiling and showing, are evident not only in Stoker's narrative technique but also in Hart's and Saberhagen's novelisation of the film. The novelisation is presented as being true to what Stoker intended, and the authors returned to his sources to unveil the 'real' story. But the occasion for the novelisation was the film, and photographs show the actors and Coppola on the set, creating the illusion which we see on the cinema screen. Hart and Saberhagen return to Stoker, but more than this, they return to the sources of his novel to show what Stoker kept hidden. They return to the film in order to re-present it in writing, but also to lift the veil on the production process and show how it was made. Thus, not only are there two origins for the novelisation (Stoker's *Dracula* and Coppola's *Bram Stoker's Dracula*), but each of these origins is itself a partial telling, which must also be peeled away to reveal the sources from which it is derived.

To add a further twist, when Stoker wrote *Dracula* he was adapting literary versions of vampirism going back at least to the early nineteenth century.[12] This impossible quest for the story's origins is alluded to in the blurb on the back of Hart's and Saberhagen's novelisation:

> A legendary evil inspires a motion picture event. The ultimate retelling of a story that has mesmerised readers for more than a century ... Here is the extraordinary story of a creature possessed of an irresistible sexuality and a powerful evil as old as time itself. This unforgettable classic of darkly erotic horror is now a magnificent motion picture from Francis Ford Coppola, featuring an internationally celebrated cast. Including eight pages of stunning colour photographs.[13]

Of course, the aim of this blurb is primarily to sell the book, and to proclaim the significance and power of the film. But there is a confusion between the authorities being appealed to within it. The 'legendary evil' is that of Dracula, whose origins are lost in 'legend' and whose evil is 'as old as time itself'. But historically the story's literary origins are relatively specific, having existed for 'more than a century' as an 'unforgettable classic', evidently a reference to Stoker. And yet the film is authorised by the name of its director, Coppola, and the authority of the film as proper conduit of the story is proclaimed by the blurb on the back of the Columbia Tristar videotape of the film, which announces that 'Coppola returns to the original source of the Dracula myth, and from that gothic romance, he creates a modern masterpiece'.[14] Coppola's role as author is also emphasised by the inclusion of the photographs which supplement the 1992 novelisation. While we continue to find allusions to the irrational fascination of the story, in its power to 'mesmerise' readers, there is also a drive to explain this power by attaching it to an authorising source. But the source is indefinitely located either in the Dracula of popular superstition and legend, or in Stoker's historically specific publication, or in Coppola's authentic realisation, which is itself recast in written form and whose production process is partially explained by behind-the-scenes photographs.

This brief look at some of the written texts of *Dracula* shows that the story (and, I would argue, Gothic in general) has an unstable position in relation to the borderline between sensational or 'popular' writing and literary fiction. The story's shifts between classic novel and potboiler also parallel the ambiguity within its modern-day status as literary work or film and television text. While it is certainly true that many more people today experience *Dracula* primarily through visual representations, the fortunes of Stoker's novel and other written reworkings have been significantly and positively affected by the circulation of Dracula films and television adaptations. Without succumbing too easily to the metaphors of infection and transformation which crop up all too frequently in critical work on the Dracula myth, it would be accurate to suggest that Dracula crosses and recrosses the boundaries between written and visual forms, and is dead in neither. His true home and origin cannot be pinned down definitively, and the attempts to fix and evaluate these 'irrational phenomena' seem doomed to remain as 'equivocal explanations'. Some of the same problems of lineage and origin will also become evident as we examine the evolution of film and television adaptations of *Dracula*.

Adaptations of *Dracula* draw not only on the novel itself but on the literary vampire tradition and theatre adaptations of these stories.[15] Many of the themes, character-types, settings and effects in *Dracula* had already been used in a variety of forms. Vampires in literature began with John Polidori's story 'The Vampyre: A Tale' of 1819, written (like *Frankenstein*) after Lord Byron, Polidori and Mary Shelley decided to write thrilling stories when bored in Switzerland in 1816. A stage version of Polidori's vampire story was produced in 1820, and an opera version in 1828. The melodrama producer Dion Boucicault produced *The Vampyre: A Phantasm* on stage in 1852, another version of Polidori's story, and this was performed as *The Phantom* in the USA in 1856. A long, melodramatic and downmarket vampire story, *Varney the Vampyre: or the Feast of Blood* by John Rymer was published in forty-five instalments from 1845–47, while a more literary vampire novel, *Carmilla* by

Sheridan LeFanu, was published in 1872. The character of Dracula was Stoker's invention, but the vampire tradition spans novel, short story, serial publication, popular theatre and opera.

There have been very many film and television adaptations of Bram Stoker's *Dracula* itself, which was first published the year after the Lumière brothers opened the first public cinema auditorium in London in 1896. According to Ken Gelder more than 3,000 films featuring vampires have been made, by no means all of them versions of Stoker's story.[16] But each vampire film needs to connect sufficiently with the viewer's knowledge of vampire lore to sustain the fiction, while also departing enough from earlier films to establish its own identity as a self-sufficient text. This process of accretion of meanings, retellings, adaptations and returns to the 'original' story leave Gothic adaptations in film and TV as open and discontinuous texts, addressing multiple audience constituencies and activating multiple references and resonances in their viewers. I shall focus on some of the better-known films which derive from Stoker's novel, rather than the genre of vampire films as a whole, though there are obviously relationships between these two groups of films and the boundary between them is sometimes not easy to establish. In 1992, the year that Coppola's film *Bram Stoker's Dracula* was finished, about twenty-five vampire films were in production. But as suggested by its title, Coppola's film was the only one which explicitly claimed to be an adaptation of Stoker's novel.

Just as we should see Stoker's novel in the context of a literary genre and its history, so too we should see Draculas on film and television in the context of the genres and histories of cinema and TV. There has been a tradition of horror film since the early decades of film production, and this Gothic horror genre has also been evident in television, not only in TV versions of Dracula and other Gothic novels, but also in 'original' dramas which are not adaptations of a text, and in the screening on television of films made originally for cinema showing. In any year's TV output in Britain, the USA or any other nation, we can find TV adaptations of texts in the Gothic tradition, TV screenings of film versions of *Dracula* and other vampire or Gothic horror films, as well as new dramas like *Twin Peaks* or *The X Files*, whose appeal is also based on 'equivocal explanation of irrational phenomena', and which make use of Gothic characteristics.

The first known film adaptation of Stoker's novel was the

Hungarian *Drakula* (1920), an unauthorised adaptation now considered a 'lost film'. Similarly, *Nosferatu: eine Symphonie des Grauens (Nosferatu: A Symphony of Horror)* (1922), was a German adaptation of the novel directed by F. W. Murnau, produced without copyright authorisation from Stoker's widow, who owned the rights to the novel after Stoker's death. She obtained a court order for all copies to be destroyed, but the film can still be seen, reconstructed from surviving prints, and is considered to be relatively faithful to the novel in its representation of character and incident. Dracula in Murnau's film is a tall, skinny, emaciated figure, with a bald head, a row of long rat-like teeth, and long bony claw-like fingers. He is far from the elegant lounge-lizard seducer portrayed in later versions of the story. The themes of infection and contagion in the novel are emphasised in this film by adding a plot component in which Dracula's arrival by ship allows a swarm of rats to invade the port (now a German town rather than Whitby) and cause a decimating plague.

The first American vampire film was *London after Midnight* (1927, also known as *The Hypnotist* and remade in 1935 as *Mark of the Vampire*) directed by Tod Browning and starring Lon Chaney Senior. The visual image we now associate with Dracula begins to be evident in this film, even though it was not an adaptation of Stoker's text. Chaney wore a cloak over top hat and tails, had long sharp teeth and inserted painful steel hoops in his eyelids to open his eyes out into large monstrous circles. The comparatively well-known *Dracula* (1931) was also directed by Tod Browning and used aspects of Stoker's novel and of Hamilton Deane's (1924) British and John Balderston's (1927) American theatre adaptations. These were hugely popular in the 1920s and continued to be performed for decades afterward. The 1931 film's dependence on interior settings and Bela Lugosi's static performance as a charming, attractive Dracula in an evening suit have become an enduring image, but Lugosi's characterisation derived from decisions made for easier theatrical staging, not from the novel.

Lugosi was cast in the film because he had played Dracula first in the Broadway stage version by Balderston. Stage versions brought Dracula on stage frequently and in drawing-room settings, in contrast to the novel where he appeared rarely and in a wide range of outside locations. The decision to turn *Dracula* into a mystery melodrama was thus the reason why Dracula was costumed in evening dress and opera cloak, making him look like the sinister hypnotists, seducers and evil aristocrats of Victorian popular theatre. Stage machinery like trick coffins, trapdoors and smoke effects also link the play to the cinematic interest in spectacle and trick effects routinely used in filmed versions. The high-collared cape we now recognise as a hallmark of Dracula was first used in the stage versions. Its function was to hide the back of the actor's head as he escaped through concealed panels in the set to disappear from the stage, while the other actors were left holding a suddenly empty cloak. In fact, Bram Stoker managed the Lyceum Theatre from 1878–98, working for and with the actor-manager Henry Irving. It is thought that Irving (famous for his mesmeric performances of sinister characters like Mephistopheles) was an inspiration for Dracula himself: he was domineering, arrogant, selfish, solemn, and financially extravagant.[17]

The first Hammer film *Dracula* (*Horror of Dracula* in the USA) was released in 1958, a British production directed by Terence Fisher and starring Christopher Lee as Dracula and Peter Cushing as Van Helsing. At a time when British films were still mainly in black and white, it was shot in a garish Technicolor, and the Hammer trademarks of copious bright blood, voluptuous maidens, as well as Lee's portrayal of Dracula as a charismatic and urbane figure, were to be consistent features in a series of six Hammer Dracula films. This series culminated in the 1973 *Satanic Rites of Dracula*, in which the Count appeared as a reclusive business magnate in contemporary settings. It was at this point that Lee quit the role, feeling that the consistency and seriousness he had brought to the part had been compromised. In 1970 *Count Dracula* directed by Jesus Franco and starring Christopher Lee (a co-production drawing funds from Spain, West Germany and Italy) presented a faithful version of the novel, but due to lack of finance it was felt to fail to do justice to its aims, even though Lee had a visual look much closer to Stoker's description than other film versions. *Nosferatu the Vampyre* (1979) directed by Werner Herzog and starring Klaus Kinski, is based on some of the visual and plot hallmarks of Murnau's version (1922), especially in the appearance of Dracula himself, and also attempts to tell the same basic story as Stoker's novel. On the other hand, John Badham's 1979 adaptation was an American film based not on the novel but on the Deane and Balderston plays, starring Frank Langella who had played the Count in an acclaimed 1977 Broadway version of *Dracula*.

In the 1970s – as censorship relaxed in Britain and the USA and the commercial possibilities of films treating sexuality directly became evident – films featuring vampires and Dracula began to exploit the erotic potential of the myth to feature nudity and lesbianism (as for example in *The Vampire Lovers* [1970]). It was in 1977 that James Hart read Stoker's novel, and was struck by its difference from the films he had lately seen based on vampire myths. Hart wrote the script for Coppola's *Bram Stoker's Dracula* (1992), which claimed in its title to be closely based on the novel. But one of the reasons for the title was that Universal Pictures still owned the copyright on the title *Dracula* used in Tod Browning's film (the same problem affected the title *Frankenstein*, so that *Mary Shelley's Frankenstein* also produced by Coppola had to use a similar formulation in its title). Costing over fifty million dollars, the film emphasised a romantic love story alien to the novel, and made use of every opportunity for visual illusion, which some have claimed overwhelms the story.[18] The disturbing events in Gothic literature are often described as 'uncanny', and critical discussion of the Gothic often refers to Freud's essay 'The Uncanny', where he remarks that, in German at least, the term 'uncanny' ('unheimlich') contains the two contradictory senses of familiar and unfamiliar.[19] In the uncanny, everything is potentially double, ambiguous, ambivalent; both good and evil, attractive and repulsive, true and false. Cinema spectatorship has been described in terms of the disavowal implicit within this ('I believe this, even though I know it is not true') – just like the mode of readership in Gothic fiction, where the reader delights in the illusion while recognising it *as* an illusion.[20] The visual style of Dracula films connects theatrical illusion, the techniques of Gothic literary writing, and the mode of spectatorship developed in cinema.

Appropriately, then, the key moment in Coppola's film – when Mina begins to be fascinated with Dracula as well as afraid of him, and recognises him as somehow familiar though she has never met him before – occurs at a cinematograph show where early films (striptease; an arriving train) are being projected to an audience entirely composed of men. Ken Gelder has pointed out that Coppola's film aligns the pleasures of filmgoing with the pleasures of this version of the Dracula story:

> We see a 'peep-show' film, with a naked woman walking towards the camera. Even at such an early point in its history, in this

account, film is thus an erotic medium which splits the audience in terms of gender: while the women are 'carried away', men are positioned voyeuristically ... This is consistent with the film's rewriting of the novel, which among other things situates almost everything that happens under the umbrella of the Hollywood romance genre – drawing romance and the experience of (going to) the cinema together. Dracula, in Coppola's film, is a romantic and 'naturally' cinematic hero who sweeps Mina off her feet: after just a little while, she simply cannot say no to him.[21]

The film returns to late Victorian London and the cinematograph to ground its historical setting and to mark its own self-consciousness as both an adaptation of a nineteenth-century English novel and a part of the cinematic tradition of such adaptations. It returns to a well-worn love-story structure to secure an identification with Dracula and Mina (as the romantic couple) rather than with Harker (the 'hero' of the novel). This notion of a return to the birth of cinema, coupled with the use of modern romance conventions, shows on one hand that desire for origins I have discussed above in relation to the written texts of *Dracula*, on the other the extent to which the novel's story has been transformed in becoming popular cinema.[22]

There have been numerous television versions of *Dracula*. In 1957 a TV version of *Dracula* was made as part of the Matinée Theater series on the American NBC network. It was apparently based on the novel rather than the theatrical version, and starred John Carradine as Dracula. However, since it was live and recording was then both expensive and rare, no copies of this production now survive. A TV version of the novel was made in Britain by Thames Television in 1969 in the anthology series of nineteenth-century Gothic fiction adaptations titled 'Playhouse: Mystery and Imagination'. It starred Denholm Elliott as Dracula, and some significant alterations were made to the story, notably an insane Jonathan Harker (Corin Redgrave) in an asylum, taking on aspects of the Renfield role from the novel. A Canadian *Dracula* (1973) in the Purple Playhouse series was close to Stoker's novel, while a year later another US TV version, *Dracula* directed by Dan Curtis, cast Jack Palance as Dracula and was the first screen version to present him as a romantic figure, seeking the reincarnation of his long-lost lover (this theme was later used in Coppola's film, and was thus not an original approach as the publicity for *Bram Stoker's Dracula* claimed).

Some of the same dashing romantic quality in Dracula can be seen in the BBC TV adaptation *Count Dracula* (1977), which cast Louis Jourdan as Dracula, but in other respects the version is very closely based on the incidents and characterisations of the novel and gained considerable critical acclaim and a large audience. In contrast to many literary adaptations of the time, the 155-minute production used state-of-the-art film and video effects to present the story as hallucinatory and nightmarish rather than static and naturalistic. In 1979, ABC television in the USA presented a made-for-TV movie version of Stoker's novel called *The Vampyre*, co-written by Steven Bochco, better known in recent years for series such as *Hill Street Blues*, *LA Law* and *NYPD Blue*. Vampire stories and original plays based more loosely on the Dracula character abound, and have often featured in anthologies of single plays like *Late Night Horror* (GB, 1968). In Britain in 1992, there was a television serial called *Vampyre: A Soap Opera*, written by Martin Hoyle and directed by Nigel Finch, and Dracula's presence in TV genres other than literary adaptation can be seen in characters like The Count in the long-running Children's Television Workshop series *Sesame Street* (where the Lugosi-like muppet obsessively counts things), and Count Duckula in the British Thames Television-Cosgrove Hall animated series of that name (1988), where the character is a Daffy Duck-like animal who sports the cape made famous by Lugosi some sixty years before.

There is a reciprocal relationship between the many film and television versions of the Dracula story and the currency of Dracula and vampire myths in other forms of popular culture. The Romanian Tourist Board offers visitors tours of 'Dracula's castle' and Transylvania, even though Stoker never visited Eastern Europe and gathered his information in the Reading Room of the British Museum from travel books and accounts of Balkan folklore. Whitby in Yorkshire, where Stoker stayed and where in the novel Dracula's ship arrives in Britain, hosts The Dracula Experience involving tours of the locations associated with Stoker's visit there and of the places featured in the text. At an uncommercial level, the Vampyre Association is a group of British devotees of Dracula and vampire fiction, people who often costume themselves in the contemporary Gothic dress code and are an organised part of a broader interest group or subculture. Some of its female members were interviewed on *The South Bank Show*'s 'Dracula Special' (London Weekend TV,

1993), and their comments suggest that, for some women viewers and readers at least, Dracula is a fantasy figure through whom they can enjoy romance, eroticism, exoticism and role-playing — elements perceived to be lacking in everyday life. 'What vampires offer is sex, death and fancy costumes, and who could ask for more?', one member of the society commented. The scheduling of this TV documentary at the point of the UK release for *Bram Stoker's Dracula* is not only an effect of public relations activity by the film's distributors, but also an acknowledgement that film versions of *Dracula* must be seen in the context of a public awareness and interest in vampires which has existed for more than a century.

Today, the Dracula myth offers an appealing mixture of nostalgia, eroticism and a sense of literary seriousness not generally available in contemporary popular culture. As studies of other subcultural groups have shown, the feeling of community, shared knowledge and insider status offered by the Vampyre Society is not simply a defensive reaction to contemporary culture but a powerful way of negotiating a relationship with it and dealing with its contradictions.[23] Another member of the Vampyre Society explained that vampires 'are erotic but in a sort of romantic sort of way. It's not like the cheap sort of sex that gets sold these days — it's more romantic, more Victorian'. To some women, the vampire myth offers licensed eroticism while holding at bay the contemporary commodification of sexuality. The injunction to define oneself through sexual practices and identities is paradoxically rejected from the standpoint of a Victorian heritage which seems romantic and authentic, but was at the time closely related to pornographic writing and to the fears and pleasures of sexual excess.[24]

It is easy to argue that the novel, film and TV versions of *Dracula* and other Gothic novels represent anxieties about gender and sexuality. Not only is sexuality itself both pleasurable and threatening in Gothic fiction, so too is the fear tied up with it. As Gelder remarks, *Dracula*'s concern with danger to the women characters is never explained in sexual terms: 'there is so much to say about sexual motivation in *Dracula* precisely because the novel's own analysts have nothing to say about it whatsoever.'[25] Part of the myth's appeal to female members of the Vampyre Society comes from the opening up of this subtext about feminine sexuality. As one of them explained in the LWT documentary, 'Mina and Lucy ... didn't have much personality at all until they turned into vampires, and then they became exciting and sexual and absolutely fantastic'. In the late twentieth century, a taste for the Gothic, and for *Dracula* in particular, is very much undead.

NOTES

1 Victor Sage (ed.), *The Gothick Novel: A Casebook* (London, Macmillan, 1990). Sage's introduction (pp. 8–28) gives a brief but rich overview of the eighteenth-century Gothic and its nineteenth-century legacy.

2 Sage (ed.), *The Gothick Novel*, p. 22.

3 Anonymous *Athenaeum* review of *Dracula*, 26 June 1897, reprinted in B. Stoker, *Dracula*, Norton Critical Editions, ed. A. Auerbach and D. Skal (New York, Norton, 1997), p. 364.

4 This issue is discussed in relation to the character of Mina in particular in J. Wicke, 'Vampiric Typewriting: *Dracula* and its media', *English Literary History*, 59 (1992), pp. 467–93.

5 Anonymous *Daily Mail* review of *Dracula*, 1 June 1897, reprinted in Stoker, *Dracula,* ed. Auerbach and Skal, p. 363.

6 See for example R. Dyer, 'Dracula and Desire', *Sight and Sound,* 3: 1 (1993), pp. 8–12, who argues that the film, like a satiated Dracula, is 'engorged' with too much allusion.

7 For a useful selection of influential critical readings of *Dracula* see M. Carter, *Dracula: The Novel and the Critics* (Ann Arbor, University of Michigan Press, 1988).

8 B. Stoker, *Dracula,* Oxford World's Classics, ed. A. N. Wilson (Oxford, Oxford University Press, 1983).

9 On contemporary relationships between high and popular culture, see H. Hawkins, *Classics and Trash: Traditions and Taboos in High Literature and Popular Modern Genres* (Hemel Hempstead, Harvester, 1990).

10 Stoker, *Dracula,* ed. Auerbach and Skal, p. 326.

11 On issues of ambiguity and interpretation in Gothic literature, see E. Kosofsky Sedgwick, *The Coherence of Gothic Conventions* (London, Methuen, 1986).

12 For the sources of Stoker's novel, see C. Leatherdale, *The Origins of Dracula: The Background to Stoker's Gothic Masterpiece* (London, Kimber, 1987).

13 F. Saberhagen and J. Hart, *Bram Stoker's Dracula* (London, Pan, 1992).

14 *Bram Stoker's Dracula*, Columbia Tristar videotape, 1993.

15 For a fascinating and detailed account of the evolution of the Dracula story from literature to theatre, film and other media, see D. Skal, *Hollywood Gothic: The Tangled Web of Dracula from Novel to Stage to Screen* (New York, Norton, 1990).

16 K. Gelder, *Reading the Vampire*, Popular Fictions Series (London, Routledge, 1994), p. 86.

17 On Stoker's relationship with Irving, see B. Belford, *Bram Stoker: A Biography of the Author of Dracula* (New York, Knopf, 1996).

18 The strengths and weaknesses of the film are briefly catalogued in A. Silver

and J. Ursini, *The Vampire Film: From Nosferatu to Bram Stoker's Dracula*, 2nd edn (New York, Proscenium, 1994), pp. 155–8.

19 S. Freud 'The Uncanny', Pelican Freud Library, vol.14 (Harmondsworth, Penguin, 1987). For an account of psychoanalytic approaches to Gothic literature, see Gelder, *Reading the Vampire*, ch. 3.

20 The classic statement of this critical approach is C. Metz, 'The Imaginary Signifier', *Screen*, 16: 2 (1975), pp. 14–76.

21 Gelder, *Reading the Vampire*, pp. 89–90.

22 I have discussed the reflexivity of *Bram Stoker's Dracula* in relation to post-modernism in J. Bignell, 'Dracula Goes to the Movies: Cinematic Spectacle and Gothic Literature', in D. Sipière (ed.), *Dracula: Insemination–Dissemination*, Collection STERNE (Amiens, University of Picardie Press, 1996), pp. 133–43, and in the context of recent American cinema in J. Bignell, 'Spectacle and the Postmodern in Contemporary American Cinema', *La Licorne*, 36 (1996), pp. 163–80.

23 On vampire fan culture, see N. Dresser, *American Vampires: Fans, Victims and Practitioners* (New York, Vintage, 1990).

24 On the relationship between *Dracula* and Victorian pornographic writing, see V. Sage '*Dracula* and the Victorian Codes of Pornography', in Sipière (ed.), *Dracula: Insemination–Dissemination*, pp. 31–47.

25 Gelder, *Reading the Vampire*, p. 67.

8

Times of death in Joseph Conrad's *The Secret Agent* and Alfred Hitchcock's *Sabotage*

Suzanne Speidel

A piece of film lore has grown up around author Joseph Conrad, namely that his works are impossible to film. There are two elements to this apparent curse, the first being that Conrad adaptations are difficult to get *on to film,* and indeed there have been a number of infamous Conrad projects which were either plagued by production nightmares, or were never completed. Both Orson Welles and David Lean were thwarted in their attempts to bring Conrad novels to the screen (respectively *Heart of Darkness* and *Nostromo*), whilst the most celebrated Conrad jinx is Francis Coppola's *Apocalypse Now*, which ran vastly over budget and took three years to complete. Eleanor Coppola's *Notes: On the Making of Apocalypse Now* relates an almost farcical catalogue of production misfortunes,[1] which seem to confirm Conrad as 'the author for directors aspiring to Kurtz-like degeneracy and derangement'.[2]

Conrad's novels are also reputed to be impossible to film *successfully,* and whilst the modern classic status of Coppola's film appears to belie this, it does seem to be the case that many Conrad adaptations (such as Carol Reed's *Outcast of the Islands* [1952], Richard Brooks's *Lord Jim* [1965], Ridley Scott's *The Duellists* [1977]) remain footnotes to their makers' high-profile careers. Some directors meanwhile (such as Nicolas Roeg, whose *Heart of Darkness* was released straight on to video in 1994) have found their encounters with Conrad to be the cause of unaccustomed critical and commercial disaster.

Consequently it is all the more remarkable that both the film and television industry should have turned to Conrad so frequently

131

for source material: Gene M. Moore's comprehensive filmography of 'films and video programs based on the life and works of Joseph Conrad' lists eighty-six entries, beginning with Maurice Tourneur's silent version of *Victory* in 1919 and concluding with Beebon Kidron's 1998 *Amy Foster*.[3] It details eight different adaptations of *The Secret Agent* (of which six were made for television) suggesting that Conrad's 1907 novel has proven no less inviting than the Conrad canon has proven a curse.

Alfred Hitchcock's *Sabotage* (1936) was *The Secret Agent*'s first big-screen adaptation (the only other being Christopher Hampton's 1996 *The Secret Agent*). It is a film which suggests the broad boundaries surrounding the notion of adaptation. Updated to the 1930s, *Sabotage* sees the Verloc family living above a cinema rather than a pornography shop, and transforms Mrs Verloc's brother, Stevie, from a retarded adult into an endearingly clumsy child, and explosives expert 'the Professor' from a psychotic anarchist to a doting grandfather and bird-shop proprietor. It also sanitises Conrad's cynical ending: both the novel and the film tell the story of how Stevie dies whilst planting a bomb for anarchist Mr Verloc, and how Mrs Verloc kills her husband in revenge, but Hitchcock's film provides Mrs Verloc with Ted, a fresh-faced young policeman, and more congenial love-interest than the novel's lecherous Ossipon (and a less conscientious investigator than the novel's Chief Inspector Heat). Rather than driving Mrs Verloc to suicide (as Ossipon does), Ted prevents a remorseful Mrs Verloc from confessing, and the couple are saved from the evils of flight, separation, imprisonment, capital punishment, or suicide by a second, fortuitous explosion which destroys all evidence of her crime.

Despite such blatant, elementary changes, *Sabotage*'s opening credits still seek to remind us of its source by including the phrase 'From the novel "The Secret Agent" by Joseph Conrad'. Admittedly the acknowledgement is imprecise, avoiding even the use of a verb to clarify the nature of the author's influence. This suggests at the outset a film in which Conrad's novel will be detectable but noticeably revised. The advantage of examining this kind of broad, unrepentant adaptation – to which we frequently apply the term 'unfaithful' – is the degree to which it makes problematic the very notions of both adaptation and faithfulness. *Sabotage* was made towards the end of Hitchcock's British career, only four years before he made *Rebecca*, his first Hollywood film. Its story of a woman and two men, and a boy and a bomb, spans two popular Hollywood genres, the love story and the thriller, and in this way Hitchcock appears to be aiming already at the same market audience targeted by Hollywood.

Consequently the decision to adapt an early twentieth-century novel can be understood in terms of a desire to take financial precautions in a competitive market – to choose a *story* which had already in some way proved itself in another medium. Thus Conrad's prominent position in the credits acts as an advertisement for the value of the entertainment on offer, drawing on his name to declare that the film's origins are respectably rooted in literary tradition. This seems to place *Sabotage* within a staple approach to narratives still practised in Hollywood today. In his book *Screenwriting*, based on the 434 graduate screenwriting class at UCLA, Lew Hunter makes the following suggestion to writers searching for initial inspiration: 'The French say it best. Pay "homage". Americans say "rip off". How inelegant. I'll say "appropriate" the plot of a classic novel or play and dress it with the clothes of whatever period you like.'[4]

This approach suggests a recognition of the pliability (as well as *ply*ability) of narratives, but it also implies that stories must have a certain solidity and resilience, in order to survive such drastic transplantations. In this respect it bears a close resemblance to the methodology of Russian formalism as well as structuralist narratology, since it views narratives as being made up of a variety of identifiable units – they have, for example, a 'plot', and also a temporal setting (or 'period') – and it is this componential nature which makes the 'classic novel or play' adaptable. Hunter recommends that the first stage in writing a screenplay should be the setting down of 'a two-page, double-spaced, two-minute movie',[5] implying that, like structuralism, the central assumption behind the Hollywood screenplay strategy is the independence of any story from its chosen mode of discourse. The story (the 'what happens' component) can be told in any number of different discourses (the 'how it happens' component), and it is this discourse which provides the narrative with, to borrow from Hunter's analogy, its extensive wardrobe of 'dressing-up' possibilities.

This connection between Hollywood policy and narratological theory is perhaps surprising. Structuralism treats texts autonomously, isolating them from their historical contexts, their authorship, their production conditions and indeed their recipients. It considers only their communicative system and process, and as such it attempts a quasi-scientific objectivity towards modes of fiction (or indeed any system of signs). Since structuralism flourished in the 1960s literary theory has moved decisively away from such declarations of detachment, in favour of exploring precisely the nature of that subjectivity that structuralism sought to circumvent. The scholarship of film studies has also adopted a more contextual approach, concerned with examining the institutions of filmmaking, and the ways in which these institutions seek to manufacture products for their consumers.

The film industry itself, however, remains firmly attached to the process of identifying and reproducing textual paradigms. Motivated by considerations of extreme self-interest, it has chosen a methodology of declared disinterestedness on which to model its own narrative approach. It does so with a view to finding prescriptive formulae within narratology's descriptive patterns – to finding that combination of narrative components which will sell, which will lend itself to mass production, and will procure maximum profit. Like structuralism, the film industry's interest in defining a narrative's constituent parts lies in a desire for security, in a desire to somehow overmaster the unpredictability of our own responses.

All this suggests a curious synthesis of contradictory elements in the commercially driven film industry's approach to adaptation. Source texts are treated autonomously, in isolation from their production and readership contexts, precisely in order that they may be fitted to the institutional requirements of cinema. However, cinema's audience is clearly not expected to treat the resulting film in this detached, abstract manner, given that we are enticed into the cinema by, amongst other things, the offer of generic familiarity. Our interpretation is expected to be based on a process of cultural association, on connecting the story (like the stars) of one film to another. Cinematic meaning is fundamentally historical, and it starts with building-blocks found outside, and before, the existence of each text's narrative components.

In this way film adaptations frequently seem to want to have it both ways. In taking textual liberties they seem to sever the cultural ties of the source text, and yet the medium of the new text thrives on precisely such connections. Indeed, as the inclusion of Conrad's name in the title sequence of *Sabotage* demonstrates, the marketing of adaptations at times exploits precisely those cultural links that its own narratological process has ignored. In this way adaptations of the kind undertaken by Hitchcock make use of structuralism's disregard for anything outside of textual organisation in a way which demonstrates an extremely astute grasp of its own cultural conditions.

What this suggests is that one way of identifying how texts have been adapted to fit such new conditions is by undertaking a textual dissection akin to that performed by both structuralist theorists and screenwriters. Consequently the approach adopted in this chapter involves the identification and examination, in both Conrad's novel and Hitchcock's film, of some of the narrative components identified by French structuralist Gérard Genette in his study *Narrative Discourse*.[6] Genette's methodology is particularly rigorous in its delineation of narrative constituents, and is most renowned for its examination of the many possibilities and characteristics surrounding the presentation of narrative time. As a result his definitions are eminently transferable on to new texts and media, and this in turn enables the identification of those narrative techniques which are not transferable from one medium to another.

Genette's approach is also precise in its adherence to the structuralist principle that the meaning of a communicative unit originates from its relationship to a binary opposition. His analysis presents us with a multifarious paradigm of splintering pairs, in which each idea is defined by its difference to its partner. Story (*histoire*) and discourse (*récit*) subdivide into story order/discourse order, story duration/discourse duration, and story frequency/discourse frequency. Mood and voice, meanwhile (defined by Shlomith Rimmon-Kenan as the question of "'who sees?' v. 'who speaks?'"[7]), subdivide respectively into distance and perspective, and narrative time and narrated time.

Structuralism has been superseded by critical thinking which sees the identification of binary oppositions as a limiting linguistic and narratological approach, since it overlooks the infinite chain – or indeed mesh – of connections and contrasts which language employs and evokes. Structuralism's advantage here lies in precisely this problematic artificiality, since the process of adaptation involves both the presumed isolation of the two texts, as well as their broader generic, canonical and cultural links. In conducting an examination which draws upon Genettean narratological distinctions the aim is to explore this contradiction, and to identify how the film's textual treatment of its source produces a movie which caters to its own extra-textual situation.

The changes made to the ending of the story are the most obvious indication of how Conrad's novel has been altered to suit *Sabotage*'s cultural context. The inclusion of the love story conforms to a commercial policy (practised principally by Hollywood studios) of offering the audience that reassuring, ordered, happy ending which it is presumed to want. However, these story alterations raise a question regarding Conrad's presence in Hitchcock's film, since the concept of adaptation seems to suggest that it is precisely the *story* which has been borrowed: the discourse, since it exists in a new medium, must surely be unavoidably altered. The separation of the notions of 'story' and 'discourse' allows us to ask and answer this puzzle of what exactly it is in an 'unfaithful' adaptation which stays the same.

Hitchcock's film retains some story elements and also some surprising discourse traces from *The Secret Agent*. The examination of the story and discourse of both texts suggests that the story of Conrad's novel is more obviously evident earlier on in the film – that portion leading up to and showing Stevie's death – but that during this section the discourse is also most markedly different. Conversely in the latter part of film – leading up to and showing Verloc's death – the novel's story is almost abandoned whilst its discourse is more detectably echoed. The reason for this lies in texts' differing treatment of narrative time, specifically in the relationship between story and discourse order.

In *The Secret Agent* the discourse requires the reader, through an elaborate series of analepses and prolepses, to piece together and recover the logic of the story during the process of reading.[8] The novel arranges its anachronies around an ellipsis so that the event around which the entire story pivots – the bomb at the Greenwich Observatory – is contained (or perhaps 'dropped through') a central hole in the discourse. In fact the discourse jumps back and forth across this gap three times, and it also engages in a laborious suturing of the elliptical breach through a series of character-motivated analepses.

In this way the novel's discourse order is employed in the rendition, and division, of a whole series of character voices and moods which are presented within the voice of the narrator. The central ellipsis serves to separate out Mr Verloc's experiences (related in chapters one to three) from those of Mrs Verloc (related in chapters eight and nine), so that the structure of the discourse makes clear the distance between the interests of husband and wife, inviting us to anticipate the moment when their two worlds meet and clash. At the same time the continuous resurfacing of the novel's subordinate analepses promotes the perfect opportunity for the parallel operation of two different narrative moods (the characters who motivate the analepses, and the narrator which introduces them), providing us with an ironic commentary on the private lives of the novel's protagonists.[9] The characters betray decidedly unheroic histories of missed opportunities, misapprehension, and deceit, making the novel's violent conclusion all the more hopelessly inevitable.

In *Sabotage* the discourse order does not follow this convoluted pattern, but instead adopts the exact chronology of the story, making its first fifty-four minutes (and especially those eight minutes in which Stevie tries to deliver the bomb to Piccadilly Circus) conform to what Lew Hunter describes as a 'time-lock'. This he explains as follows:

> The train is rolling in with the bad guys at noon (*High Noon*). The bomb goes off in eight hours (any dramatic TV series). We only have an hour's worth of air in this submarine (*Run Silent, Run Deep*). Tomorrow morning everyone either goes off to college or stays here (*American Graffiti*).[10]

Like *The Secret Agent*, Hitchcock's film uses discourse time in order to manipulate our response to the story's characters, as we can see from an explanation Hitchcock was later to give to François Truffaut, regarding the difference between audience surprise and narrative suspense:

> Let us suppose that there is a bomb underneath this table between us. Nothing happens, and then all of a sudden, 'Boom!' There is an explosion. The public is surprised, but prior to this surprise, it has been an absolutely ordinary scene, of no special consequence. Now, let us take a suspense situation. The bomb is underneath the table and the public knows it, probably because they have seen the anarchist place it there. The public is aware that the bomb is going to explode at one o'clock and there is a clock in the decor. In these conditions this same innocuous conversation becomes fascinating because the public is participating in the scene. The audience is longing to warn the characters on the screen: 'You shouldn't be

talking about such trivial matters. There's a bomb beneath you and it's about to explode!'[11]

Sabotage's rearrangement of the discourse order ensures that the bomb sequence is reinstated as the centre of our attention. This suggests that the film's discourse order is unfaithful to its source here in order to exploit the full visual and narrative potential of the story's action sequence. We are offered the spectacle of the explosion, and we are also invited to engage in apprehensive sympathy for Stevie (who, unlike his novelistic counterpart, does not know he is carrying a bomb). In this way the reader's dispassionate judgement of characters is replaced by the viewer's compassionate concern about what will happen next.

Sabotage replaces the novel's guessing game (regarding what happened when the bomb went off) with a waiting game, putting us in a position of knowing powerlessness. As Hunter's time-lock explanation implies, the time-bomb scenario offers cinema the opportunity to show off its own peculiar discourse capabilities, and, as with Conrad's novel, these capabilities involve the ingenious arrangement of narrative temporality. What is particularly exploited here is the unavoidable playing out of both story and discourse time against what David Bordwell terms 'projection time'.[12] This refers to the running time of a film, as dictated by the combined effect of all filmic technique (the *mise-en-scène*'s shot composition, shot duration and montage; the recording of the soundtrack; and the set projection rate of twenty-four frames per second).

During the scene in which Stevie carries Verloc's time-bomb the film manipulates the fact that, whilst we know the time the bomb will explode in the story (1.45 p.m.), we cannot be certain when the discourse will enact this moment in the real (and 'reel') time of projection. Consequently we are treated to a playful (and heartless) montage of crosscutting between Stevie's progress through London, the bomb he is carrying, and the clocks he passes on the way. The cutting is rapid (with no less than thirty-nine shots depicting Stevie's two-minute bus ride), but the closer we get to 1.45 in the story, the longer the discourse seems to require to dramatise the event (with each new clock we see, the size of the fraction that the minute hand has moved has decreased), so that the explosion becomes alarmingly imminent and frustratingly delayed. In a final acknowledgement of the shameless manipulation being practised,

Hitchcock actually makes us wait until the minute hand has moved, slowly and in close-up, on to 1.46, at which point the bomb, Stevie, a small dog, an old lady, and the bus containing all four, finally explode.

The treatment of Stevie's death in the novel and the film both boast a sophisticated handling of discourse time, but it is noticeable that our response to this manipulation is markedly different in each case. This is because the discourse of the first fifty-four minutes of Hitchcock's film occupies a different position in our awareness of the textual strategy, than does the discourse of Conrad's novel. Though historically at the inception, and stylistically on the fringe, of the literary Modernist movement, *The Secret Agent* was written when the narrative operations of the novel were moving from confident, realist convention to experimental creativity and crisis, and the discourse temporality of Conrad's novel reflects this. The repeated shifts in discourse order produce a preoccupation with the question of who is speaking (since we constantly reassess whose mood is focalising, and which voice is narrating, the story). The narrative voice seems itself absorbed with the awkwardness, difficulties, and failures of language – and with the problems and possibilities of its own chosen discourse.

Sabotage meanwhile displays considerably less unease about the techniques of its medium, and given its location within Hitchcock's career, and the history of cinema, such preoccupation would be surprising. By 1936 Hollywood cinema was engaged in a process of creative consolidation – its introduction of variation was conducted within the parameters of recently established patterns of technical and generic repetition. Hitchcock's later British films share this confident assertion of mature yet evolving conventions, and the explosion sequence in *Sabotage* typifies this. Its ingenious manipulation of discourse time does not subvert the practices of *mise-en-scène*, but rather celebrates them with gleeful extravagance.

In this way Hitchcock's film adapts, not only the novel's story and discourse, but also the relationship between the two, and it does so in order to cater for its own institutional and cultural context. Rather than encouraging an examination of its discourse *Sabotage* invites our investment in the action of the story. Our anxiety about the bomb's imminent explosion offers us the illusion of participation in another world – which is a primary objective of an industry requiring we buy a ticket to enter, and hoping we will visit often.

By switching our attention from narrative discourse to story Hitchcock's film clearly changes the novel's discourse radically. In so doing, however, it also ensures that we can still see clearly the connection between the adaptation and its source, because the story we recognise as Conrad's becomes visible, more visible in fact than it was in the original. Paradoxically the story of Stevie's death, robbed of the obstacles presented by *The Secret Agent*'s discourse, seems to be 'purer' when told in Hitchcock's film.

Lissa Schneider has pointed out that *The Secret Agent* and *Sabotage* are both genre 'hybrids', divided between the 'spy story' and the 'maternal melodrama'.[13] Because *Sabotage* 'straightens out' the novel's discourse order this generic division takes on a temporal partition, with the first fifty-four minutes of the film showing us the results of Verloc's spy mission, and the remaining twenty-two minutes demonstrating the effects this mission has on the Verloc household. This latter portion of the film contains the story's second death sequence, and this is in fact the only direct scenic correlation between the novel and the film. What this suggests is that it is towards the end of the film, when the novel's story undergoes its most radical alterations, that we find more noticeable echoes of the novel's discourse. Once again these traces are most readily identifiable within the texts' temporal properties.

In Conrad's novel Verloc's death is recounted as follows:

> He was lying on his back and staring upwards. He saw partly on the ceiling a clenched hand holding a carving knife. It flicked up and down. Its movements were leisurely. They were leisurely enough for Mr. Verloc to recognise the limb and the weapon.
>
> They were leisurely enough for him to take full meaning of the portent, and to taste the flow of death rising in his gorge. His wife had gone mad – murdering mad. They were leisurely enough for the first paralysing effect of this discovery to pass away before a resolute determination to come out victorious from the ghastly struggle with that armed lunatic. They were leisurely enough for Mr. Verloc to elaborate a plan of defence, involving a dash behind the table, and the felling of the woman to the ground with a heavy wooden chair. But they were not leisurely enough to allow Mr. Verloc the time to move either hand or foot. The knife was already planted in his breast.[14]

This passage contains a characteristically Conradian split in the narrative mood which both upholds and exploits the discourse's temporal ambiguity. Written in the third person, and excluding the mood of Mrs Verloc, the narration uses free indirect discourse to suggest a contamination of its own voice by the mood of Mr Verloc. This is achieved by the colloquialness of phrases like 'raving mad – murdering mad', and 'that armed lunatic', the placement of which within the measured voice of the narration offers an ironic, grotesquely comical comment on the rapid deterioration of Mr Verloc's spousal affection.

Verloc is also mocked in death by the furtive insertion of a discourse ellipsis ('The knife was already planted in his breast'), as well as a playful manipulation of discourse duration. The narration's detailed, repetitive account (with its recurrent phrase 'They were leisurely enough ...') allows the discourse to ape the 'magnified' perceptions of Mr Verloc, who is witnessing the final moments of his life in an exaggerated, 'slow-motion' form. However, the narration also alerts us to expect an abrupt switching back to the 'real' time of the story (we anticipate the phrase 'but they were not leisurely enough'), and the passage ends in comical cadence, since Mr Verloc's 'elaborate plan' is cut off by the speedy planting of the knife. The temporal properties of the discourse again provide an ironic commentary on the deluded, 'out of sync' perceptions of the character.

This passage also contains the kind of precise allusion to visual detail which may account for Orson Welles's surprising comment that 'I don't suppose there's any novelist except Conrad who can be put directly on the screen',[15] and it is not hard to imagine how a number of elements here could be 'put directly' into film. The moving shadow on the wall, for example, evokes the chiaroscuro, anti-realist *mise-en-scène* of German Expressionist cinema, and Hitchcock did in fact borrow from this style when presenting the murder sequence in *Blackmail* (1929). Here a young woman stabs a would-be rapist, and we see the struggle of the attempted rape in a shadow-play on the wall in much the same way that Conrad's Verloc witnesses the murderous approach of his wife. Subsequently the woman is framed wielding the knife in an image of wronged but deadly femininity, which is far more reminiscent of the novel's Mrs Verloc than anything we see in *Sabotage*.

In showing Verloc's death *Sabotage* studiously avoids the sensational, and it rejects much of the novel's story as well as some crucial elements of discourse. In discarding Conrad's pictorial detail *Sabotage* again demonstrates a concern for the audience's involvement with the characters, since it enables the film to, as Hitchcock puts it, 'make the murder inevitable without any blame attached to the woman'.[16] In other words the effect of watching a woman murdering her husband is minimised – and this is done in order to redeem Mrs Verloc in time for the commercially advisable happy ending. The film is so successful in salvaging Mrs Verloc's character that François Truffaut even went so far as to argue that 'the scene almost suggests suicide rather than murder'.[17] *Sabotage* achieves this by again exploiting the medium's temporal properties, and Hitchcock later cited Verloc's death-scene as an illustration of his own preferred approach to montage. He described the scene as follows:

> I showed her hand dropping the knife ... and then having to pick it up again because more meat needed carving – and then dropping it with a clatter. Then immediately a close-up of the man hearing the clatter. Then the woman's hand clasping and unclasping over the handle of the carving knife. All we saw was a foreground of table ... and her hands hovering. Then back to him. He got up, and the camera tilting with him. He realises his danger. I never bothered to show the room, and I allowed that man to go right past the camera towards the woman; and then again he comes to her and he looks down, and the camera goes right from him, following his thought, down to the knife ... And then he makes a grab and she gets it first. Then the two hands: her hands win. And then all you see is two figures, and the man gives a cry and falls.[18]

In this scene Verloc's culpability is suggested in part by the *mise-en-scène*'s construction of character point of view (or more accurately physical viewpoint), since the sequence avoids using the over-the-shoulder, shot/reverse-shot convention, whereby both characters are allowed to occupy the same shot at once. Here we are shown each character in turn, and this practice is brought to its logical conclusion when Mr Verloc goes 'towards the woman', since the camera now replaces Verloc's position within the scene. He and we move towards a stationary and seemingly helpless Mrs Verloc, making her the object of a threatening, potentially victimising gaze.

Hitchcock's account, although impressionistic (and occasionally slightly misleading), makes clear how the sequence's temporal properties – specifically its editing – shape our understanding of events. As Hitchcock explains 'to have shot all that in long view would have been useless. It had to be made up of these little pieces'.[19] As in the earlier death sequence the technique of crosscutting is crucial, and here the singling out of the man, the woman, and the knife seems reminiscent of the apocryphal Kuleshov experiment. Soviet film-maker Lev Kuleshov, having cut together three different montages involving a close-up of an actor's expressionless face (one crosscut with a child, the second with a bowl of soup, and the third with a dead woman), claimed that audience reactions to such sequences demonstrated how cinematic meaning is communicated chiefly through montage. Whilst the experiment has never been satisfacto-rily verified or repeated, Hitchcock's montage does clearly demonstrate the power of presenting carefully selected detail in concise temporal juxtaposition.

Projection time also plays an element here, since its relentless-ness requires that the moment last much longer than its split-second duration in the novel's story time. The scarcity of actual action during this prolonged enactment colludes with the montage in drawing our attention to the abstract – to the moment's surreal nightmarish quality, and also to what might be going on inside the characters' heads. The *mise-en-scène*, as it crosscuts between wife and husband, performs here in miniature the discourse order of Conrad's novel, inviting us to interpret the story as one of a doomed marriage between violently opposed temperaments, whose emotions we share alternately.

Tom Ryall argues that at this point in *Sabotage* we become aware of Hitchcock's presence as a manipulative force behind the camera, of Hitchcock as *auteur*.[20] The sequence forces us into an interpretative act regarding character intent not required by the time-bomb montage, and its reliance on the specifically filmic process of selecting and juxtaposing scenic detail prompts us into an awareness of how the discourse operates. Consequently *Sabotage* begins to display a Conradian self-consciousness of the properties and possibilities of its chosen medium, and in so doing it briefly restores that relationship – in which the story is subordinated to the discourse which presents it – which exists in *The Secret Agent*. In this way the film's rejection of some aspects of the novel's discourse results in the unexpected recuperation of others. At the same time a characteristically Conradian moment of narration is transformed here into a quintessentially Hitchcockian moment of cinema.

Lissa Schneider, disagreeing with Truffaut's verdict on Verloc's death, argues that 'there is little filmic evidence on screen to suggest that Verloc's death is either self-willed or inadvertent'.[21] Her comment is perhaps unintentionally precise, in that we are in fact never shown the image of the death wound being inflicted. *Sabotage* offers an oblique allusion to the novel's temporal ellipsis ('The knife was already planted ...') in the form of a spatial omission: when the stabbing takes place we are shown a two-shot of husband and wife, during which the struggle for the knife takes place below the line of the frame. The *mise-en-scène* takes advantage of the spatial limitations of framing in order to avoid elaborating on the question of character culpability.

Schneider's and Truffaut's differing interpretations of this ambiguity suggest how, when watching adaptations, our response to what we see on screen may be influenced by a number of different cultural connections. Schneider argues for the similarity of the novel's and the film's generic hybridity, and in searching for Conradian traces within the film she detects that moral deficiency in Mrs Verloc, which the novel depicts as common to almost all its characters (indeed it is common to almost all the characters in almost all of Conrad's novels).

Truffaut's assessment, meanwhile, may well derive from a different, typically Hitchcockian, moral ambiguity. If we accept even a partial exoneration of Mrs Verloc then Ted's protective chivalry towards her looks increasingly like an act of sexual blackmail. This interpretation aligns *Sabotage* with later Hitchcock films, such as *Vertigo* (1958) and *Marnie* (1964), in which 'guilty' women are either punished or saved by dashing lovers, who are also manipulative father-figures. Both Robin Wood and Tania Modleski have pointed out the disturbing tension in such films between the ostensible restoration of order and the ruthless misogyny which brings about such conclusions.[22] Neither Sylvia Sidney, as Mrs Verloc, nor John Loder as Ted, can compete with quintessential Hitchcock stars like James Stewart, Cary Grant, or Grace Kelly. Yet the adaptation of Conrad's *The Secret Agent* does seem to have provided a blueprint story for the tales of icy, but tormented blondes, and strong but ruthless heroes, which helped to make such stars household names.

What this suggests is that no matter how autonomously an adaptation treats its source, the cultural ties of neither work can really be severed. *Sabotage* adapts both the story and the discourse of *The Secret Agent*, and it does so in order to construct a narrative which will conform to cinema's commercial requirements. The resulting film has shaped the development of Hitchcock's filmography – a film-ography which in turn feeds back into our current assessment of the film. Ultimately even structuralism cannot subvert these connections, particularly since the proposition that meaning requires pairs tempts us to assume that interpretation requires comparisons. The discernible traces of Conrad's novel within Hitchcock's film encourage us to search for more such traces, and this suggests that two particular pleasures which adaptations can offer us are the detection of the process's own narrative ingenuities, and the discovery that the source text somehow 'still applies' – even in movies. Comparing *Sabotage* to *The Secret Agent* provides a reassurance as to the resilience of cultural continuity: neither time, nor cinema, nor murdermeister Hitchcock have managed to 'kill off' Conrad.

Adaptation is a process which draws attention to its own reproductive act, seeming to invite the expectation that the 'offspring' live up to its 'parent' whilst simultaneously establishing an identity of its own. Conrad's experimental discourse, coupled with his status as a Polish writer of English literature (suggesting another possible institutional conflict) place him in something of a marginal position within the literary tradition, whilst Hitchcock is now central to the history of cinema's stylistic and institutional development. Echoes of *Sabotage* re-emerge in many later Hitchcock films: the technique of crosscutting for the purposes of suspense recurs, most memorably in the crop-dusting sequence of *North by Northwest*, whilst the use of temporal juxtaposition and spatial selection to imply murderous violence was used in *Psycho* to create the 'slasher' sequence which changed the manipulation of *mise-en-scène* for ever.

Consequently the way in which this pairing of texts define each other has been reversed. Conrad is clearly no longer needed to advertise Hitchcock, but Hitchcock's film may be said to perform something of a cultural 're-animation' of Conrad's novel. Clearly this is a minor Hitchcock movie of a major Conrad work, but the institutional, generic, and canonical strings attached to each text set up a tug of war in which the two sides appear increasingly evenly matched.

NOTES

1 Eleanor Coppola, *Notes: On the Making of Apocalypse Now* (London, Faber and Faber, 1995).

2 Hugh Herbert, 'The Horror! The Horror!', *The Guardian* (17 July 1995).

3 *Conrad on Film*, ed. Gene M. Moore (Cambridge, Cambridge University Press, 1997).

4 Lew Hunter, *Screenwriting* (London, Hale, 1994), p. 27.

5 Hunter, *Screenwriting*, p. 44.

6 Gérard Genette, *Narrative Discourse*, trans. Jane E. Levin (Oxford, Blackwell, 1989).

7 Shlomith Rimmon-Kenan, *Narrative Fiction: Contemporary Poetics* (London, Routledge, 1989), p. 72.

8 Genette uses the term 'anachronies' to refer to 'the various types of discordance between the two orderings of story and narrative', Genette, *Narrative Discourse*, p. 36. The definition is subdivided into the binary opposition analepsis/prolepsis, the former referring to those moments when the discourse jumps backwards in story-time (more commonly known in the cinema as a 'flashback'), and the latter referring to a discourse jump forwards (a 'flashforward').

9 Genette distinguishes between 'anachronies that the narrative takes direct responsibility for, and thus stay on the same narrative level as their surroundings', and 'subordinate anachronies', which 'one of the characters of the first narrative takes on', Genette, *Narrative Discourse*, pp. 47–8.

10 Hunter, *Screenwriting*, p. 50.

11 François Truffaut, *Hitchcock* (London, Granada, 1978), p. 80.

12 David Bordwell, *Narration in the Fiction Film* (London, Routledge, 1988), p. 81.

13 Lissa Schneider, '*The Woman Alone* in Conrad and Hitchcock,' in Moore, *Conrad*, pp. 61–77.

14 Joseph Conrad, *The Secret Agent* (London, Penguin, 1963, repr. 1990), ch. 11, p. 234.

15 Orson Welles and Peter Bogdanovich, *This Is Orson Welles*, ed. Jonathan Rosenbaum (London, HarperCollins, 1993), p. 262. Given Orson Welles's own failure to put Conrad on the screen this statement is questionable. It is a comment which is best explained as a reference, and compliment, to Conrad's pictorial style of prose and, as Gene M. Moore points out, Welles seems to contradict himself, remarking in the same interview that 'There's never been a Conrad movie, for the simple reason that nobody's ever done it as written,' Welles and Bogdanovich, *This Is Orson Welles*, p. 32. See also Moore, *Conrad*, p. 2.

16 *Hitchcock on Hitchcock*, ed. Sidney Gottlieb (London, Faber and Faber, 1995), p. 186.

17 Truffaut, *Hitchcock*, p. 120.

18 Gottlieb, *Hitchcock on Hitchcock*, p. 187.

19 Gottlieb, *Hitchcock on Hitchcock,* p. 187.

20 Tom Ryall, *Alfred Hitchcock and the British Cinema* (London, Athlone, 1996), p. 160.

21 Schneider, in Moore, *Conrad*, p. 69.

22 Robin Wood, *Hitchcock's Film's Revisited* (New York, Columbia University Press, 1989); Tania Modleski, *The Women Who Knew Too Much: Hitchcock and Feminist Theory* (New York, Methuen, 1988).

9

'Lids tend to come off': David Lean's film of E. M. Forster's *A Passage to India*

Neil Sinyard

He was never quite the man to come to terms with Forsterian subtleties.[1]

One other thing, I've got rid of that 'Not yet, not yet' bit. You know, when the Quit India stuff comes up, and we have the passage about driving us into the sea? Forster experts have always said it was very important but the Fielding–Aziz friendship was not sustained by these sorts of things. At least I don't think so – the book came out at the time of the trial of General Dyer and had a tremendous success in America for that reason. But I thought that bit rather tacked on. Anyway, I see it as a personal not a political story and I want people to argue about what happened in the caves through their understanding of the characters involved.[2]

The most successful screen adaptations of literature have, I would argue, one or all of three main characteristics. They aim for the spirit of the original rather than the literal letter; they use the camera to interpret and not simply illustrate the tale; and they exploit a particular affinity between the artistic temperaments and preoccupations of the novelist and filmmaker. To embroider this a little, I would say that an effective film adaptation is not afraid to diverge from the original if it feels such divergence is either true to the feeling/ethos of the original, or can be justified in terms of an alternative (possibly superior) narrative or thematic strategy, or is necessitated by the communicative difference of the two mediums (i.e. what works in novelistic terms might not work on film). Moreover a film should surely make *some* changes to the original structure, for if it is merely duplicating the plot in visual terms, why make the film at all? However, the most interesting adaptations are those which, through these changes, disclose a personal interpretation of the text, so that the film becomes part critical commentary written by the camera, and part palimpsest – that is, a fresh creation is revealed under the skin, as it were, of the original.[3] It seems to me that David Lean's 1984 film version of E. M. Forster's *A Passage to India* fulfils all these criteria to a greater or lesser extent, but certainly with sufficient intelligence and craftsmanship to make it by far the most cinematically satisfying of all the Forster film adaptations to date.

Coincidentally, it took fourteen years for Forster to write *A Passage to India* (*Howards End* had been published in 1910, *Passage* in 1924) and it took fourteen years for David Lean to complete another film after the critical mauling of *Ryan's Daughter* (1970). It was Forster's last novel and it was Lean's last film. It seems more than coincidence, however, that brought novel and filmmaker together for Lean's films reveal a cluster of themes and preoccupations that occur in *A Passage to India* and would ostensibly make him the ideal director for the subject: for example, the metaphor of hallucination and mirage for confused states, that one finds in *Lawrence of Arabia* (1962); the spirit of place that intoxicates and eroticises the foreigner, as in *Summer Madness* (1955); British repression, sexual frustration and consequent delirium, that Lean explored in *Brief Encounter* (1945), *Great Expectations* (1946) and *Ryan's Daughter*. 'What visions! What consummate craftsmanship!' exclaimed fellow filmmaker Dusan Makaveyev on seeing the film, before adding darkly, 'but then Lean is a genius and perhaps audiences don't want that!' It was not so much audiences as the English critical intelligentsia who found Lean wanting as the ideal Forster interpreter.

There is no doubt that part of the critical hostility shown to the film in this country was due to two main causes: a literary sensibility amongst critics that was far more developed than a cinematic sensibility (something which has bedevilled British film criticism over the years); and a reverence for Forster as literary icon which would resent any free play with their idol's creative imagination, a reverence which, I should declare, I do not happen to share. It may be that my high estimation of the film is attributable to (or at least not inhibited by) an estimation of the novel which is less flattering than the critical norm and is therefore less outraged by Lean's changes and omissions. Indeed, to contextualise this argument, it may be necessary to spell this out in a little more detail. 'Never quite the man to come to terms with Forsterian subtleties', says Penelope Houston of Lean in *Sight and Sound* in this chapter's opening extract, the word 'quite' giving an ineffably patronising tone to the judgement – as if the poor soul aspires to such sophistication but has not 'quite' got the breeding. (It reminds me of Frank Swinnerton's vicious parody of *Aspects of the Novel* to convey what he saw as Forster's intellectual snobbery: 'Some of us were at King's College Cambridge, the rest, oh dear yes, not.')[4]

I have to say that although there are many qualities I admire and identify in Forster as a writer (the gentle humour, the decency of his liberal values, the humane and often heroic hatred of racism, nationalism, intolerance) 'subtlety' has never been one of them. Forster's novels are often disfigured by narrative and symbolic clumsiness, as he grapples with the aspect of the novel form that he finds least congenial: namely, the telling of a story. I am thinking, for example, of that moment in *The Longest Journey* (1907), when at the beginning of chapter five he disposes of an expendable character by having him killed playing football. 'Gerald died that afternoon. He was broken up in the football match.'[5] To which one's reaction is not 'How subtle!' but 'Some match!'; and Forster's bathetic, unathletic phrase 'broken up' makes the effect seem even worse. Or take *Howards End*, where the crushing effect of learning on poor Leonard Bast is thunderously symbolised by the alarmingly literal device of having a bookcase fall on top of him. The symbolism of *A Room with a View* (1908) is even cruder than that, almost diagrammatic in its obviousness, where a room with a view signals its occupant as 'enlightened' whilst a room without a view indicates its occupant as 'blinkered': a cramped, limited character is even called Vyse.

Even the poise of Forster's highly regarded authorial voice sometimes wavers between evasiveness and obviousness. 'Visions are supposed to entail profundity,' he says in *A Passage to India*, but then adds, with a lame sub-Victorian apology, 'but – wait till you get one, dear reader!'[6] When he says in *Howards End* at one stage that 'indeed Margaret was making a most questionable statement',[7] one thinks of Brahms's response when people insisted on pointing out thematic similarities between his First Symphony and Beethoven's Ninth: 'Any donkey can see that.' When he asserts about Mrs Wilcox in the same novel that 'it is odd, all the same, she should give the idea of greatness',[8] the reader feels obliged to correct the author and respond that it is not odd, it is frankly incredible, given Forster's inability to dramatise this 'greatness'. Some of us, who admire Forster's emphatic statements in other contexts, still have difficulty with the blatant insensitivity of the opening of chapter six of *Howards End* that blights the whole novel: 'We are not concerned with the very poor. They are unthinkable, and only to be approached by the statistician or the poet.'[9] (Dickens would have shot him for that: think of how much more human curiosity and compassion there is in that author's perception of the 'mystery' in the 'meanest of them' in *Hard Times*). Of course, there is much more to Forster than these lapses of artistic judgement and the cumbersome melodrama of his plotting (murder in *A Room with a View*, alleged rape and sexual hysteria in *Passage to India*, seduction, illegitimacy and manslaughter in *Howards End*, child–death, fatal accident, violent assault in *Where Angels Fear to Tread*), but I remain singularly unconvinced that 'Forsterian subtlety' is an adequate critical club with which to beat David Lean and his film. What I prefer to do is trace the evolution of Lean's approach to the text and explore both what it tells us about the novel in narrative and symbolic terms, and what it illuminates about the work of one of England's premier directors.

In a long letter to Santha Rama Rau, who had written a popular adaptation of *A Passage to India* for the theatre and was involved in the early stages of the writing of the screenplay, Lean has some very interesting perceptions about the novel and about the specific difficulty it presents in adaptation for the screen – difficulties that, in some cases, have to do with the different natures of film and novel.[10] It is a fascinating document because it gives some major clues about Lean's approach to, and interpretation of, the text. The core of the adaptation, he argues, must hinge on what happened at the caves. Some critics might dispute the centrality of that episode to the novel as a whole (though in a Penguin Modern Classics edition of the novel published in 1961 the synopsis on the back cover devoted more than half its length to this single incident), but for Lean to establish this event as the top priority of his adaptation seems entirely sensible and convincing. It is what the narrative leads to and from, and it parallels, for example, Harold Pinter's brilliantly direct strategy for the seemingly intractable problem of adapting *The French Lieutenant's Woman* – you start at the work's indisputable, inexorable core (in that case, Sarah Woodroff's monologue about the French

Lieutenant) and work your way backwards from its implications. Lean argues persuasively that Forster 'found himself out of his depth in this scene' – I would argue that Forster is out of his depth both physically and metaphysically in this scene – 'and changed it, rather carelessly, into a sort of mystery.'[11] He goes on to say that he dislikes the cheap Agatha Christie-type detail of the binoculars with the broken strap, though he will actually keep that detail in the film as a piece of incriminatory evidence against Aziz; and he feels that the guide as 'suspect rapist' is a red herring.[12] He insists that any adaptation must decide what happened, and Lean's view is to see it as a hallucination. Having decided that, he must then work back and think what light that might shed on the character of Adela Quested. 'For the first 150 pages of the novel,' Lean says, 'I don't know and can only guess at explanations for her behaviour ... I have a strong feeling that Forster didn't care for her and was only interested in using her as a somewhat tiresome tool in the plot.'[13] By interpreting the Marabar Caves incident as a hallucination and from that reconsidering and reconstructing Adela's character, Lean transforms her into a heroine who has tantalising connections with some heroines of his other films, which might offer another explanation for his being drawn to this material. In the process, he makes the character of Adela an infinitely more interesting personality in the film than she is in the novel.

In adaptation terms, then, for the film, two problems are thereby solved: the clarification of the Marabar mystery; and the transformation of the dreary Adela. Lean identified three other particular problems with the novel for screen purposes, in interviews prior to the film that thereby probably only succeeded in antagonising Forsterians before they even saw the finished product. Firstly, he felt Forster had too much of an anti-English bias in the novel, and he would try to balance it a little more, be more even-handed, which disquieted some critics who felt the novel's politics would be gutted and its anti-imperialist message lost.[14] I must say that I have never experienced this with the film: the hypocrisy, arrogance and insensitivity of the Anglo-Indians come through with undiminished force. Secondly, he felt the final part of the novel would need tightening and tidying for the film. Again he was criticised for this, particularly for his omission of the last scene between Fielding and Aziz on horseback – a diminution on a visual as well as political level, it was said – but again Lean felt it would not work cinematically and was rather 'tacked on' in the novel. Certainly part of the interest of the scene in the novel is its prophetic power – the prediction of the end of British rule in India – and Lean no doubt felt it would be pointless for him to make a display of being prophetic *after* the event. His emphasis, anyway, he said, was on the personal not the political story and, even there, that is hardly a betrayal of Forster's intention, since the novelist said the work was more about the failure of human communication than the horrors of imperialism. Thirdly, Lean felt that Forster's narrative structures did not lend themselves to cinema without some adjustment:

> Forster doesn't – *as you have to do in a film* – have a well-defined thread going through it. One of the difficulties was not to be tempted by side-tracks. He is a wonderful side-tracker. His side-tracks are the most entertaining reading, but I don't think they're necessarily film material.[15]

Forster's dislike of the prominence of a plot in a novel – 'The novel tells a story. Oh dear yes, the novel tells a story'[16] – is famous, and is perhaps the most stark contrast to Lean, who was one of the cinema's master storytellers. He recognised that the film needed a strong narrative line, leading to and from the caves, so that Adela, as he said, should be 'almost impelled *from the outset* towards her appointment at Marabar. This is the eavesdrop. Only we will know about it.'[17] The feminising of the novel in this way might not be to everyone's taste, but at least it is carried through with unerring logic and coherence to the film's very last frame; if it ducks the novel's homo-eroticism it at least undercuts its misogyny; and it is absolutely consistent with some key preoccupations of the director from the very outset of his career. It would be impossible in this brief analysis to elucidate all the nuances of Lean's adaptation, but in teasing out some of the slight or significant deviations from the novel by focusing on key scenes, I hope to uncover Lean's interpretive slant on the material and what the differences tell us about their respective art forms.

Unlike the novel, the film begins in England: rain, umbrellas, Adela (Judy Davis) in the travel bureau buying her passage to India. By beginning the film here, Lean clearly intends to highlight the contrast – physical, psychological, political – between the environment the English are used to and that which they will encounter, which in turn serves as preparation for the hallucination that will take place at the narrative's heart. Adela will leave England in the rain, as Lean puts it,

> pale and pure. Then the sun comes out. Suez, the desert, the heat of the Red Sea. India. I've often wondered why Europeans first arriving in the East either like it or hate it. Lids tend to come off.[18]

Adela gazes at the model of a ship and then, with particular intensity, at a picture of the Marabar caves. The hypnotic pull of this picture in the first scene is evidently laying the ground for later narrative developments but is also suggesting that Adela might develop into another of those heroines of particular fascination to Lean – women such as Laura in *Brief Encounter*, Jane Hudson in *Summer Madness*, Rosie Ryan in *Ryan's Daughter*, who in Steven Ross's phrase, possess 'a romantic sensibility attempting to reach beyond the restraints and constrictions of everyday life'.[19] In another marked difference from the novel, the film will end with Adela back in a rain-soaked England, a neat cyclical structure that emphasises her centrality in Lean's scheme of things. This in turn solves a narrative problem in the novel that Lean identified: namely, that Adela fades out of the narrative too early, and that the film would have to find some way of keeping her going to the end. He does this through judicious use of a detail Forster refers to incidentally in his final chapter: Aziz's forgiving and conciliatory letter to Adela some years after the event.

The train journey with Adela, Mrs Moore (Peggy Ashcroft) and the Turtons (Richard Wilson and Antonia Pemberton) is a useful addition to the adaptation, concisely introducing and indicating character – the Turtons' prejudice, Adela's naivety, Mrs Moore's directness – and serving as a metaphor for the emotional and psychological journeys that Adela particularly, and Mrs Moore too, are to undergo. Trains never lost their magical attraction for Lean, and scenes in or around them in his films – for example, the business around Milford Junction in *Brief Encounter* or the magnificently filmed journey across a revolution-torn Russia in *Dr Zhivago* (1965) – are invariably important. In *Passage*, they loom significantly, because they are progressively menacing: later we will have the train journey to the caves, then Mrs Moore's last train journey prior to her death. They are met at Chandrapore by Adela's fiancé, Mrs Moore's son, Ronny Heaslop (Nigel Havers). 'I had no idea he [Turton] was so important,' says Adela, to which Ronny replies, surprised: 'You hadn't?' Cut to the miniature British flag on Turton's official car that is to force Dr Aziz (Victor Bannerjee) and his friend Mahmoud Ali (Art Malik) off the road. British symbols and icons are to be a form of significant shorthand in this film: emblems of power, different cultures, different values. Inspecting the damage to his bicycle, Aziz will hiss, contemptuously: 'English!' In *Lawrence of Arabia*, Ali (Omar Sharif) will similarly shout 'English!' at Lawrence (Peter O'Toole) when Lawrence is at his most stubborn and exasperating. Both Forster and Lean share a fascinated horror with Englishness – the arrogance and oddness of the English and what Forster memorably called their 'undeveloped hearts'.[20] Forster and Lean are fascinated by what happens when you take them from their usual habitat and put them somewhere hot where they can lose their inhibitions, shed a skin as it were, but where they come face to face with themselves. As Mrs Moore will say in the film: 'India forces one to come to terms with oneself. It can be very disturbing.' In Lean, there is a dual impact of their Englishness on their environment and their environment on their Englishness, as can be seen also in *Lawrence of Arabia* and *The Bridge on the River Kwai* (1957). The impact leads not simply to tension but to near breakdown, even madness, as they lose sense of where they are and who they are. In Lean's phrase, lids come off.

On arriving at Ronny's house, Adela is immediately drawn to the window and a view of the fateful Marabar caves; Lean is remembering his narrative thread here and the sense he wants to convey of Adela's almost unwitting, magnetic attraction to the caves as if she there senses her destiny. Later, when Ronny knocks at her door but then says, 'Good night' without coming in, Adela's disappointment is registered in a mirror shot (Judy Davis superb here, as elsewhere): a hint of sexual frustration but also of an insecure sense of her own identity, attractiveness. Dissolve to a sign of the court of the city magistrate – what Ronny represents, a depersonalised symbol of office, a statement of his position in that society which is more important to him than anything else and quite dissolves more personal feelings.

In the first meeting of Dr Aziz and Mrs Moore in the mosque, Lean sticks closely to Forster's own dialogue. The visual composition is masterly, though: the moon reflected in water, wind stirring the leaves, Mrs Moore appearing like a ghost – a premonition of her later death perhaps and an anticipation of her spirit that will live on after death. This is a tender conversation in whispers, sensitive to setting, superbly acted: the crucial bond between these two characters is indelibly established. When Mrs Moore returns to the play in the Club, she says to Adela: 'I've had an *adventure.*' Adela is looking for adventure, but the adventure she has will change her life. In the club, they all stand for the National Anthem: British solidarity and conformity (an anticipation of the moment when they will later all stand for the stricken Ronny, except, pointedly, Fielding), punctuated by the moment when Mrs Moore, her mind straying from English decorum and thinking of her meeting with Aziz, looks over her shoulder towards the river. There is a shot of the Ganges in all its moonlit majesty and then, in a thrilling moment at the heart of the film's meaning, crocodiles plop suddenly to the surface – the animalistic and the primitive rising unbidden out of the darkness, like the return of the repressed.

Lean's rendering of the Bridge Party and Fieldings' more modest gathering are mostly faithful to Forster, the former scene emphasising Mrs Moore's irritation at English condescension and the tepidly British music ('Tea for Two,' 'Roses of Picardy,' 'In a Monastery Garden'), the latter emphasising the talk of mystery and muddle. Godbole (Alec Guinness) seems noticeably to discomfort Mrs Moore, as if he sees through her and senses her vulnerability and unease; and when he defines the Marabar Caves as 'empty and dark', Lean cuts to Adela (her sexual state?) and Mrs Moore (her spiritual state?). Forster's 'into this Ronny dropped' is perfectly conveyed by Lean's abrupt, precisely timed close-up of the character, flushed and rude. When Adela, partly because of this behaviour, later breaks off her engagement while they are watching a game of polo, Lean indicates Ronny's response through a witty visual trope: a shot of a polo player as he falls off his horse, but then picks himself up, dusts himself down, and starts all over again. It is a lovely laconic observation of the English way of accepting misfortune and emotional upset with equanimity and dignity. 'We're being awfully English about this, aren't we?' says Adela (Forster says 'British' in the novel). 'I suppose that's all right.' The *limits* of the English temperament are to be tested in the film's following scene, which is its first major departure from the novel and in some ways the most radical and interesting in the entire adaptation.

Adela has gone for a ride on her bicycle and, in straying from the path, has come across a deserted temple with erotic statues.

Investigating further, she finds the statues surrounded by monkeys which chase her off. Forster purists were particularly offended by this scene. Although dismayed at first that she had not been more involved in the writing of the film, Santha Rama Rau later expressed relief because, she said, 'I think I would have had a fit if I had known in advance that the film was going to contain the sequence of a lonely 'brave' Memsahib cycling about the Indian countryside and coming upon erotic sculptures only to be scared into flight by a pack of shrieking monkeys. This sort of vulgarity was so remote from Forster's oblique, equivocal approach to Adela's sexual malaise.'[21] Still, Rau's 'oblique' and 'equivocal' might be another person's 'muddled' and 'evasive': I agree with Lean that Adela's lurid fantasy in the Marabar Caves is not adequately prepared for in the novel and needs to be if the film's central event is to convince. Whereas Forster can only hint tentatively at Adela's state, Lean boldly ventures into territory where the novelist could not – dare not – go. Lean's stress on the sensual and erotic impact of India on the heroine is very much in the tradition of such works as Paul Scott's *Raj Quartet* or Powell and Pressburger's most delirious melo-drama, *Black Narcissus* (1947). The scene will anticipate the moment of crisis at the Marabar Caves (an indefinable threat, followed by panic and hysteria) and also prefigure an unnerving moment during Adela's drive to the trial, when a native, disguised behind a monkey's face, pushes his head inside the car, as if pushing this earlier incident to the forefront of her consciousness and linking the two events.

The scene is centrally concerned with what Lean calls Adela's 'as-yet-untapped sexuality', which is expressed purely through visual suggestion. Having just broken off her engagement in a very English manner (i.e. restrained, polite) to a very English gentleman (i.e. dull, unemotional), and now straying from a regular path, she has suddenly come upon a temple of love whose imagery of sexual fulfilment is in direct opposition to her frustrated emotional state. She is being brought sharply face to face with a very different culture of worship – erotic and emotional rather than reverential and restrained. She is also being compelled to confront something behind her romanticised view of India which she cannot come to terms with or control, because it touches on her own sexual uncer-tainty and neurosis. It is a walk into old places, brimming over with sexual heat and crawling with animal vitality and it puts her to flight:

running away from her inner self and straight back into the arms of Ronny, with whom she resumes her engagement. Is this because he will fulfil her sexual yearnings or, more likely, being a dull prig, he will subdue them, protect her from them?

What seems to me incontestable is that Lean's motivation of the heroine's renewed engagement is immeasurably more persuasive and intriguing than in the novel, where Ronny and Adela are reunited through an arbitrary accident involving their car and an animal (a tired old narrative contrivance Forster had already deployed in *Howards End*). Lean continues with a wicked joke: Ronny and Adela at a dance together where the main tune is 'Lady be Good'. But alone in her bed, accompanied by Lean's nature imagery (flowers opening their buds), Adela dreams of those statues. In narrative terms, the scene is a crucial block in Lean's careful construction of Adela's emotional passage to the Marabar Caves. In symbolic terms, the scene has a wholly appropriate eroticism and sexuality that a D. H. Lawrence would not have shied away from (think of Ursula's encounter with the horses in *The Rainbow* when she is in a state of emotional trauma) but an E. M. Forster would: it is his central limitation as a novelist.[22]

The Marabar Caves episode in *A Passage to India* is Forster's equivalent to the Box Hill episode in *Emma*. Nothing is wanting except to be happy when they get there: a civilised set-piece in which everything goes steadily, horribly wrong. The sequence is introduced by a superb, typical cut by Lean from a shot of a hawk crossing the caves to a shot of Mrs Moore from inside the cave, as if challenging her to enter. The film gives an explicit aural charge to the echo of the cave (a distorted baby's cry, a roar, Mrs Moore's name rocking in amplified mockery across the walls) that Forster's flat, impoverished vocabulary – 'the echo began in some *indescribable* way to undermine her hold on life'[23] – cannot match. In his review of the film in *Sight and Sound*, Gavin Millar has argued that the film gets Forster's echo disastrously wrong, the film's serving to celebrate Mrs Moore's identity rather than annihilate it, as Forster's does, in the utterly dull 'boum'.[24] Millar's elaborate argument tends only to emphasise the contrivance of Forster's device: one is never quite convinced that an echo – particularly as he describes it – could have as much meaning as he insistently ascribes to it.[25] Cinematically, Lean could not give Forster's echo the nullity that Millar demands because it would simply come over as anti-climactic. He opts for something less mystical, more powerful, more personal – an amplification of Mrs Moore's name that reverberates with hollowness, which understandably shakes her, and a distinctive roar that sounds like the rush of the express train that hurtles past Laura in *Brief Encounter* as she contemplates annihilation.

There has been a false dawn and now, when Adela looks towards Chandrapore through her field glasses, she says: 'It's almost a mirage.' Much of the film can be felt in that moment: mirages, imprecise perceptions, distortions of scale. Has any film made more over an incident in which 'nothing happens' – except, perhaps, Lean's *Brief Encounter*? The brief dialogue between Aziz and Adela before she goes into the cave is more focused than in the novel: a delicate discussion of love, arranged marriages and instinctive sexual feeling between man and woman which is enough to disconcert Adela about her own sexuality and her engagement to pompous, sterile Ronny. So that when she goes into the cave, what follows her – and how well Lean has marshalled all this – is her prim English upbringing, the impact of India, her hostility to imperialism and the Anglo-Indians, the influence of Mrs Moore, her doubts about her fiancé, the touch of Aziz's hand as he helps her up the cliff. All are gathered to that moment when a man stands in the opening of the cave and Adela's English reserve cracks wide open under the pressure of the echo of her sexual frustration. Bold shock cut to a shot of masturbatory running water; Mrs Moore's sudden 'What's happened?' is an inimitably Lean-like reaction of premonitory doom;[26] there follows in rapid succession the shot of Adela's hat tumbling down the cliff, a long shot of Fielding's arrival, Aziz's careering down, Adela's savage scratches.

The aftermath of the incident yields some fine cinematic moments. When Mrs Moore is leaving on the train Godbole appears under an archway, like Aziz at the mouth of the cave, making a sign that terrifies her, as if he has foreseen her death (the casting of Alec Guinness as Godbole was much criticised, but the authority and aura he gives to this scene alone would justify it). Cut to Adela on her way to the trial, encouraged by the Turtons and passing a statue of Queen Victoria, as if the whole of the British Raj is propelling her towards the courtroom.

In the courtroom scene, Lean respects key details of the novel – the Indian pulling the fan, Adela's hurt expression at the reference to her physical unattractiveness. There is a moving dissolve to the sea and Mrs Moore, the sound of the former seeming to harmonise with the terrifying, fatal roar of her heart: the chant of her name outside the courtroom is heard over her burial at sea. One of the great moments of the film is Adela's walk to the witness box, dream-like but not slow motion to suggest a mind still in shock, and accompanied by an evocative soundtrack of voices and the cave's echo. The Bible comes into the film frame at such an odd angle that it looks something quite alien and the shot gathers up several motifs in the film – English piety, Mrs Moore's *loss* of belief, Adela's upbringing ('I've been brought up to tell the truth'), the different religions and customs that might have precipitated this crisis. Lean's magisterial editing during her testimony – flashes of the moment when she and Aziz clasped hands, of lighting the match in the dark – suddenly transforms the cave into the inside of Adela's head. When she refuses to incriminate Aziz, she is asked by McBride: 'Are you mad?' a question often posed of Lean's heroes and heroines.[27] She looks up. The monsoon is beating a tattoo of release on the courthouse window, preparing us for our last shot of her.

To summarise: although the film might be said to soften the satire and savagery Forster directs at the Anglo-Indians, it tightens the narrative structure and does better by its female characters, particularly Adela, who is a dry stick in the novel but transformed in the film into one of Lean's most poignant repressed romantics. Lean diverts Forster's droll omniscient commentary essentially into the consciousness of a central character – the only way to do it, he would argue – and rises to the story's central visual challenge: the vague, visionary events of an ill-fated expedition during which the tremulous trickle of subdued English emotion will explode into hallucination and hysteria. I would argue further that the film's two finest scenes (Adela's encounter with the erotic statues, Mrs Moore's train departure) are of events that do not appear in Forster but are nevertheless legitimate, imaginative flights derived from the text, its hints, its possibilities, its absences. Their inclusion is comparable with, say, Orson Welles's brilliant opening of *Othello* (1952), with Iago suspended in mid-air in an iron cage, which is not in Shakespeare but which has, in Grigori Kozintsev's phrase, 'a dynamic, visual reality'[28] that justifies the addition.

I am conscious that this is a very *auteurist* reading. Given that Lean not only directed the film but also wrote and edited it, I do not apologise for that, though obviously this leaves open numerous

Neil Sinyard

other avenues for exploration. The strategy of this, though, is partly to insist that a film adaptation of this text, or any text, cannot properly be expected simply to be the original in pictures, as it were, and must become both something else and someone else's. Derek Malcolm in his review of the film in *The Guardian* put this rather well:

> There's no such thing as a faithful screen version of a literary classic if by faithful you mean literal. The best a film maker can do is to take an intelligent view and pursue it logically to the end. That logic is better expressed in images than in words. David Lean's *A Passage to India* does precisely this supremely well. It isn't Forster's *Passage,* it's Lean's. And that's no bad bargain.[29]

The very act of adaptation is an appropriation of a text from one medium to another and, in the best cases, from author to *auteur*. In his writings on film and stage versions of Dickens, Grahame Smith has described adaptation as a dual process, whereby an act of possession, in which the original material is taken from its creator, is followed by an act of recreation, in which this material now appears in a completely new form. And why not? As Orson Welles used to say: 'If Verdi did it (i.e. make operas of Shakespeare), why can't I'? (i.e. make films of Shakespeare). Indeed E. M. Forster himself did it, adapting Herman Melville for operatic purposes in his libretto for Benjamin Britten's *Billy Budd*. So, whatever Forsterians might say, David Lean is surely entitled to take the raw material of *Passage* and make of it a highly personal study of the passion beneath the probity of the English character, of the disorientating imperialist legacy which both aggrandises and alienates a sense of national identity, and much else besides. Never quite the man for Forsterian subtleties? Lean was always the man for Adela, India and the Marabar Caves. He does not catch Forster's tone of voice? But how could he, or any film director? Novels describe: films depict. At their best, adaptations from one to another should not be seen as travesty but translation, not a reductive illustration of an inimitable masterpiece but an imaginative retelling of classic material in a new form and for a new audience.

NOTES

1 Penelope Houston, *Sight and Sound*, spring 1985, p. 82.
2 *The Guardian*, 23 January 1984, p. 11.

3 Adaptation as a form of palimpsest was explicitly alluded to on the credits of Jean-Jacques Annaud's film, *The Name of the Rose* (1987), when the adaptation by Andrew Birkin, Gerard Brach, Howard Franklin and Alain Godard was described as a 'palimpsest' of Umberto Eco's novel.

4 Frank Swinnerton, *The Georgian Literary Scene* (London, Hutchinson, 1935), p. 311.

5 E. M. Forster, *The Longest Journey* (London, Penguin Modern Classics, 1960), p. 56.

6 E. M. Forster, *A Passage to India* (London, Penguin Twentieth-Century Classics, 1985), p. 213.

7 E. M. Forster, *Howards End* (London, Penguin Modern Classics, 1961), p. 55.

8 Forster, *Howards End*, p. 73.

9 Forster, *Howards End*, p. 44.

10 The letter is quoted at length in Kevin Brownlow's monumental biography, *David Lean* (London, Faber and Faber, 1997), pp. 646–51.

11 Brownlow, *David Lean*, p. 647. In *The Manuscripts of A Passage to India* (1978), edited by Oliver Stallybrass, the editor has shown that Forster's earlier version was much more explicit about the sexual assault and also made clear that Aziz was responsible.

12 Cicely Havely, 'End of Empire' booklet (London, Penguin, 1991) for the Open University's Literature in the Modern World course. Cicely Havely is much more scathing about Forster's evasiveness on this point, and takes particular offence at the agreement between Adela and Fielding to 'let us call it the guide – it will never be known' (p. 261). Havely comments: 'Forster allows a calumny to remain alive, like a half-killed snake. When there is no explanation, when no one can be accused, 'Let us call it the guide' – and blame an Indian.' Forster thus manages to be both enigmatic and racist. Havely goes on: 'It is not just that Adela Quested does not know whether she was attacked; the narrative does not know either; the author has refused to know. This is shocking in a fiction where nothing else is withheld from us, and where the narrator assumes an unusually godlike stance' (p. 70). I agree with this. Forster's defence of his vagueness as a legitimate trick 'because my theme was India' (letter to G. L. Dickinson, 26 June 1924) is quite inadequate for the reason Havely indicates: it is stylistically inconsistent with the rest of the novel. This is muddle, not mystery.

13 Brownlow, *David Lean*, p. 649.

14 See *The Guardian* interview, p. 11. Also 'Return Passage: An Interview with David Lean', *Stills*, March 1985, p. 30.

15 'Return Passage', *Stills*, p. 30, my italics.

16 E. M. Forster, *Aspects of the Novel* (London, Pelican, 1962), p. 34; first published 1927. 'Yes – oh dear yes – the novel, tells a story,' says Forster, and goes on, 'and I wish that it was not so, that it could be something different – melody, or perception of the truth, not this low atavistic form.'

17 Brownlow, *David Lean*, p. 649, my italics.

18 Brownlow, *David Lean*, p. 649.

19 Steven Ross, 'In Defence of David Lean', *Take One*, 3: 12 (1972). There

is an interesting discussion of this, and other aspects of Lean's themes, style and reputation, in Richard Combs's 'David Lean: Riddles of the Sphinx', *Monthly Film Bulletin*, 52, (April 1985), pp. 102–6.

20 E. M. Forster, 'Notes on the English Character', in *Abinger Harvest* (London, Edward Arnold, 1936), pp. 33–5; first published 1920.

21 Brownlow, *David Lean*, p. 655.

22 I would like to express my indebtedness for some of the ideas about the significance of the temple scene to my teenage daughter Natalie, with whom I discussed the scene and who seemed to me to have a better understanding and appreciation of Lean's intentions and achievement than most English film critics.

23 Forster, *Passage to India*, p. 160, my italics.

24 *Sight and Sound*, spring 1985, p. 139.

25 Forster, *Passage to India*, pp. 160, 213. Forster is at his most religiose and strained here, and his use of words like 'indescribable' and 'unspeakable' recalls F. R. Leavis's criticism of Conrad's style in *Heart of Darkness*: that he is trying to make a virtue of not knowing what he means.

26 It recalls the moment in T*he Bridge on the River Kwai*, when Major Warden (Jack Hawkins) wakes up and says 'What's happened?', instinctively sensing that something is wrong – the tide has gone out.

27 'Are they both mad?' asks the Doctor of Saito and Colonel Nicholson in *The Bridge on the River Kwai*, 'or am I going mad?' Lawrence is asked, 'Are you mad?' in *Lawrence of Arabia*. One of Lean's most evocative titles is *Summer Madness*.

28 Grigori Kozintsev, *The Space of Tragedy: The Diary of a Film Director* (London, Heinemann, 1977), p. 54.

29 Derek Malcolm, *The Guardian*, 14 February 1985, p. 11.

10

Watching manners:
Martin Scorsese's *The Age of Innocence*,
Edith Wharton's *The Age of Innocence*

A. Robert Lee

> Whatever other qualities the historical novelist has, the essential one is the visualising power ...
>
> Edith Wharton, undated fragment[1]

> my problem was how to make use of a subject – fashionable New York – which, of all others, seemed most completely to fall within the condemned category. There it was before me, in all its flatness and futility, asking to be dealt with as the theme most available to my hand, since I had been steeped in it from infancy, and should not have to get it up out of note-books and encyclopaedias – and yet!
>
> Edith Wharton, *A Backward Glance* (1934)[2]

> This was a love story requiring fineness and finesse, set among the first families and old order of New York. It was not something we were born to, but then, that might be an advantage. We could come to it without an agenda.
>
> Jay Cocks, 'Introduction', *The Shooting Script: The Age of Innocence, Screenplay and Notes by Martin Scorsese and Jay Cocks* (1993)[3]

Edith Wharton meets Martin Scorsese? A novel of 'Old New York' 1870s WASP high manners like *The Age of Innocence* (1920) made over for the screen by a director best known for Italian American *film noir* like *Mean Streets* (1973), *Taxi Driver* (1975) and *Goodfellas* (1990)? Barely had the word been mooted than chins wagged, warnings sounded. Here was filmmaking *chutzpah* to a fault, an oddity too far, a case of colliding or, at the very least, unlikely (and unlike) sensibilities brought together under the commercial aegis of Columbia Pictures.

In the event Scorsese not only honoured the craft of Wharton's novel but created a wonderfully exact and expressive film as, from the start, might always have been foreseen from one of America's most accomplished contemporary directors. He had 'pictured' the novel with style, measure, fidelity, yet also, and throughout, with a quite surest sense of how to make the camera yield its own distinctive film language – from the opera-house panorama as Gounod's *Faust* is performed to mark the beginning of the social season in *haut bourgeois* New York through to the sight of Newland Archer's last, wistful decision (a lifetime later in the story's terms) not to climb her apartment stairs and resee Countess Ellen Olenska in Paris.

'With *The Age of Innocence*, I wanted to find a way of making something literary – and Americans are cowed by the tyranny of that word – and also filmic.'[4] So Scorsese himself looks back on his own ambition in adapting the novel. In part, he goes on to explain, he had in mind the technical difficulty of making complex period film in America ('we no longer have the studios that have all the props and sets').[5] He also remarks about how much more of a tradition such filmmaking is in England, with an eye to adaptations like John Schesinger's *Far from the Madding Crowd* (1967), and its grasp of the vernacular scenic idiom of Hardy's Wessex, or Stanley Kubrick's *Barry Lyndon* (1975), albeit largely shot in Ireland, whose use of Thackeray's novel of epic 'impetuosity' virtually makes landscape into time.

To these he adds the record of the Merchant–Ivory films, adaptations from E. M. Forster to Kazuo Ishiguro, 'where they make use of English settings'.[6] Similarly he invokes European filmmaking of a related vein, whether the Visconti '*Leopard*' trilogy (1954, 1963, 1977), with its sweeping portraiture of Sicilian aristocratic wealth and dissolution, or Truffaut's *Jules et Jim* (1961) as a modern period movie full of 'elegaic eroticism' and which, reflexively to a degree, 'reveled in cinema'.[7]

Nor, as Jay Cocks, his co-writer of the screenplay, yet further bears out in their shared list of twenty or so cinema sources for *The Age of Innocence*, is that to underplay Scorsese's abiding admiration for American 'literary' film. Typically, and perhaps most of relevance, Cocks and he invoke Orson Welles's *The Magnificent*

Ambersons (1942), taken from Booth Tarkington's 1923 novel of social manners and snobbery (whatever the vexations of the studio's change to a less sardonic ending), and William Wyler's *The Heiress* (1949), a reworking of Henry James's *Washington Square* (1881) with its oblique, powerful currents of eroticism and constraint in the figure of Catherine Sloper.[8] All of these, to which they themselves add cinema pieces like Vincente Minelli's *Madame Bovary* (1948) – the note runs 'Ellen Olenska must surely have read Flaubert', and Roger Corman's *The Tomb of Ligeia* (1965) – glossed as a 'canny adaptation ... of Poe's malarial imagination', give working coordinates, a screen context.[9]

To be sure, too, *The Age of Innocence* has the advantages of being beautifully cast and acted, especially the principals of Daniel Day-Lewis as Newland Archer, Michelle Pfeiffer as Ellen Olenska and Winona Ryder as May Welland. Each stays meticulously in character while at the same time contributing to a genuine flourish of ensemble playing: Archer as indulged, moneyed, gently dissenting New York son and brother, Ellen as Old World returnee 'European' American and May as New World American *ingénue*-wife. Décor, dress, etiquette, all given diligent research, add to the exactness as does the considerable use of paintings (barely a domestic interior is shown without its complement of portraits, landscapes and still lifes) with, to follow, London and Paris seen first as impressionist canvases and then in terms of the Louvre and Faubourg St Honoré. Scorsese also uses momentary whole screens of red or orange to reinforce this pictureliness, feeling as held within a field of colour and hue as in a Mark Rothko canvas. The largely British–Irish cast, one assumes, was chosen not only for actorly prowess but in part also to carry the punctilious 'high' New York accent.[10] Joanne Woodward, in turn, as the voice-over, echoes not only the novel's narrator but a kind of subtly fugitive, evidentiary Edith Wharton herself.

Scorsese's especial care with his location shots also paid clear dividends. The New York town of Troy supplied him with persuasive simulacra of the three-storey brownstones of fashionable late nineteenth-century Manhattan. Philadelphia's Academy of Music, aptly baroque in its vaulting and gilt embellishment, doubled for the Opera House. New York's National Arts Club became the imposing, many-chambered Beaufort Mansion. Newport, Rhode Island, virtually plays itself in the summer scenes, a playground in pastel of lawns and coastline parties, sporting competitions, sailboats and the vacationing rich. The New York patroon cottage where Archer goes to see Ellen has about it the contrasting look of 'American primitive', a spare architectural simplicity to frame Archer's excited dream of Ellen. A touch of exoticism, however, and not a little iron-ically, runs through the Florida episode set against the cages of a parrot-filled white aviary where Archer seeks to persuade May into an early marriage.

A literal enough Paris supplies the screen version for what Wharton's novel calls 'one of the avenues radiating from the Invalides' and, within it, the isolated 'little square' under 'a soft, sun-shot haze' from where Archer will look up to Ellen's 'awninged balcony' and finally shuttered *appartement*.[11] The film, here, too, acts scrupulously on the novel's suggestion of Ellen's life and its passage as enclosed in another world, 'this rich atmosphere', but which, for Archer, finally remains best to be 'seen' only in imagination (the novel describes him as having missed 'the flower of life' as if to imply that, were he to meet Ellen again, it would re-emphasise all he has foregone as a life with her).[12]

The sets designed by Dante Ferretti, for their part, again insist not only on period authenticity but on a continuing play of inner signification as much as outward show. Of those especially built for the film, Archer's study-library, his retreat, is made to flicker in half-lights, shadows from the fire, curtained windows (in the interview with May he tries to open a window), and the patina of heavy furni-ture and leather-bound books. Could he, against this weight of affiliation, ever have seized the chance offered in the person of Ellen to make good on his longing? The Beaufort Ballroom supplies a geometry clearly as social as physical, a painterly or embossed world caught in its own determining frame. The hall of the Metropolitan Museum, where Archer and Ellen meet, the screen version fills with appropriate Gothic resonance – the preserved bones, the darkness, as a context for passion, transgression. Scorsese uses this chiaroscuro as a correlative of how the two see themselves and are seen by others.

Likewise the film's music enters and surrounds the action with a near-perfect auditory feel, from the inaugural Gounod aria to the Strauss waltzes, from Beethoven's 'Pathétique' sonata to the Mendelssohn Quintet and 'Marble Halls'. This insistence upon appropriate sight and sound, in fact, might have been better recog-

nised as a long-established Scorsese signature and as carrying over
the precision of the 'Little Italy' of *Mean Streets*, the night-time
Manhattan of *Taxi Driver* or the East Brooklyn of 1955 in the early
sequences of *Goodfellas*.

The final claim, however, as it always must be in film of quality,
lies in Scorsese's integration of each working source and part, the
film as held within the one defining style. In this regard we also need
to take especial note of his resolve to make *The Age of Innocence* go
well beyond 'the usual, theatre-bound film versions of novels'.[13] He
would, in other words, try to establish a visual or scenic match for
Wharton's dense, meticulous irony, her command of nuance.

What kind of novel, then, had Scorsese taken upon himself to make
over for the screen? The conventional response would be to say a
work of manners borne of the history Wharton herself describes
autobiographically in *A Backward Glance*:

> Our society was, in short, a little 'set' with its private catch-words,
> observances and amusements, and its indifference to anything
> outside of its own charmed circle; and no really entertaining social
> group has ever been anything else.[14]

Certainly the circumstantial show of 'our society' is given with
an insider's touch – the contrast of long-gentrified old as against
financier new money (the 'patroon' van der Luydens at one end and
the banker parvenu Julius Beaufort at the other), with the Mingotts,
Archers, Wellands, Chiverses, Leffertses et al. as branch players.
Perhaps, too, only Henry James or Marcel Proust ever made a fuller
effort to capture the alliances and courtships, the rhythm of the
social seasons, the circles of mutual observation, the talk, the requisite dress codes, and the dinners and soirées of so self-enclosed a
circle of caste.

For Wharton that also embraces the townhouse social elite for
which the fleshly, appetitive Mrs Manson Minott ('Old Catherine'
or 'Catherine The Great') provides a gossipy centre (its downstairs
walls covered in dog portraits); the 'professions' in which Archer
plays lawyer at the genteel, Dickensianly named 'Letterblair,
Lamson and Low' ('Old Mr Letterblair' has served as 'the accredited
legal adviser of three generations of New York gentility' p. 81); and
the myriad servant underclass of maids, footmen and the drivers of
each ever-waiting landau and brougham.

Which novel, or film in its wake, also better offers a social 'language' of foodways (or a male coterie world in the form of each loudly snipped, lit and deeply inhaled cigars which only the 'European' Ellen dares challenge by lighting a cigarette for herself and Archer)? Sillerton Jackson struggles comically over his beef at the Archer dinner table, a marker for the provincialism of appetite represented by Mrs Archer and Janey. The lavish van der Luyden banquet becomes a culinary reprimand, a state of the art show of social power replete with ill-dressed English Duke, the best plate and the Roman Punch, to those who have snubbed the Mingott invitation to meet Ellen. Archer dines with his bachelor employer on fare as unappetising as the message he finds himself called upon to deliver to Ellen about her need to abandon thoughts of divorce (and which, in another irony, will make her unavailable to him). On honeymoon, at a Paris dinner, Archer meets in Rivière a man of interesting mind but not fortune; it will point up his growing sense of having settled for only half with May.

The 'family council' meal at Newport leads, in a yet further irony, to Archer's encounter in Boston with Ellen (where, as the film nicely underlines, he initially sees her as the subject of a painting). The 'first dinner party' given by the Archers, a bitter last irony, will be to bid farewell to Ellen, which the film captures as an occasion of conspiracy, silence, more genteel code and which shows Archer, as for the first time, obliged to 'see' himself in the true regard of his peers as philanderer, a strayed and wayward husband.

Wharton's *The Age of Innocence* possesses the two strands left out from the film, the bohemian writer-artist coterie personified in the down-at-heel journalist Ned Winsett and, embodying just a right hint of social eccentricity, Medora Manson and her infatuation with the fake community apostle of love Dr Algernon Carver. They both underline how full and circumstantial a story Wharton in fact wrote, but reasonably cut for Scorsese's purposes.

So far, so familiar. Wharton's novel, however, at its centre turns on a human equation both older and richer: that of the heart's affections, desire in all its contradictory pulls of dream and sublimation, resolve and evasion. What does Archer most seek in Ellen or she in him? What gain, what loss, slowly emerges for Archer in his betrothal to May? For all his own assumption of subject not object as he seeks to win over May's parents for an accelerated engagement, or aids the Mingotts in their rehabilitation of Ellen, or contrives each feverish encounter with her in Boston and New York, does he not himself become increasingly uncentred, in part caught out by his own Bovaryist or dilettante's lack of self-understanding and, in equal part, by May herself in the calculated untruth she tells Ellen about her pregnancy and her subsequent dispensation as wife and mother? Will not, finally, his dream of Ellen always prove too rich as she in fact tells him, too extravagant, for (in the resigned phrase he uses to his son Dallas as they approach Ellen's Paris home) 'old-fashioned' blood like his?

These and associated questions Wharton builds one into the other, rooted in their own time and place and yet always indicative of greatly more perennial fare. She gives to each, too, not only the power of setting, of social ethos, but of a complex narrative vantage point. Archer's every turn she has us see ironically from behind his own shoulder and so to be held up (anything but intrudingly) for judgement. At the same time, and a mark of her own Modernist turn, she also leaves gaps, unwritten parts of the story left to the reader to fathom. Foremost among them are Ellen's (and May's) own interior thoughts, Ellen's actual relationship with both the Count and then his secretary, the role of Beaufort in Ellen's life and, latterly, her times in Washington and then (and allowing for her mentioned help to Annie Beaufort), over three decades, in Paris.

'Can't you and I strike out for ourselves, May?' (p. 74) Archer asks shortly after their engagement. In her own way the conventional May indeed will (straight back into the world she has come from), whereas, in their own way, he and Ellen, who hover at the edge of unconvention, extrication, will not. Wharton's achievement, in 'a world balanced so precariously that its harmony could be shattered by a whisper' (the film's voice-over), is to tell, to watch – and have us watch, the flows and contraflows of the lives entailed in that paradox.

As Jay Cocks recalls it, Scorsese had a working 'charter' for the film, *The Age of Innocence* as period reprise but free of clutter, any 'thick layer of dust'.[15] 'It's a love story', Cocks has him saying. 'What's important is the feeling, not the setting. Just nail the emotion and everything else will follow.'[16] The challenge, accordingly, Scorsese took it upon himself to suggest, lay in giving due and full weight to the Archer–Ellen–May triangle as the essential drama being played out within this upper-echelon New York and all of its class ritual.

The film, too, like Wharton's novel, would show, or watch, 'feeling' as an unfolding rhythm, each exterior locale correlated to a locale deep within. It can little be said not to have delivered on that promise.

That is, from the start, Scorsese recognised Wharton for infinitely more than some mere custodian of an American Age gone by, a kind of from-the-source archivist – the onetime Edith Jones whose Knickerbocker mercantile-genteel family had given rise to the phrase 'keeping up with the Jones's.' For all the 'novelist of manners' tag, and Wharton's command of a historic American era given over to sumptuously genteel or as she calls it 'airless' claustrophobia, he rightly saw *The Age of Innocence* (to which could readily have been added *The House of Mirth* (1905), *Madame de Treymes* (1907) and the quartet of novellas she called *Old New York* (1924)) as indeed endemically, and throughout, a novel of deepest, at times near-ravening desire.[17]

Wharton had written, and Scorsese would seek to recreate, nothing other than a species of passion play, and that the more powerful for being situated inside Old New York as 'slippery pyramid' (p. 48), an enclosure. A world of strictest 'form', thereby, so much itself given to disguise, contextualises Archer's own disguised and divided love of Ellen over May. In this the film sets out its own stall of visuality, as it were, right from the outset, a screen 'narrative' reflexively taken up with seeings and seen, watchings and watched.

As the titles come up, the screen moves from framed handwriting to a pink, indelibly sexual or vaginal rose opening and closing as though a palimsestan lace, its pistil caught for a moment then surrounded in the swirl of petals with all their suggestion of fragility yielding to would-be ecstasy. This floral sequence (flowers rightly become a major stock of the film) in turn gives way to the more mundane yellow daisy plucked by Mme Nilsson, in clearly seeable heavy make-up ('extravagantly painted' according to the shooting script), as she sings from *Faust* 'M'ama . . . non m'ama' ('He loves me . . . he loves me not'). Hers, the focus insists, is indeed performance, opera as set-piece gesture, stylised set, with Mme Nilsson in brocaded white dress and her male co-singer/lover in maroon hose and doublet. Similarly the later leavetaking scene between the costumed lovers in *The Shaughraun*, which Archer reveals always draws him to the play, could not more silhouette the passion he denies to himself feeling for Ellen.

Scorsese's camera lifts and pans out to the whole opera house and we become aware of how the one stage implies the other, that of 'society', too, as a choreography of footlights, boxes and house-seats, tuxedos and gowns, and with a fast, almost blurring serial shot of each dutiful cufflink, jewel, brooch and watch-chain. Crucially it settles on the binoculars passed by Larry Lefferts whose word on 'form' ('I didn't think the Mingotts would have tried it on' he pronounces on the appearance of Ellen, p. 19) is as definitive as that of the older Sillerton Jackson who performs a similar service on 'family'. This, indelibly, as, alongside, we see through the binoculars to Ellen and her Mingott–Archer clan, is a world of gaze and predatory watchfulness, and in which any deviation from the norm implies not only risk, gossip, but, at worst, removal from sight or, as in Ellen's case, seemingly complete erasure.

Archer (visually immaculate in tails and button flower) moves from the men's box to that of Mrs Welland (in matronly dark green), May (in *ingénue* white) and Ellen (in exotic blue). His become the 'eyes' which alight upon May's lilies of the valley, upon the Countess's hand Europeanly offered but which, Americanly, he shakes rather than kisses. Later the film will invite us to watch him kiss, unglove, that same hand as though in de-accelerated, fetishised close-up, nowhere more intensely and freightedly than in the carriage which takes him and Ellen from the Jersey City train terminus to Manhattan. His gaze at the opera, and ours with it, then moves outward to the seated assembly – faces, costume, couples, Old New York as *tableau vivant*. In this masterly opening vignette Scorsese so effects a kind of double curtain-up, an invitation to see a 'start' of the season and a 'start' of the kind of story and the feelings it will pursue to follow.

The sequence pauses, too, to settle upon Regina Beaufort as she leaves in the third act for her ball and then moves to the waiting carriages outside. The Beaufort Ball we also so anticipate as continued over performance, 'society' as a kind of sanctioned dance within fixed rules of motion. We watch Regina as grandee and matron (yet another guise which will be reversed when Beaufort's bank fails and, in widow's black, she appeals to Catherine for clan solidarity and causes her to suffer a stroke), then step towards her carriage, her arm held by liveried manservant. This is money gentrified into high social style with Regina, as against Beaufort who will eventually take off with the actress Annie Ring, its loyal, spousely icon.

The ball itself Scorsese shoots first as an unused ballroom caught under rays of sunlight. Its stillness (dustcovers and the like as props) then dissolves into animation, the initial fast-moving quadrilles, the talk of each social group, the salutations and drinks and the display of manners as tactics of offence and defence. Archer adds his own white gloves to those conformistly already upon the table before making his way through the various ante-rooms (the voice-over, citing Wharton's text, calls them 'boldly planned') before reaching the main floor. The camera could hardly better suggest a gallery of both custom and consciousness.

Mrs Beaufort is seen as placed like a live sentinel beneath her own youthful portrait, with to follow the sight of Beaufort's 'audaciously displayed' Buguereau nude ('Return of Spring'), the swirling waltz seen in vertical as well as horizontal shots, Julius Beaufort's sauntering entrance, and May, still with her lilies of the valley (a sprig of which Scorsese has Archer break off suggestively when he has a moment alone with her in a bower to the side) and her news of Ellen's withdrawal 'at the last minute'. The 'dance' indeed can be said, and be seen, to have been launched.

The camera tracks Archer's movement from opera to ball, then through the different drawing rooms to the ballroom, as following a man wholly at one with the ritual. For all his professed *ennui*, he belongs utterly within this overall décor, servant as much as imagined master of convention. Whatever will be his eventual turbulent shift of feeling from May to Ellen, from sanctioned marriage to illicit passion, the opening scenes have visually located him for all his longing as no serious nay-sayer to pre-emptive rules which, having made him, can as easily unmake him.

Thus May, too, in all her ingenuousness, is also caught (amid her circle of young women companions) as fully knowing of what is expected of her. The camera links her sprig of flowers to her very body, both innocent blooms, which Scorsese further emphasises in her lowered glance and coquettish play with Archer. The later archery scenes will build on these lingerings over her lithe huntress body, May as chastity yet with just the hint that she may not always prove the wholly ingenous Diana. Film, like text, invites us to see her as the world most sees her, virginal daughter, genteel fiancée and soon to be dutiful wife.

Ellen, by contrast, and although the opera scenes afford but a glimpse, we encounter as the 'dark' woman of Polish title who has moved outside the circle and who Scorsese has turn to look upon Archer at the opera with a perfect movement of eyes. Her gaze, whatever the accommodating banter, the camera draws attention to as that of quite 'other' experience, of a sexually knowing woman from beyond New York and deepened by a failed, true aristocratic marriage and the knowledge of Europe's greater social and artistic historicity.

Archer, throughout, is shown to believe that he sees all, the man of his family (for whom mother and daughter deny themselves house space), the kindly courtier of May, the caring prospective kinsman of Ellen. In fact, and for as much as the film has him look, or ponder or scrutinise, he 'sees' (in the sense of understand) too little too late, whether about himself, or the world his marriage to May will perpetuate and which will judge him Ellen's lover, or, indeed, Ellen and all that she had seen.

Scorsese's visual cues and juxtapositions, faithfully seeking their own version of Wharton's narrative, so build into a composite 'take'. Little more might be asked in the way of exposition, the unfolding written word made over, enfigured in its equivalent screen imagery.

This lavish visual furnishing, Scorsese's grammar of watching and seeing, runs right through his *The Age of Innocence*. If one stresses a number of key sequences, that is not, accordingly, to underplay the whole but to emphasise how each carries the implication of the whole. Nor is it to divert attention from how Scorsese keeps in view the carried through motifs, from flowers (including the lilies of the valley sent daily to May as against the roses for Ellen) to domestic interiors (few more eccentric-comic than Catherine's with her 'French' downstairs bedroom), or from scenes of explicit conceal-ment (Archer's guilty, meticulous placing of a key in its envelope for his assignation with Ellen) to those of exposure (Ellen and Archer seen in the street by Larry Lefferts and judged, or misjudged, accordingly).

The film's visualisation of how Archer first recognises his own feeling for Ellen the film locates within her Manhattan house. Archer enters before Ellen, his eyes drawn first to the 'new' art – an impressionist's faceless woman with parasol upon a beach and a bold, linear, portrait of sea and littoral, then to the mask upon her table. An Italian maid enters. He watches Ellen through the window say farewell to Beaufort. We witness not only an incipient jealousy but his growing doubts as to his own custodial 'family' stance by his overlapping show of art and life from so far beyond, outside, Old New York.

On entrance she speaks of her 'odd little house' and the 'little pieces of wreckage' she has brought from Europe. And as they turn to talk of the van der Luyden dinner (with her own nice irreverence at the expense of the hypochondriacal Mrs van der Luyden or 'Cousin Louise'), he revels in the display of cushions, rugs and artefacts all sumptuously blended into what he half-acknowledges is a small palace of art. As for the first time he begins to see in Ellen herself, as she pours tea, lights cigarettes for them, and as the fire blazes and ebbs, the living emissary of a world beyond the New York he has hitherto believed a 'labyrinth' but she 'straight up and down'. The roles of adviser and advised reverse or, at the least, and as Scorsese has them look and estimate each other, come under interrogation.

In their talk of fashion, right and wrong etiquette, the ways of family, Scorsese's direction implies that everything they do or discuss carries its own dark, exquisite counter-current. Ellen wonders where 'truth' lies in a social order so abundantly given over to appearance or face. Tears come. And as Archer takes her hand Scorsese has us see the contract between Archer and Ellen become all the more intense for what it holds back, feeling at the edge of becoming articulate and, thereby, dangerous. It is feeling, too, scrupulously 'seen',. each gaze, glance, smile, gesture, built into an unravelling visual continuity.

Their relationship, thereby, is at once explicit yet also figurative or subliminal, and to recur in exactly that form in nearly every subsequent encounter between them. This is sight and touch as the promise of passionate life, a necessary contrast with the sculpture of May's kindly but unpassionate hands – those of the archer who will eventually triumph as the kindly but inexorable guardian of decorum. The image of embracing hands continues, too, when Archer fantasises Ellen's hold of him at the patroon house (Scorsese's own contribution); when, at Archer's next visit to Ellen's house, he kisses her literally hand and foot only to be confronted with May's letter confirming an early marriage; when they meet in Boston and grasp hands across the table; and in his last, claustrophobically intense ride with her in the carriage from Jersey City.

This first Archer–Ellen encounter, however, lays down the

pathway. Scorsese appears to have done it as a single take, the flows of feeling seen and watched as discrete in themselves and yet, typically, and by directorial design, to be enfolded into the film's ongoing and larger narrative.

A necessary contrast lies in how Scorsese renders the archery scene in which May plays a serene, ingenuous Diana. Scorsese opens with a panoply of linen-clad figures, blue and white awnings, the sight of arrows landing in targets, and May to be seen beatifically against the backdrop of a tree in full leaf. Only Beaufort hints of a flaw in the idyll with his observation that this is the only kind of target May will ever 'hit'. May is then seen with her quiver of arrows, her winner's smile, being photographed, and finally wearing the silver archery brooch (donated by Beaufort) as she sits in an athlete's triumph with Archer and Catherine.

The visual language again serves perfectly. This is May's world, everything as it seems and in which light, and lightness of being, prevail. The summer pastels – whether as dress, picnic apparatus, bonnets – all bear an iconography of undeliberated ease and openness. Even Archer is seen to smile and bear May off in her winner's pleasure. But the whole image of archery, arrows targeted and then aimed, makes for a residue which will be called upon when May 'wins' her husband back from Ellen. Scorsese gives the process its own screen metaphoricity, May as transparent yet in her competitor's recognition of Ellen, somehow, and at the same time, not.

No more intensely visual a scene occurs in *The Age of Innocence* than that of Archer's gaze upon Ellen at the water's edge in Newport; it summons up Monet or Cézanne, a veritable call to contemplation. We are a year on from Archer's marriage to May and the voice-over tells us of how he has heard of Ellen's life but not seen her. Sent to find Ellen by Catherine, he strolls as indeed once again a figure in a picture urgently across manicured lawns, along a seaward path, through the leafy greens and browns of summer trees, and on to a bridge, unseen as he thinks (though in fact, as she later tells him, 'seen' by Ellen), the watcher from afar.

The sheer beauty of the scene is given conscious emphasis. The idiom is one of seascape, almost a live re-enactment of the painting he first saw in Ellen's house. Each component scintillates, Scorsese's own filmic 'text' of life as art: a reddish and blurred sunlit sea, the slightest ripple of waves, Ellen herself with her back to Archer at the end of the pier in stunning white dress and parasol (he will mistakenly think it the one at the Blenkers home), and the lighthouse and gently billowing sailboat. As he watches, and then gives himself the wager of whether or not she will turn to him before the boat passes the lighthouse, we see in him literally the will to an apotheosis always held in check by the life he has contracted with May (she will speak on his return to the house of a 'changed' Ellen).

Little wonder it is to this beauteous, memorial scene of desire that Scorsese has the film revert in Paris, Ellen at the horizon not only of a blithe, warm, beckoning Atlantic ocean but of dream become memory. When Archer turns from going up to her apartment at the end, his words in the novel are '"It's more real to me here than if I went up"' (p. 286). Scorsese again acts on cue. He departs from Wharton's text in making Archer's memory of Ellen at the water's edge a kind of sublime haunting to accuse and pursue the companionable but quotidian family (and even political) round which has become his life. For the film it provides the perfect after-image, Archer's own epitaph.

Although less abundantly 'visual', Archer's journey with Ellen from Jersey City to New York carries a shared configuration of meanings. 'It happens to me all over again', Archer tells Ellen. Scorsese's camera picks up on that intensity. He films them pressed towards, almost into, each other in the carriage as if to physicalise the lifetime represented by those two hours (a comparison with Archer and May in their Paris carriage is inevitable). Their hands, first gloved, and then lingeringly ungloved, join and yield to a larger embrace, the implication of an unrealised, unrealisable, consummation. He speaks of a realm in which words like 'mistress' don't exist; she reproves him, and speaks of what life lived on the moral run, and so out of view, is really like ('It's no place for us'). In anger, loss, he stops the carriage and leaves her with one last despairing gaze – 'I should not have come today.'

The power of the scene lies in Scorsese's use of the carriage as exquisite prison. The trot and neigh of the horse, the rocking movement, the brief glimpse of the driver, all play against a will to step away from time (one key shot lingers over the turning wheel of the carriage). Even the rustle and thickness of Ellen's coat, her furs and bonnet, and Archer's topcoat, signal enclosure, restraint. The camera moves with utter exactitude from one body to the other, from Archer's closed eyes to his embrace of her to her ready response. When, as they talk, she reminds him of how he has always obeyed convention, and he abruptly exits from the carriage, the screen with reason might seem to imply sexual rise and fall, stolen bliss followed by post-coital sadness.

Ellen moves off in the carriage with an almost frozen return of his gaze, his own lost secret sharer headed for another order of time and place. At this point Scorsese pulls his camera back to pass on to a subsequent drawing room scene of May doing embroidery and Archer poring over prints of Japan. Fantasy has indeed replaced fact, a compensatory would-be travel of mind over feeling. His life, now, will be May, decorum, order, his own first son and subsequent family, and, by dint of telephone (typified in his Chicago–New York conversation with Ted) and the like, a 'new' New York which still carries, in essence, his own 'old' New York. As both novel and film imply, it might for Archer have been destined to be that all along, with desire, with Ellen, as always for him, and at whatever cost, his own grand illusion.

Scorsese's *The Age of Innocence* will not likely be judged his best film. That rarely occurs for a director who achieves *auteur* status. It may be, too, that to adapt texts entrammelled in their own thickly allusive narrative language is to inhibit a same or equivalent power as film. Is not *Taxi Driver*, or any of Scorsese's best-known films, more 'cinematic', more purely an upshot of his own writer-director's camera and imagination?

His version of Wharton's novel, even so, remains a superb effort. In large part that has much to do with not trying to obliterate the literary original, both playing the narrator's voice into the film and yet, at the same time, finding for the story told by that voice a right visuality or screen language. The upshot is that in watching Scorsese watch Wharton, as in any great adaptation, we experience doubly: a text relived in film, a film become its own 'text'.

NOTES

1 From an untitled fragment in Edith Wharton's Yale papers. Quoted in Blake Nevius, *Edith Wharton: A Study of Her Fiction* (Berkeley, California, University of California Press, 1953), p. 43.

2 Edith Wharton, *A Backward Glance* (New York, Appleton-Century, 1934), pp. 206–7.

3 *The Shooting Script: The Age of Innocence, Screenplay and Notes by Martin Scorsese and Jay Cocks* (New York, Newmarket Press, 1993) 'Introduction', p. vi.

4 David Thompson and Ian Christie (eds), *Scorsese on Scorsese* (London, Faber and Faber, 1989), '*The Age of Innocence* – A Personal Journey', p. 185.

5 *Scorsese on Scorsese*, p. 187.

6 *Scorsese on Scorsese*, p. 187.

7 *The Shooting Script: The Age of Innocence*, p. 132.

8 *The Age of Innocence: Screenplay and Notes*, pp. 127–35.

9 *The Shooting Script: The Age of Innocence*, respectively p. 133 and p. 135.

10 Besides Daniel Day-Lewis as Archer, the cast includes Richard E. Grant as Larry Lefferts, Alec McGowen as Sillerton Jackson, Geraldine Chaplin as Mrs Welland, Miriam Margolyes as Mrs Mingott, Sîan Phillips as Mrs Archer, Michael Gough as Henry van Luyden and Jonathan Pryce as Rivière.

11 Edith Wharton, *The Age of Innocence* (New York, Signet Classic, 1952), pp. 284–5. For ease of access all page references are to this edition.

12 *The Age of Innocence*, p. 275.

13 *Scorsese on Scorsese*, p. 179.

14 *A Backward Glance*, p. 79.

15 *The Shooting Script: The Age of Innocence*, pp. vi–vii.

16 *The Shooting Script: The Age of Innocence*, p. v.

17 Edith Wharton, *The House of Mirth* (New York, Scribner's, 1905); *Madame de Treymes* (New York, Scribner's, 1907); and *Old New York: False Dawn; The Old Maid; The Spark; New Year's Day* (New York, Appleton, 1924).

11

Brideshead Revisited revisited: Waugh to the knife

Fred Inglis

Granada broadcast *Brideshead Revisited* as an eleven-part serial across the winter of 1980/1. It looked like an enormous risk. For years, conventional producer wisdom had been that the fixities of fifty-minute programme slotting together with the congenital inattention of audiences meant that the extended rhythm of the novel must be subject to the most violent compressions and excisions if the thing were to be represented on television. What are now thought of as not undistinguished, even classic moments of cinema – the Merle Oberon/Laurence Olivier version of *Wuthering Heights* (1939) or Olivier's duet with Greer Garson in *Pride and Prejudice* (1940) may be good enough romantic period-and-wardrobe comedies in their way but they can hardly pass as translations of their great originals.

To put things this way is to arrive with a bump at the nub of this collection. What is an adaptation of a novel for? Even more sharply, what is an adaptation *for* of this peculiarly licensed kind of novel – the novel freed from the competition to resist superannuation by the newer novel (novelty being inscribed in its very etymology) in virtue of its segregation as a classic?

All novel-writing societies appoint certain works, sometimes temporarily, to classic status. By the same token, all narrative-making societies (which is to say all human societies) maintain the continuity of a list of Old Favourites. There has been a little *frisson* in that section of the strictly academic division of labour which studies stories for its living to see such lists as instruments of social oppression, ways of keeping down those who are looking up, weapons of class struggle among peoples for whom class struggle hasn't been much of a cut-throat business for a couple of centuries. These worthies light upon great traditions of canonical novels as secret agents of a police appointed to patrol the boundaries of social power and status.

No doubt canonicity is indeed so used, from time to time, by *bourgeois gentilhommes* and *femmes savantes*, but as a political weapon the novel stands to political action in something of the same relation as a flyswat does to the latest fashion in automatic rifles. All of which is not to say that canonical traditions tell us nothing about the meanings of lives; only that they will hardly do to hold up the grand arch of either radical or reactionary historiography.[1]

What they will do, however, returns us to the moment in Granada's programme planning when Derek Granger the producer and Charles Sturridge and Michael Lindsay-Hogg, the two directors of *Brideshead*, persuaded the people with the money to let them go ahead with a twelve-hour, actionless travelogue, adapting for a mass audience a minor branch of the one true canon which describes, as Evelyn Waugh himself had put it, 'the operation of divine grace on a group of diverse but closely connected characters', an operation taking the form of 'a fierce little human tragedy'.[2]

It must have looked an unlikely choice. It had its harbingers. Against the *bien-pensants* who supposed that no narrative longer than the single play or movie could hold a television audience, the BBC had broadcast in 1978 and 1979 its extended versions of John le Carré's cold war spy novels, *Tinker, Tailor, Soldier, Spy* and *Smiley's People*. They had been substantial successes, commanding, across each of their five-and-a-half-hour length, audiences of over seven million[3] and, even better for the small, prominent, glamorous and intensely self-referential world of programme-making, figuring very largely indeed in the broadsheet and weekly review pages.

Brideshead was, of course, well on the way by 1979, as was another gigantic version of a less-than-giant title in the canon, Paul Scott's four-decker about the dying politics of the British Raj, *Jewel in the Crown*. Both adaptations, like le Carré's two novels, were to star beknighted heroes and heroines of the national stage. Alec Guinness dominated the two spy stories as George Smiley; Peggy Ashcroft was the subdued but omnipresent force of *Jewel in the Crown*; around them were grouped utterly dependable, strong and upright pentameter-pronouncers of the Royal Shakespeare

Company: Ian Richardson, Geraldine James, Bernard Hepton, Ian Bannen, Charles Dance.

The point was well, even elaborately taken. *Brideshead* famously caught the conscience of the King of British Theatre, Laurence Olivier, in its net, together with his inevitable regent, John Gielgud, as well as the honorary stepdaughter of both men, Claire Bloom. Brilliantly, Granger cast as *Brideshead's* two *ingénus*, the light and the dark of upper-class English theatrical manhood, Anthony Andrews and Jeremy Irons. Behind them followed a line of perfectly envisaged, magnificently played supporting cast – Diana Quick as Lady Julia Flyte, Jeremy Sinden as 'Boy' Mulcaster, Jane Asher as Celia Ryder, a tiny masterpiece by John le Mesurier as 'the gentle and unyielding old Jesuit', Father Mowbray.

The intelligence and sensitively accurate casting alongside the shamelessness with which two vastly celebrated septuagenarians were chosen to play fathers in their fifties betoken the seriousness of the venture. But something else was at work at the moment of conception. The credits of the first le Carré rolled across a lovely shot of Oxford spires; the music on the soundtrack was a haunting setting of the *Nunc Dimittis* by Geoffrey Burgon sung in a pure and piercing choirboy treble. The historical moment of *Jewel in the Crown*, bitter and caustic as was its treatment, was nonetheless the moment of Allied victory over Fascism, the moment at which the whole legacy of Empire – soldiers and brass bands and bungalows – came up for judgement at the joined hands of Clement Attlee, Labour architect of New Britain in 1945, and the Lord Mountbatten, Attlee's last Viceroy in India.

Brideshead comes out of that sudden, powerful and protracted surge of feeling. Its television authors were all Granada recruits from Oxford; the choice of adaptor and scriptwriter catches up all the themes adumbrated by the coincidence on the screen of John le Carré, Paul Scott and Evelyn Waugh, to say nothing of Fay Weldon's version of *Pride and Prejudice*.

John Mortimer was a striking combination of barrister and playwright. The public school and Oxford son of the grandly hateful and lovable blind lawyer-father he celebrated in *A Voyage Round my Father*, he embodies the cultural moments of both 1945 and – let us say – 1979, when *Brideshead* went into production and Margaret Thatcher came to power. All his adult life, Mortimer has been an active member of the Labour Party, strong in support of its genteel, comprehensive reforms, amused and bemused by its lapses into oafish sectarianism and the inanities of socialism in one country, cheerfully hostile to and understanding of the viciousness and stupidity of his country's appalling class symbolism. At the same time, no man of his class and generation could escape feeling the penetrative force of British imperialism – 'Lion and Women and Lord Knows What' – right through him, body and soul.

So Evelyn Waugh would be a crux to such a man, especially so to such a writer. The concise, ribald, shocking Waugh of *Scoop* and *Vile Bodies* – bitter Fool at the expense alike of ruling-class adulteresses, press barons, black princes – would be as congenial as the poet of the Oxford and Venetian townscapes, of Inigo Jones and *Clos de Bèze*. At the same time, Mortimer – translator of Feydeau and of *Der Hauptmann von Köpenick*, creator of Rumpole and author of his middlebrow polemic against Mrs Thatcher *Paradise Regained* – understands for what it is Waugh's flagrant misogyny, his dedicated mimicry of caste, his lovable and repugnant snobbery, the absolute sincerity and irrelevance of his Catholicism.

The studied contradictions of men, moment and production are hauntingly harmonised by Geoffrey Burgon's theme music where he plays off in a perfect, unironic kitsch resolute chords from the public school hymnal against strong echoes of baroque orchestration, settling between each the melodic line of plaintive German *Lieder* and English folksong: Benjamin Britten's legacy, as it were, combining Purcell, Schubert, Cecil Sharp and the popular sentiment of *Abide with Me*.

It is usual these days to dismiss such a combination with the swearword 'nostalgia'. Nostalgia is named by Theory as the defining presence of contemporary culture and its structure of feeling.[4] If we think of nostalgia as being a strong yearning for past membership (Freudians would say, for the beatitude of 'oceanic bliss' during preweaning), then there is no necessary reason for our pejoration. Such a yearning may as well be a prompt to progressive action as not. It is Walter Benjamin who points out that in our dreams of a better social order for the future we turn back to images of a prehistoric because classless past, in order to imagine how the wretched world might be transformed into utopia – hence *News from Nowhere*.[5]

Waugh's novel is candidly reactionary. He wrote, as he said, when 'it seemed that the ancestral seats which were our chief national artistic achievements were doomed to decay and spoliation like the monasteries in the sixteenth century. So I piled it on rather, with passionate sincerity.'[6] In the magnificent opening to Book One 'Et in Arcadia Ego' (words first spoken by Death Himself), Waugh yearns to rejoin the past membership of the perfect friendships provided by an imaginary Oxford in 1923. That membership turned upon the all-male, monastic, delightfully irresponsible collegiality of the city whose beauty gave that debonair life its religious foundation and its suppressed gravity. All those lucky enough to have been students with a company of friends at Oxford and Cambridge this century will recognise and perhaps share the depth of Waugh's love for the place. Set aside what Raymond Williams called their 'sheer cold bloodymindedness',[7] and the bleak solitude in which those who were excluded by disposition or poverty from the golden youth used to live. History, politics, aesthetics and sociology (so to speak) combine from time to time to make Oxford a happy circumstance where champagne and plovers eggs, low doors in the wall and enchanted gardens, tearing high spirits and a chance meeting with a perfect stranger may teach Waugh's own lesson that 'to know and love one other human being is the root of all wisdom'.[8]

John Mortimer may therefore be taken to stand for much in grasping the significance (and enjoying the delights) of this version of *Brideshead Revisited*. Men of his class and generation – of the next two or three generations no doubt – went to Oxford, as Waugh put it for 1923 when *he* went,

> in search of love, and ... full of curiosity and the faint, unrecognised apprehension that here at last I should find that low door in the wall, which others, I knew, had found before me, which opened on an enclosed and enchanted garden which was somewhere, not overlooked by any window, in the heart of that grey city.[9]

Mortimer quotes these lines in full during the production and I cannot doubt that producers and directors, actors too for all I know, shared a recognition of all they meant. Rather than Catholicism, the heart of this translation of Waugh's ruined but classic folly is the theme of friendship and the love of place. It is a theme dear to the hearts of the cultural fraction of the English bourgeoisie which made the film, and stands up well enough as the meaning of life after the fall of Anglican Christianity.

Some of the more delirious custodians of that conservative Marxism which passes in Britain for cultural critique have seen such celebration of friendship as mere ideology, and lumped together a cluster of recent Anglophile movies as expressing what Tom Nairn has called a banal 'Ukanian nationalism'.[10] Ukania, by this token, is a sort of post-seventeenth-century Spain in which new Money and old Property combine to maintain a deathly powerful hierarchy of caste and monarch. Its peculiar achievement is to magic together 'the crass and the faery', the ordinary and the transcendent, in a 'bogus sentimental unity of extremes'.[11]

Brideshead, as both novel and television, works this magic. Indeed, Waugh is explicit about this as his purpose. The novel opens in a bleak, drearily wartime army camp outside Glasgow. When Charles Ryder arrives in the dark small hours at a new camp many hours of directionless train journey later, he neither knows nor cares where it is. Only in the morning does he ask, 'What's this place called?'

> He told me and, on the instant, it was as though someone had switched off the wireless, and a voice that had been bawling in my ears, incessantly, fatuously, for days beyond number, had been suddenly cut short; an immense silence followed, empty at first, but gradually, as my outraged sense regained authority, full of a multitude of sweet and natural and long forgotten sounds: for he had spoken a name that was so familiar to me, a conjurer's name of such ancient power, that, at its mere sound, the phantoms of those haunted late years began to take flight.[12]

As he said, Waugh 'piled it on rather'. In the film, this passage is read out pretty well uncut over the action, Jeremy Irons walks past the ordinary, messy doings of the civilian army of early 1944 until he gazes at the splendid silhouette of Vanburgh's great Anglo-Palladian masterpiece at Castle Howard in North Yorkshire.

It is a magic moment all right, and it deploys one of the classical tropes of modernism. A noble image from the past is contrasted, to our disadvantage, with a mean and squalid image from the present. Eliot's *Waste Land* is a casebook of such effects, and it is no accident that the poem is quoted by Anthony Blanche, 'part Gallic, part Yankee, part, perhaps, Jew; wholly exotic', twenty minutes later on screen.[13]

The hard nuts of the Old Left would call this a Ukanian effect, in which the egalitarian new army personified by Ryder's favourite target of contempt, Lieutenant Hooper, is cancelled by recollections of the lost and lovely regime which lived in the antique and Catholic baroque of Brideshead. At a later date, they'd say, soapy serials like *All Creatures Great and Small* and *Heartbeat* cast the same spell over a stupefied citizenry whose favourite bedtime story is one in which once upon a time happy friends bound all parts of their little local community in a gregarious chain of 'familial' being.

We might say instead, in Mortimer's more loving way, that the great poetic themes of friendship and solidarity are best completed by loved and lovely places. By catching and – in a moral sense – placing Waugh's powerful conjunction of a hateful, at times vicious caste snobbery and his love of hard art and life's sweet and anguished ephemerality, the production team pays on both sides something both beautiful and ugly in recent English history. They then leave it behind.

After all, the choice of the novel was hardly self-evident in 1979. It was Clive James, reviewing the production at the time, who called the novel 'magnificent ruin',[14] but his test of the adequacy of the film was its fidelity to the words on the page. Mortimer was enough of the same view to decide to have Jeremy Irons read the text over much of the action, so much so that James asked why he didn't just read the whole novel aloud on television and have done with it.

But of course a television adaptation is, as I suggested, a translation of the original. Andrew Davies, probably the best known of contemporary adaptors of classic texts, described his famous 1995 version of *Pride and Prejudice* as 'like a critical and interpretative essay' of what was, in any case, his 'favourite novel'.[15] If we think of an adaptation as a translation, it should be with Davies's remark in mind, as well as our recollecting Robert Graves's observation that poetry is what gets lost in translation.

We still keep trying. Translation happens everywhere, and every translation is first of all an attempt to represent its interestingness to those who have not met the original before. It is also, in the case of a move from page to screen, an attempt to fix a story on a less shadowy screen than the imagination.[16]

The danger is then, as many people have said, that the vividness and irresistibility of the screen supplants and dominates our individually imagined versions, so that we cannot ever see Brideshead other than as Castle Howard, nor the slender waif Julia as other than the beautiful if tubby Diana Quick. The joy, however, lies in being able to recognise the completeness and accuracy of visualisation, never more so than in the topography of such a work as *Brideshead*, where the known and loved beauty of Oxford and Venice and London figure so largely.

His commitment to fidelity to the text is declared by Mortimer's decision to use Irons's slightly sleepy, pleasantly uninflected voice to read so much of Waugh's prose aloud. There were many though much slighter precedents, the best-known perhaps being John Mills reading fragments of Pip's narrative in David Lean's 1951 version of *Great Expectations*.

Lean, however, used Dickens's prose as *continuo*; Mortimer uses it as leitmotif. It was a daring move, for the convention has been much disparaged. On the other hand, for all Waugh's title-page disclaimer, 'I am not I: thou art not he or she: they are not they', there is an inescapably clear and keen sense that narrator and author are constantly superimposed; that Charles Ryder is – as Waugh knows – a (sentimentally) idealised other picture of himself, in both 1923 and 1944. Irons-reading-Waugh-aloud is a simple and winning device to keep adaptor subservient to author. It might also be added that the device is damnably quick and easy to use; every time you get stuck for a transition, go back to what the chap actually wrote.

Fidelity-to-the-original is an absolute value of the production team. *Jewel in the Crown*, the only twelve-hour rival, is a compression of four long novels; *Smiley's People* is a five-hour version of three hundred-odd pages. *Brideshead*, singularly, takes twelve hours to picture 315 pages. Nothing is left out. Infidelities to the detail of the novel are paid, heavily, in cash: the thing must be told in the United States to recoup its stunning costs; hence the cast of stars much adored on both sides of the Atlantic, and never mind the ludicrousness of Olivier in his seventies explaining that he plays tennis at the Lido with the local pro. Gielgud as Ryder's father, on the other hand, is playing a fifty-year-old who himself played an old gent with 'the shuffling mandarin-tread which he affected'; 'in his late fifties ... it was his idiosyncrasy to seem much older than his years; to see him one might have put him at seventy, to hear him speak at nearly eighty'.[17] Gielgud does him splendidly, with a fine delight in the weirdness of human self-presentation which serves to remind us that Waugh is a comic writer who learned much both from Dickens and from P. G. Wodehouse; either of his great mentors would have delighted in Anthony Blanche, Rex Mottram or Mr Samgrass. Respectively, Nicholas Grace, Charles Keating and John Grillo do them proud. George Santayana once observed of Dickens that 'when people say [he] exaggerates, I think they must have neither eyes nor ears',[18] and Grace's version of Blanche's 'self-taught stammer', his glaucous eyes, his inviolable allegiance to an art that shall be truthful is one of the keys with which Mortimer unlocks the secrets of the novel.

At this point Mortimer and Waugh are at one. We are well into Book Three, and Charles Ryder has returned from a painting tour of Latin America to a triumphant exhibition of his paintings in Bond Street, attended by the Duke and Duchess of Clarence. At the end of the evening Anthony Blanche, whom he has not seen for a dozen or more years, comes to tell him what he thinks of the pictures.

> 'Then I came back at the unfashionable time of five o'clock, all agog, my dear; and what did I find? I found, my dear, a very naughty and very successful practical joke. It reminded me of dear Sebastian when he liked so much to dress up in false whiskers. It was charm again, my dear, simple, creamy English charm, playing tigers.'
> 'You're quite right,' I said.
> 'My dear, of course I'm right. I was right years ago – more years, I am happy to say, than either of us shows – when I *warned* you. I took you out to dinner to warn you of charm. I warned you expressly and in great detail of the Flyte family. Charm is the great English blight. It does not exist outside these damp islands. It spots and kills anything it touches. It kills love; it kills art; I greatly fear, my dear Charles, it has killed *you*.'[19]

Charm, correctness, 'the English zest to be well-bred', 'English snobbery is more macabre to me than English morals', these are the native qualities Blanche so detests; these are also and exactly the qualities out of which Waugh himself fashioned an elaborate persona which he would take up, drop, and reassume at will for most of his life.

The television production leaves the contradiction where it belongs, rooted in the text. Insolent and heartfelt snobbery is liberally sprinkled throughout – the snobbery of the devout social climber Waugh always was (while Waugh the novelist took and gave so much pleasure in kicking away in his work the social ladder

he climbed so ardently at play). One scene will have to do to indi-
cate it.

Halfway through the second book, Charles Ryder believes
himself to have broken with the Brideshead family after he has
disgraced himself in Lady Marchmain's eyes by giving the alcoholic
Sebastian money on which to get drunk. He has quit his studies in
Oxford and gone to Paris to become an art student on the way to
his career as an architectural painter patronised by aristocratic
society. Rex Mottram, then courting Lady Julia, has been put in
charge of the young drunkard on the way to a Swiss clinic. Sebastian
pinches Rex's gambling money and vanishes to drink it away. Rex
comes to find Charles and tell him the tale over dinner somewhere
grave and gourmandising in the Sixth *arrondissement*.

Waugh himself was in later years a decidedly heavy eater and all
his life loved wine and heavy drinking. In the preface to the 1960
edition of the novel he confessed that, sixteen years after its composition, he found the book 'infused with a kind of gluttony, for food
and wine ... and for rhetorical and ornamental language, which
now with a full stomach I find distasteful'.[20]

The Parisian dinner scene is done with a slow relish of the food
and wine and even greater relish for the revelation of Rex
Mottram's ignorant lack of appreciation of both. Mottram is, great
heavens, the sort of man who would suggest adding chopped onion
to caviar ('chap-who-knew told me it brought out the flavour'); he
failed, poor sap, even to notice the 'simple and unobtrusive sole'
and, rejecting the delicious and youthful brandy Charles is drinking,
insists on a 'balloon glass the size of his head' so that the restaurant
staff, who know a blackguard when they see one, 'wheeled out of
its hiding place the vast and mouldy bottle they kept for people of
Rex's sort'.[21]

Rex is a central agent in the decline of England which was
Waugh's lifelong theme, a harsh motif in the threnody he sings over
her degeneration. Julia says later to Charles, as their love affair starts
to flower aboard their Atlantic liner,

> I thought he was a sort of primitive savage, but he was something
> absolutely modern and up-to-date that only this ghastly age could
> produce. A tiny bit of a man pretending he was the whole.[22]

The detail and finesse of the restaurant scene – the thin, green sorrel
soup beneath their spoons, the tulip-shaped brandy glasses, the plain,

sombre décor – take the measure of something strong and wistful, new in the culture of the 1980s, likely to last some decades yet. It is a taste for the solid certainties of class taste set at the very rim of adult life of a dying parental generation. Revivals of consumer taste and even of political vision, I think, are often like that. The settled past for which the storyteller reaches back is that happiest time of which grandparents spoke, when the social order was settled and explicit and yet when there was a flair and a savour of the change to come. The 1920s have carried this aura on both sides of the Atlantic for some time now, and the television words and images punctiliously sustained it. The production team used as its restaurant *La Belle Epoque* in Knutsford, a mile down the road from the gorgeous Paxton conservatory at Tatton Park which serves for the Brideshead Eden where the two young fauns play. The effect was faultless.

Paris also, of course, is of a piece with this feeling. Paul Fussell points out, in his study of English travel writing, what Paris connoted for the 1920s: solid bourgeois values, hotels, food, furniture, naturally; but also recklessness, the new dances, sexual and sartorial freedoms, all the complex associations of the noun 'gaiety', which started to take on its new life round about the turn of the century.[23]

Waugh himself intuited the new significance of hedonistic travel. The television *Brideshead* candidly wallows in its vast extension to the mass tourism of today. The imagery of the production is insistently and consistently architectural: quite right, too. Painting the buildings is Ryder's job. But the domes of Vanburgh and of Wren, of Castle Howard and the Sheldonian were inspired by Florence and Venice, and the elegiac televisual passage devoted to the boys' stay with Lord Marchmain in Venice is, along with the transatlantic crossing, one of the two climaxes of the production. Justice is done, for sure, to Waugh's professed theme – 'divine grace' and so forth – but for the humanist-consumerist producers and audience, the real thing is the deeply innocent and sexless love of two very young men on a perfect holiday, followed by the deeply serious and prurient observation of the consummation of adulterous love between a very beautiful young woman and a ditto young man.

Waugh wrote, and the television production quoted:

My theme is memory, that winged host that soared about me one grey morning of wartime ... These memories, which are my life –

for we possess nothing certainly except the past – were always with me. Like the pigeons of St. Mark's, they were everywhere.[24]

It is an unhappily indulgent paragraph, for he was never at his best when being conscientiously sincere, and it is, to say the least, contestable as to certitude. But his adaptors are faithful nonetheless to the theme of memory. Of necessity, faithfulness notwithstanding, the memories are also theirs.

Like any adaptation which is any good, the television *Brideshead* is a new work of art. It is so not only in the sense that any new production of classic play or opera aspires to be a new work of art; it is also a new work of art as Canaletto's careful copying of the Grand Canal from his *camera obscura* is a great new work of art. Canaletto organised his copy intensely, shaded and reflected it, chose which shadows to deepen and highlights to exalt, set green and gold and lapis lazuli just as they were, and just so.

The television *Brideshead* has its clumsinesses and foreshortenings, but no one can doubt that its production team were artists. To take the lesser example first, they turned Waugh's chilly and calculating copulation into the sort of loving sex you'd expect from someone as sad and lovely and unselfconsciously gracious as Diana Quick. In Waugh's hateful image, which Mortimer quotes, Ryder goes to bed with her 'as though a deed of conveyance of her narrow loins had been drawn and sealed. I was making my first entry as the freeholder of a property I would enjoy and develop at leisure.'[25]

The cold observation speaks eloquently of the misogyny apparent throughout the book and epidemic in Waugh's life and art. The screen pictures a little decorous heaving, and then Diana Quick lying serenely half-naked, talking fondly to her lover as the boat pitches and rolls about her calm centre. By now and perforce, the television story has had to give up on Charles as a bad job ('a dry stick' as Waugh conceded) and learn a present-day lesson about the easiness and gladness of straight sex. In a pleasant touch, Charles leaves Julia's room in the early hours and gives a guiltless good morning to the passing steward as he goes.

The Venetian episode is done far more sumptuously but with just as firm a pedagogic hand. It is none the worse for that.

Readers will recall that Charles overdraws his account at Oxford and is driven home penniless to find the muffled teasing of his father as unyielding as his bank. To his joy, he is suddenly called to keep Sebastian company at Brideshead after a trifling accident and Sebastian, due to stay with his father who has decamped to Venice in the company of an amiably stolid Italian dancer in order to escape the prying and sanctimonious virtue of his wife, shares his ticket price with Charles so that they can travel third class to Venice. The switch to Italy is preceded by a heart-lifting moment as the boys shout with sheer excitement as they run down an echoing corridor of the vast house: it is one of the many such touches with which the producers recapture all such boyhoods.

Now the producers bring their heroes to the unforgettable pleasures of a perfect holiday while, pleasantly conscious of their own appropriate puritanism, they make sure that the perfect content of such a holiday is art, for art has the place in their hearts that God has in Waugh's. Indeed, Mortimer quotes Lord Marchmain as asking, 'And how do you plan your time here? Bathing or sight-seeing? ... You can't do both, you know.'[26]

The boys do the sights in wobble-dissolve with a fine disregard of topographical verisimilitude. They cruise up in a gondola to the Palazzo di Polignac where the Marchmain household greets them but which inside turns out to be the Palazzo Barbaro where Monet and Sargent painted, and Browning and Henry James wrote.

The television Venice, like the television Oxford, is handsomely regilded and restored, its canals clean and green, its stones golden, its pastels freshly pink and pale blue. Nothing here of Thomas Mann's foetid waters, decadent desires and lurking, odorous plague. In a delicious cameo, the movie shows the two boys and Cara in front of the overwhelming Tintorettos in the Scuola Grande, before Titian's golden, scarlet and stupendous Assumption, where the calm and lovely Virgin ascends gracefully up from the people to the Father. Jeremy Irons gazes admiringly upwards at the painting; Anthony Andrews looks coyly sideways, as who should say, 'I know *you* think it's wonderful and I'm enjoying myself, but it's not really my cup of tea, you know'. It's a very tricky bit of acting, and finely brought off.

So, too, is the intercalation of seeing such sights as these with the travelogue shots of the amazing city, the endearing high jinks of their stay and the dutifully brochure-illustrating moments: an ominous shot of Sebastian drinking wine too eagerly at a fountain-side; coffee at Florian's; the gorgeous glass, mirrors and chandeliers in the Palazzo Pisani Moretta; the dazzling white façade of San Moise against the night sky; sunshine shattered on the canal waters; paddling in a sudden shower off the Lido, a scene which gracefully mutates into rain in Green Park as the pair go home.

It's a delightful sequence, an architectural-tourist theme dear to the heart of the production team. The value offered to us is the art-pilgrimage: Oxford, Yorkshire, Venice, Portmeirion, varying masterpieces all. Thereafter, surprisingly, but Waugh pointed the way, Gozo-pretending-to-be-Fez (perfectly well, too), and Gozo pretending-to-be-Guatemala as well. In each case the walled medina, the narrow windowless streets and stairs, the sudden tranche of light from an open door, the glimpse of greenery and palms behind tall gates contrast memorably with the English landscape prospects and the huge windows of Castle-Howard-as-Brideshead.

The serial is an architectural education and a celebration of cultivated tourism such as Waugh would have despised, yet which he in much of his writing inaugurated. It is extremely charming and, as Anthony Blanche warned us, the charm spots and diseases the art from time to time. For the art is slight, too slight, one might say, for eleven hours of television. It sustains, in spite of itself, a view of conduct in which loyal and passionate friendship together with admiring admirable paintings, architecture and poetry, keep a body upright and a spirit fulfilled, especially if you have the luck from time to time to find serious sex with a very good-looking woman. Such a life will bear up well enough in the teeth of certain disappointment, disillusion, boredom and occasional despair.

This view of the world is sufficiently Waugh's own, without the accession of divine grace. It is certainly contemporary. It is probably that of the production team. It is, one has to say, irremediably masculine but not just oppressively so. It belongs to a man who, as the millennium approaches, sees fall across it the shadow of his own death. The authors – Waugh first, then Sturridge, Granger, Mortimer, correct Englishmen from Oxford, hardworking lovers of art and travel and life – experiment with depriving Ryder of what ought to be the gifts reserved for age, as honour, love, obedience, troops of friends. They endorse Waugh's decision to deprive him of the woman he loves, for it is a straightforwardly intelligible and absolute rule of television adaptations that the story may not be altered in its essential line. Julia renounces Charles in the name of her duty to God. His solace is to find God.

It is a meaningless consolation to the millions who watched *Brideshead* devotedly. It was largely meaningless to Waugh's own readership in 1945 as the poet Henry Reed, reviewing the book, complained at the time (he also complained vigorously about Waugh's snobbery, 'testiness at other people's bad taste having a special vulgarity of its own'[27]).

Renunciation of earthly happiness in order to do one's duty to Catholic precepts, themselves a direct apprehension of the presence of God, is almost disappeared from English culture, even among Catholics. It is certainly no part of John Mortimer's world-view. That he presents the action with such a delicate sympathy is a token of his good manners and of adaptor's aesthetics, such that the better the original the more one must be faithful to it. (Andrew Davies put the same point differently when, speaking of Michael Dobbs's *House of Cards* he said, 'it's much easier to adapt a bad book than a good one'.) This is also a lesson which sorts happily with a quite new strand in contemporary ethics, whereby the mysterious beliefs of other people are respected simply for their otherness however incomprehensible they are to us.

One might make a little test case of Julia's renunciation, of Sebastian's holy idiocy in the depths of his helpless drunkenness, above all of Lord Marchmain's deathbed reconversion to the church. *In extremis*, as Catholic liturgy has it, and while the almost too lovable, inevitably Irish Father Mackay (done to a treat by Niall Tobin) conducts the Last Sacrament, the motionless body on the bed stirs and, with, it must be said, a ham hand the Almighty Father of English Theatre marks a slow, enormous and quavering crucifix upon his forehead, torso and outstretched arms.

It is a *coup de théâtre* of pure superstition: God in the room, reconciliation with Him in the last nick of time, the veil of the temple rent, a strong shiver all the way down your spine. But unless you deeply share the metaphysics, the aesthetic effect is, as I say, like those worthy, far from inadequate efforts of latterday anthropological theatre to reconstruct the strangeness and distanciation of, say, Sophocles or ancient Indian drama.

If, as for worse and for better, our culture does, you see the world in humanist and not religious ways, Lord Marchmain's cross is a mere comfort for the bereaved, and Julia's renunciation of marriage to someone she loves an act of austere self-denial to make us wince with that kind of admiration which refuses emulation.

This is not *homme moyen sensuel*, saying 'good for her but not for me'. It is a case of seeing things quite differently. One respects the fierce serenity of principle in the other's world-view, but one will not imitate it exactly because one could not see the point.[28]

This cuts across the new principle of comparativity in human understanding. What we recognise in this alien world of devout Catholicism is difference. But domestic television drama, of its small-scale, homely nature, its punctual serialisation and familial ethos, depends utterly on our sympathy with its realism. No one recognises this better than programme directors. In that case, to take *Brideshead* so bravely as your chosen text, is to appeal to your audience in terms not of its hope of Christian redemption, but in the larger, more unkillable hope that a good yarn will keep the promise of happiness implicit in all art, never more so than when the grateful tears greet tales of the happiness of others lost to time and chance.

Hence, I think, the power of a story based on love and friendship circumscribed by travelling holidays. The time at Oxford is presented, as well it might be, as a kind of holiday and so too are the sojourns at Brideshead. Indeed time itself is in this production (and specifically not in the novel) marked out by the frame of feeling peculiar to holidays. (These people are, after all, the idle rich; Ryder apart, the war gives them their first chance of meaningful labour.) That is to say, each segment of the action is framed by particular expectations of its end. The question which tantalises our sympathies is whether tremulously temporary happiness, or the purposefulness or intensity of this segment of time will find satisfactory resolution. Oxford, Brideshead, Venice; Paris, the 1926 General Strike, Fez; Portmeirion-dressed-as-Cannes-in-sepia, the *Queen Mary* in mid-Atlantic, Brideshead again; finally, the calm coda of desolation, the best words of love in book or film, '"I don't want to make it easier for you," I said; "I hope your heart may break; but I do understand."'[29]

In these three simple sonatas, each movement recapitulates the rhythm of the holiday sojourn, even retaining by a masterly touch something of the holiness left in the etymology of the word. Each is situated in a magically picturesque place, breathing out the invitation to love and luxury, the compounds of art. Each offers novelty:

of encounter, of domestic timetable, of geography and climate (nothing like a storm to go with sex, as every bad-weather kitsch-artist knows). Change the place and change the rules; exotic places make new self-definitions imaginable. Holidays pretend that fantasy may become action, even when all is said and done about the filthy beaches, the used syringes, the dead babies.

In *Brideshead*, each narrative segment is charged with the exotica of history: the 1920s, the Riviera, Cunarder travel, theatrical class struggle, all ineffably clad in Armani versions of historical wardrobe, silk dresses, linen suits and cream shoes unreally smoothed by steam-iron and artificial fibres and celestial dry-cleaning.

Memory, not God, is Waugh's first theme and that of the television production and its extremely intelligent, forgivably sentimental authors. This is the open secret of *Brideshead*'s success. What is remembered and enacted are the adventitious conjunctions of place and person which make deep feeling and fulfilment possible. When this simple frame is dressed in the stylish clothes of a departed ruling class and its glowing light darkened by the background of impending world war; when its personae are played by the youthful beauties and parental familiars of the National Theatre; when the whole sequence is suffused by the never-very-bitter sweetness of intense happiness and love lost and lovingly recollected – the wonderful unbearable legacy of Wordsworth and Schubert; when all this is leisurely and gracefully orchestrated as eleven hours of television, why then you have a masterpiece in a new genre.

Of course, your originators have to be men of rare audacity and unusual dedication – you might as well say, of genius – to see how all this might be done. The awful thing is that television drama is of such saturating ubiquity that the bright star of something as marvellous as *Brideshead* is soon put out.

NOTES

1 As they are required to do in much contemporary pedagogy, as illustrated in Franco Moretti's *The Way of the World* (London, Verso, 1983) or, more inanely, in the Open University course written by Michael Rossington and entitled *A Study Guide to British Poetry 1950–1980*.

2 All quotations are taken from the Everyman edition of Evelyn Waugh, *Brideshead Revisited* (Chapman and Hall, 1960; Everyman's Library, 1993), ed. and with introduction by Sir Frank Kermode.

3 *BBC Handbook* (BBC, 1982).

4 I am developing here some remarks of mine in *Popular Culture and Political Power* (Brighton, Harvester Wheatsheaf, 1988).

5 See his *The Lyric Poet in the Era of High Capitalism* (London, New Left Books, 1974), p. 221.

6 Waugh, Preface to *Brideshead*, p. 2.

7 In his obituary for F. R. Leavis, *Times Higher Education Supplement*, 12 June 1978.

8 Waugh, *Brideshead*, p. 153.

9 Waugh, *Brideshead*, p. 26.

10 Tom Nairn, *The Enchanted Glass: Britain and its Monarchy* (London, Verso, 1988).

11 This latter phrase is taken from an obedient application of Nairn's thesis to present cinema. See Paul Dare, 'The Bourgeois Paradigm and Heritage Cinema', *New Left Review,* 224 (July–August 1997).

12 Waugh, *Brideshead*, p. 14.

13 Waugh, *Brideshead*, p. 27.

14 *Clive James on Television* (London, Picador, 1991) p. 614.

15 In conversation with me, February 1996.

16 It is Sartre, in his celebrated essay *The Psychology of the Imagination*, who notes the usual poverty of that faculty.

17 Waugh, *Brideshead*, p. 54.

18 George Santayana, *Selected Writings*, ed. N. Henfrey (Cambridge, Cambridge University Press, 1968), vol. 1, p. 195.

19 Waugh, *Brideshead*, p. 246.

20 Waugh, Preface to *Brideshead*, p. 1.

21 Waugh, *Brideshead*, p. 161.

22 Waugh, *Brideshead*, p. 182.

23 Paul Fussell, *Abroad: English Literary Travelling between the Wars* (Oxford, Oxford University Press, 1980).

24 Waugh, *Brideshead*, p. 203.

25 Waugh, *Brideshead*, p. 235.

26 Waugh, *Brideshead*, p. 87.

27 *New Statesman*, 23 June 1945.

28 I am here developing some ideas broached in my *Cultural Studies* (Oxford, Blackwell, 1993), first prompted by Richard Norman's 'On Seeing Things Differently', *Radical Philosophy*, 1: 1 (1972).

29 Waugh, *Brideshead*, p. 308.

12

'Piecing together a mirage': adapting *The English Patient* for the screen

Bronwen Thomas

Anthony Minghella's adaptation of Michael Ondaatje's novel won nine Academy Awards in 1997 and went on to become one of the most successful British independent films ever made. The critical response to the film ranged from the reverent to the positively ecstatic, but was nearly always tinged with a sense of sheer relief that an adaptation of a literary text still has the capacity to compete with the Hollywood blockbusters. For example, in *The Guardian* Derek Malcolm celebrated the fact that 'the film is an epic, and adult, tale of doomed romance – of the kind Hollywood used to make but now doesn't dare in case its core audience of 17- to 25-year-olds get bored'.[1] The film may even be said to have spawned, or at least tapped into, a mythology powerful enough to excite almost a cultish following. Articles and documentaries about the 'real' Count Almásy (the 'English' patient of the title) have appeared,[2] and according to the *Independent on Sunday* the film was responsible for a growth in the tourism market for the African deserts.[3] Perhaps most important of all, the words 'epic' and 'romantic' have once again been spoken by critics of film without embarrassment or irony.

Many of the reviews heralding the release of the film in Britain portray Anthony Minghella as engaged in an almost heroic effort to adapt a 'difficult' novel. First published in 1992, *The English Patient* won the prestigious Booker Prize, and firmly established Ondaatje's reputation as a novelist.[4] Born in Sri Lanka, but based in Toronto, Ondaatje had successfully built a reputation as a poet, before turning to fiction and, for a short while, filmmaking. Between 1970 and

1974 Ondaatje made three films, two documentaries and a five-minute fictional piece.[5] The films have hardly contributed to the enhancement of Ondaatje's reputation, but several critics have pointed to the ways in which the experience of working with film has influenced his writing. For example, Testa argues that Ondaatje's predilection for juxtapositioning, polyphonous narration and heterogeneous stylistics emerges from his work with film, although he also adds the proviso that in the hands of the novelist, such techniques often represent an imaginary reinvention of filmic techniques rather than an uncomplicated borrowing.[6] Undoubtedly, Ondaatje is a writer who is fascinated by film. This was evident from his enthusiastic participation in the making of *The English Patient*: he was a familiar figure on set. It is also clear from his frequent references to film in his fiction, as in *The English Patient* where Kip regards Hana 'as if a camera's film reveals her, but only her, in silence'.[7]

Anthony Minghella turned to filmmaking after a successful career as a playwright. Prior to *The English Patient*, his best-known film was *Truly, Madly, Deeply*, a romantic tale of love beyond the grave, which avoided the sickly sentimentality of the similarly plotted *Ghost*, largely because of the tone of sardonic, often black humour which characterises the dialogue. His adaptation of Ondaatje's novel continues a successful run of bringing Booker Prize-winning fiction to the screen. As Philip French has noted, out of 160 novels short-listed for the prize since 1969, about twenty-five have been turned into films.[8] Minghella's adaptation boldly departs from its 'original' in many ways. This appears to be unapologetic on Minghella's part, for as Anne Billson puts it, the director 'uses the original as a launch-pad ... it turns out less like a slavish rendering of the book than a partially remembered dream of it'.[9] Minghella has spoken of how, when he read the novel, it seemed to remind him of a film he had seen.[10] Several of the more visually striking tableaux come straight from the novel: a burning man falling from the sky; a man carrying his lover's body across a desert; a garden lit by hundreds of candles housed in snail's shells. During the shooting of the film, Ondaatje was never less than fully supportive of the 'vision' which the director brings to the novel. Indeed, he has claimed that it is readers, rather than writers, who are likely to be offended by adaptations, since it is they who invest most in interpreting how the characters might appear.[11] Certainly, the collaboration between the two men seems to have been especially harmonious, and must be the envy of many an adapter.

In the novel, the central figure of the English patient[12] is spellbound by the stories of Herodotus, a writer whom he describes as 'piecing together a mirage' by seeking out 'cul-de-sacs within the sweep of history'.[13] This could also be taken as a description of Ondaatje's narrative technique, eschewing linearity and completion in favour of plot-lines which are fragmentary and characters who remain enigmatic. A mirage is described by the *Oxford Concise Dictionary* as an 'optical illusion caused by atmospheric conditions, esp. appearance of sheet of water in desert or on hot road; illusory thing'. In Ondaatje's novel, as I shall argue later, the image of the mirage is far from being confined to the scenes in the desert. At times the characters appear to lack control over their own destinies, and even their own dreams and memories. This may be through the influence of love or affection, disorientating the characters by thrusting them into unfamiliar territories. Alternatively, the characters may be forced to exist within a mirage which is not of their own making, for example in wartime where propaganda and myth provide the reassurance that the horrors of war are necessary evils in pursuit of a 'just cause'.

But the image of 'piecing together a mirage' implies a voluntary, conscious effort to construct the illusion, rather than an involuntary deception brought about by external circumstances. Many of the characters appear to construct their own 'mirages' to escape reality, whether this is through injecting oneself with morphine (Caravaggio), or reverting to the world of childhood (Hana).

Yet there is also the impulse, voiced by the maverick Caravaggio, whereby 'we want to know things, how the pieces fit',[14] and in order to do this we have to step outside the mirage and acknowledge that it is illusory. As I shall argue later, the desire to tell stories, to piece together events into some kind of narrative structure, is shared by many of Ondaatje's characters, especially the English patient. But this inevitably involves a distancing from the events and persons being depicted, so that the act of storytelling may itself be a mirage, erected on fast-fading memories and half-remembered images. The presence of the third-person narrator in the novel would seem to represent the possibility of 'piecing together the mirages', providing just enough impetus for the reader to seek out connections and links between the various fragments. But it is often far from clear just who is narrating and difficult to assert with any certainty whether the narration is located inside or outside the mirage.

The mirage is most commonly associated with the visual, and with the sensation that what is seen cannot necessarily be believed. There are many scenes in the film where characters appear to be taken aback by a *trompe l'œil*, for example where the English patient regains consciousness after the plane crash in which he has been burnt. Adopting his perspective, the camera presents us with a dazzling display of kaleidoscopic lights and colours refracted from a Bedouin healer's medicine bottles. The immediate effect is one of disorientation as we try to establish just what it is that we are seeing. This is a cinematic convention with which we are familiar, the reawakening of a character often being accompanied by sensations of disequilibrium. But, like the novel, the film does not offer us the reassurance of fixed and determinable boundaries between the mirage and the real. Throughout, the cutting between scenes, and the use of flashback, constantly forces us to reorientate ourselves in relation to what we are seeing.

What I wish to explore in this chapter is the extent to which Minghella's adaptation retains the sense of fragmentation and precarious vulnerability which is so characteristic of Ondaatje's novel, or whether he pursues a mirage of imposed coherence and continuity. I shall do this by examining in depth the ways in which place, time and point of view are represented in novel and film, and by outlining the ways in which Minghella's narrative departs from, or adds to, Ondaatje's.

Plot

The English Patient has been described as 'a magic carpet of a novel',[15] covering in its sweep a vast panoply of landscapes, characters and time-frames. At its core is the story of four characters, each 'damaged' in some way, who are thrown together by the hazards of a war in a ruined villa in Italy. The English patient, we gradually learn, is in fact a Hungarian aristocrat and desert explorer, Count Laszlo de Almásy, whose life was thrown into turmoil when he embarked on a tempestuous, sometimes violent affair with his English colleague's wife, Katherine Clinton. When the husband,

Geoffrey, discovers their affair, he tries to kill them all in a plane crash, but in the process only succeeds in killing himself and fatally injuring his wife. Almásy sets off across the desert to find help but is mistaken for a German spy and captured by the Allies. It is only by going over to the Germans and helping their campaign that Almásy is able to return to Katherine, to find that she has died. He sets off on a symbolic, but inevitably doomed, attempt to return her to her beloved England, but the plane catches fire. Almásy survives the fall, but is badly burnt, and his life is only saved by the ministrations of a Bedouin healer. He claims not to be able to remember who or what he is, leaving others to attempt to piece together the fragments of his life.

The English patient is tended at the villa by a Canadian nurse called Hana, who has remained behind after the Allies' victory. She has been scarred by the death of her father and by having to witness the deaths of so many young soldiers. Soon afterwards, the occupants of the villa are joined by the opportunistic and seemingly amoral Caravaggio, a sometime thief and spy who, it emerges, was a friend of Hana's family. Caravaggio has been tortured by the Germans, leaving his hands mutilated, and he blames Almásy for his fate, believing that the count became a traitor. The final addition to the quartet is the Indian sapper, Kip, who arrives at the villa as part of a bomb-disposal unit, and who becomes Hana's lover. We later learn that Kip too has been scarred, both by being branded a traitor by his brother for serving with the British, and by the death of his English mentor and friend, Lord Suffolk.

The various narratives of these individuals' lives are interwoven throughout the novel so that the 'facts' only emerge piecemeal. Moreover, each of the characters is profoundly affected by their encounters with the other residents of the villa. The last we see of Caravaggio, he is suspended in mid-air halfway across a rope bridge. We never learn whether he successfully makes it across, nor where he is going. Meanwhile, the English patient stoically awaits his inevitable death. But we only experience this longed-for release as it is foreseen by Kip, who supposes that 'In the future, if and when the patient dies, Caravaggio and the girl will bury him'.[16] Kip leaves the villa to start a new life, grief-stricken at the death of his comrade, Hardy, and disillusioned by the 'betrayal' of the Allies in dropping nuclear bombs on Hiroshima and Nagasaki. At the close of the novel we learn that he has become a doctor and is married with children, but that he still thinks of Hana and their time at the villa. Hana, too, embarks on a new life, but her future seems less assured, since we are told that she 'has not found her own company, the ones she wanted'.[17]

To describe the plot of Ondaatje's novel in this way is misleading, because it implies a chronology and a logical progression. In fact, reading *The English Patient* is a very different experience, as the narrative teases us with by-roads and subplots, and seems to change voice, location and period on almost every page. The experiences of the characters while they are at the villa are mainly narrated chronologically and provide some point of stability in the narrative. However, the novel is in some senses like the copy of Herodotus which Almásy cherishes: a collection of stories, some of which have a recognisable structure and lead to some kind of closure, others of which are inserted into the novel as if from different hands who inhabit different worlds. The novel has at its core recurring images and themes which might be deemed central to its understanding. For example the literal act of map-making in which Almásy and his colleagues are engaged becomes a symbol for the efforts of the characters to try to make sense of the circumstances in which they find themselves, and to try to lay claim to landscapes, people and aspects of themselves which require charting in order to solidify their 'reality' . Another recurring theme is that of betrayal, both private, as when wife betrays husband, and public or historic, as when the Allies drop their nuclear bombs on Hiroshima and Nagasaki. Yet to isolate one image or emotion as representing the 'essence' of the novel would be to risk over-simplification.

In addition to the convolutions of the plot and the complexity of its narrative structure, the novel contains so many intertextual references that to try and map its sources and loci of meaning would seem as demanding as the project facing Almásy and his fellow cartographers in the desert. Along with Herodotus, reference is made to the writings of Pound, Milton and Kipling, while contemporary popular songs by the likes of Hart and Rogers provide another dimension through their sounds and images. With the adaptation of the novel for the screen, these intertextual resonances proliferate. Billson has claimed that the sensuousness of the film and its refusal to bow to realism owe much to Powell and Pressburger.[18] But the most frequent comparison is with David Lean, and in particular his *Lawrence of Arabia*. Tom Shone has even suggested that it is 'as if David Lean had made *Lawrence of Arabia* and *Brief Encounter* but not waited in between, instead making them as the same movie'.[19] Such comparisons have led to the promotion of the film as an old-fashioned romantic epic. As Kevin Jackson commented,

> *The English Patient* retells some of the old stories movies have always liked to tell – about the hard, lonely man melted by passion; about the glacial beauty with an incandescent heart who forsakes her husband for this brooding solitary; about ardours which end in death and noble self-sacrifice.[20]

The most prominent image in the publicity material promoting the film focuses on the solitary figure of Almásy set against a desert backdrop, and a prospective viewer would have little indication that there is any more to the film than the story of his tragic love affair. But as Jackson goes on to say, the film also tells us stories that are not so familiar, striking notes seldom permitted by the Hollywood industry.

Minghella's script departs from the plot of the novel in several significant ways. The film focuses much more closely on the relationship between Katherine and Almásy than does the novel. This means that the story of Hana and Kip's relationship becomes secondary – for some, even marginal. To the cynical, this might smack of knee-bowing to the Hollywood machine, and the commercial wisdom that a relationship between a Sikh and a French-Canadian might not have the same appeal as that between a swarthy European and an English rose. In the publicity material for the film, the actor playing Kip (Naveen Andrews) is given second billing alongside several of the film's minor characters, and behind Ralph Fiennes (Almásy), Juliette Binoche (Hana), Willem Dafoe (Caravaggio) and Kristin Scott-Thomas (Katherine). However, for many critics, too, it is the relationship between Almásy and Katherine that constitutes the heart of the story. As Scobie argues, 'It is in their affair, presented in a series of short, intense, almost hallucinatory scenes, that the fire of the heart burns brightest'.[21] Also, as we shall see, Minghella goes some way towards deconstructing myths such as that of the 'English rose', so that they become more problematic.

Despite the length of the film version (around two hours, forty minutes), some elements of the plot are omitted, notably the scenes in England involving Kip's mentor, Lord Suffolk. Nevertheless,

Billson's claim that Minghella has 'ironed' out some of the complexities of Ondaatje's plot would seem unjustified.[22] The film remains
highly complex and the sheer pace of the narrative places great
demands on the viewer's concentration.

There are several minor changes to the plot which nevertheless
are highly significant in terms of our interpretation of the characters
and their actions. In the novel Geoffrey and Katherine are described
as having met in the Oxford Union Library, but in the film Geoffrey
proudly relates that they had been friends since childhood. This
subtle change means that their relationship is couched in a kind of
innocence, like brother and sister, thereby throwing into sharp relief
the fervent, often violent passion shared by Katherine and Almásy.

The relationship between Hana and Caravaggio is also altered.
In the novel there is an immediate mutual recognition of their
shared past in Canada (part of which forms the subject of Ondaatje's
novel *In the Skin of a Lion*), whereas in the film the relationship
between them is unclear, and more distant. In addition, the death of
Hana's father is overshadowed in the film by the insertion of a
highly dramatic scene in which Hana's friend is blown up by a land-
mine. This enables Minghella to portray the degree to which Hana
is 'more patient than nurse'[23] with more immediacy and dramatic
tension than is evident in the novel, where her emotional scars are
more deep-rooted.

Another significant alteration involves the death of Madox,
Almásy's colleague and friend. In the film, Caravaggio torments the
English patient by telling him that Madox committed suicide as a
direct result of learning of his friend's treachery. In the novel, the
motive for the suicide is not as clear-cut, being portrayed as the
result of the gnawing sense of malaise Madox experiences with the
onset of the war. The effect of this departure is to emphasise the
enormity of Almásy's actions and the sacrifice he makes to honour
his promise to Katherine. However, it might also be said to gloss
over the extent to which the war is seen as an intrusion into the lives
of the characters, so that while in the film the brutality of the war
may be evident, its necessity is never really brought into question.

Many of the more memorable scenes and lines in the film do
not take place in the novel. In the film it is implied that Geoffrey
learns of his wife's affair when he sees her and Almásy setting off in
a taxi together. The scene excites complex emotions, creating
considerable tension but also inviting some sympathy for the morti-

fied Geoffrey. Ondaatje has expressed his delight with this scene, commenting in a typically disingenuous fashion that when others had complimented him on the scene, which he agreed was intrinsic to the film, he had had to remind himself that it did not in fact appear in the novel at all.[24]

Perhaps one of the most significant of Minghella's contributions is the addition of considerable dry humour to the narrative. Minghella displays great dexterity in orchestrating the emotions of his audience, moving them from laughter to tears and back again in an instant. We feel a degree of warmth for the enigmatic patient because of his propensity for humming popular tunes to himself almost unawares, and because even though he is in constant pain he is able to find humour in the most mundane things. One of the most memorable vignettes in the film comes when Hana feeds ripe plums to the English patient and he at once heightens and deflates the sensuality of this act by commenting wryly that 'It's a very *plum* plum.' The tortuous end to the affair with Katherine is similarly not without its painful, sometimes bitter humour. Almásy's descent into drunkenness provides some moments of slapstick humour as he tumbles and breaks all sorts of social taboos. But it is also deeply moving, representing as it does the emptiness and confusion he feels once the mask of phlegmatic detachment has been ripped away by his passion for Katherine.

Minghella seems highly adept at stretching the audience's taut sensibilities to excruciating but at the same time exquisite climaxes. In the novel, as Katherine finally breaks off the affair, 'her head sweeps away from him and hits the side of the gatepost'.[25] In the film the audience's reaction to this scene is a nervous laugh, unsure as to whether this clumsiness is the actor's or the character's. Literally, it seems, we do not know whether to laugh or cry, and this produces an uncomfortable sensation of uncertainty, confusion and frustration which brings us closer to the two characters. The supreme poise of the English rose is disturbed for a split second. And during that same instant the viewer's poise is disturbed, as the pleasurable mirage of the romance is momentarily lifted and replaced by a profound uncertainty as to the meaning of what is being viewed. As a result, this seemingly inconsequential moment takes on a supreme significance, prompting a reassessment both of the relationship between the characters, and of how we as viewers are being positioned by the narrative.

The ending to Minghella's film ties up some of the loose ends of Ondaatje's plot. In one of the most moving scenes in the film, we see the English patient pleading with his eyes for Hana to end his suffering, and witness her administration of the fatal overdose that will grant him peace. Both Kip and Hana are shown departing from the villa to carve out new lives for themselves, in contrast to the ambiguity surrounding their fates at the end of the novel. It might appear, therefore, that Minghella opts for closure where Ondaatje provides a much more complex leave-taking. But it does not necessarily follow that the viewer emerges from the film feeling that all of its enigmas have been resolved, nor that the emotions it evokes are any less complex.

Place

One of the challenges of adapting *The English Patient* involves the attempt to 'map out' for the viewer the often dizzying shifts in location (and time) that are represented. One of the many symbols which recur in the novel is that of the bridge, constructed to provide a stable and fixed connection between disparate places and peoples. However, while the artistry and the idealism behind such enterprises may be celebrated, we are never allowed to forget that, especially in wartime, such constructions are vulnerable and destructible.

Amongst the places that we visit in the novel are the desert, South Cairo, London and rural Devon. But if we are ever '*in situ*' as Kip is, briefly, when he is stationed with Lord Suffolk, then it is in the Villa San Girolamo in Italy. This is where the novel begins, and it is where we return in the narrative when our explorations into other worlds, other times, are suspended. Yet at the villa, we are told, 'there seemed little demarcation between house and landscape, between damaged building and the burned and shelled remnants of the earth.'[26] It is also a building (now ruined) which has been built upon the ruins of other, forgotten buildings. Thus any sense of stability or 'place' which we are offered seems entirely temporary and fragile.

The villa is a forgotten place, and a place where people who want to forget can find a haven. Overlooked or abandoned in turn by both retreating and advancing armies, it is set apart from the outside world in place and time, much in the vein of a mythic lost world or Shangri-La. This sense of isolation is important for the four characters because here they were shedding skins. They could imitate nothing but what they were. There was no defence but to look for the truth in others.[27]

To some extent, the characters are able to 'shed' the trappings of nationhood, the sets of cultural norms and beliefs which set them apart from one another. But if this offers them a sense of freedom, it is a precarious one, as the blurring of boundaries does not safeguard against betrayal nor provide uncomplicated access to the 'truth in others'. Like the characters who inhabit it, the villa is a place of contradictions and dualities. Described at one point as a place made up of 'daylight darkness',[28] its dense greenery and its shadows may provide shelter and repose, but they always threaten to become claustrophobic. It is a place where release is only possible for two of the characters through frequent injections of morphine, and where, ultimately, the relief of pain and the healing of wounds can only be achieved fleetingly.

Minghella's villa (filmed in Tuscany) is a lush but ramshackle habitation which we only ever catch in glimpses. Each of the characters is given her or his own space – the English patient his room, Hana her garden, Kip his outhouse, Caravaggio the shadows. In addition, there are strong images of regrowth and revitalisation. This is perhaps most evident in the scene where Kip, Hana and Caravaggio 'refresh' the English patient, body and soul, by taking him on a madcap tour of the villa's grounds during a thunderstorm, accompanied by the strains of an Irving Berlin number. After the traumas of the war, and the oppressive heat of the Italian summer, the scene provides an almost tangible sense of relief, and the audience cannot fail to be delighted by the child-like euphoria of the characters.

But Minghella's villa is far from being an innocent or paradisal playground for the characters. One of the ways in which the film captures the duality of the villa is through subtle manipulation of the lighting. For example, Kip's arrival at the villa is couched in symbolism, as he enters into the room where Hana is playing the piano surrounded by a halo of sunshine. In addition, the English patient's room is often depicted bathed in golden sunlight, symbolising the healing balm of Hana's attentions, and also providing a visual link with the golden sands of the desert. But much of the action takes place in the shadows or in semi-darkness, as when Hana plays hopscotch in the moonlight, or Kip woos her with his display of candles set in snails' shells.

In the novel the lush vegetation and seclusion of the villa contrast starkly with the barren landscape of the desert. It is Almásy who is most closely linked with the desert, since he exults in the ways in which its shifting landscapes frustrate attempts at ownership and possession. Again, the word 'demarcation' is used as he asserts that 'In the desert it is easy to lose a sense of demarcation',[29] but for Almásy this is something to celebrate rather than fear. This is why he is better able than some of the other characters to deal with the upheavals and reversals of the war. During the war, factions and allegiances between different peoples shift and realign like the sands of the desert. In addition, whole landscapes may be altered, as bombings and troop movements change the contours and the characters of town and countryside.

In many ways the desert is the one place where we do not appear to encounter mirages, or at least do so mainly through legend and myth. In the desert, the Europeans come into contact with different versions of the 'civilised', so that they come to recognise the mirage of cultural imperialism for what it is. One result of this is a relaxing of the stifling and hypocritical morality of their world. But the exhilaration that this freedom brings may verge on the kind of madness that we associate with the mirage, a sense that here 'anything goes' because the usual laws and moralities are suspended. Thus the German explorer Bermann is discovered concealing an Arab girl in his tent and, more disturbingly, Almásy appears to confess to breaking the taboo of 'intimacy ... between the dead and the living' when he returns for his lover's body.[30] Minghella steers clear of controversy by avoiding any hint of such intimacy between Almásy and Katherine in the film. But he also alters the plot-line involving Bermann, depicting the German flirting with one of the young Arab men accompanying the cartographers. The sole purpose of this change must surely have been to highlight the extent to which the characters feel able to express themselves more freely in the desert.

Minghella's film devotes more narrative time to the desert than does the novel. Through Almásy's words, we come to appreciate its nuances – the traditions of those whose home it is, and the different characters of the breezes and winds that shape its contours. But the film also brings us close to the physical reality of the desert. When

Katherine and Almásy are caught in a sandstorm, we can almost feel the sand in our hair and beneath our fingertips as much as we feel the growing intensity of their feelings for one another.

Minghella's film begins and ends with aerial shots of the desert, exploiting to the full the cinematographic potential of this backdrop. This reflects the extent to which his adaptation foregrounds the Katherine/Almásy relationship and its tragic *dénouement*, and locates that romance in an exotic landscape which Derek Malcolm characterises as 'pretty toothsome'.[31] It also locates us firmly in the mind-set of the world of the mirage, since the shapes that we think we see in the sand shift and mutate from frame to frame. The desert may well provide a visual 'feast' but it, too, has a history which has the potential continually to surprise us. The more the desert is explored, the more mysteries it throws up, and the more certainties it subverts. For example, once the secrets of the Cave of Swimmers are made known, we can no longer regard desert/water as mutually exclusive.

The Cave of Swimmers is important within the desert landscape as virtually the only point of stability from which the explorers (and the viewers) are able to orientate themselves. Minghella departs slightly from the novel in portraying the discovery of the cave as a personal triumph for Almásy, casting him in the same heroic mould as a Lawrence or a Livingstone. In the film, we experience this discovery along with Almásy because its wonders are revealed to us by the light of the torch he carries as he ventures further into the cave. As the shapes become recognisable, we are taken back to the opening sequence of the film in which a hand is seen painting and recording the figures depicted on the cave walls. Interestingly, however, this figure is painted from the feet upwards, so that its meaning only emerges piecemeal, and recognition is only possible when the whole figure is finally revealed. When we revisit the cave for the final time, as Katherine is dying, it has taken on a familiarity which provides some comfort. A fitting final resting place, the cave is decked out with reminders of other worlds, other times: in addition to the figures painted on the cave walls, the camera picks out the copy of Herodotus, Almásy's torch and perhaps most poignantly for Katherine, tinned provisions from 'home'.

In the novel, it is only when the explorers decamp from their desert base to Cairo that the affair between Katherine and Almásy is able to flourish. Under the cover of the city's network of streets and alleyways, and its vast population, deception is easy. In some senses, therefore, it is over-simplistic to portray the desert as the place where the characters truly come to know themselves and others, or the city as the place where they once again revert to their 'civilised' selves. Especially during wartime, the stability which the city seems to offer is shown to be a precarious one. Moreover, the bargaining and the haggling which flourish in the back streets and the bazaars, continually remind us that appearances are deceptive, and that nothing should be taken at face value.

In the film, the scenes set in Cairo are full of bustle and noise, and serve as a stark contrast to the silence and emptiness of the desert. Yet Almásy's room becomes a haven in this maelstrom, the only window on the outside world shielded by a lattice blind, so that even the light has to enter stealthily. In this room time seems to stand still for the lovers. As Tom Shone has argued, Minghella is content to build up the love story patiently and gradually,[32] and once it has been established he is no hurry to depart, 'sticking around' to show us Almásy sewing the dress which we saw him tear from Katherine at the beginning of their love-making in a gesture which is symbolic of the kind of piecing together which the characters all seem to seek.

Cairo is also a place of play and relaxation for the characters after the asceticism of their existence in the desert. Minghella has said that his depiction of the legendary Shepheard's hotel was intended to introduce an element of luxury to the film.[33] The hotel features twice, the first time as Katherine and Almásy are drawn together in the city, and the second after the relationship appears to have come to an end. In the first scene, as the explorers appear decked out in formal wear, and dance in set patterns and moves, there is some sense of relaxation as they slip back into their 'civilised' guises. But as Almásy cuts in to dance the foxtrot with Katherine we sense some awkwardness and frustration with these rituals and a tension between the characters which, it seems, the order and intricacy of the dance moves will be powerless to contain.

The second scene set in the hotel reveals this tension in a darker light as Almásy stumbles around drunkenly and broods in the shadows. The thrilling tension of the earlier scene is here replaced by a sense of danger as Almásy threatens to lose control completely. Almost in parody of the earlier encounter, he suggests that he and 'Mrs Clifton' should dance the 'Bosphorous hug', a private reference to their shared term for the 'place' on Katherine's body which Almásy claims as his own, but a reference whose crudity and inappropriateness is nonetheless painfully apparent amongst the stuffed shirts and ball gowns which surround them.

The place which is notable by its absence from the film is England. In the novel several scenes are located in England, such as when we are given a fleeting insight into the twilight world of the mapmakers and their gentlemen's clubs in London. But much of what we see of England in the novel is filtered through the eyes of the outsider, Kip. This has led Scobie to argue that Englishness is written out of the novel, so that there is a gaping hole at its centre.[34] Minghella appears to have taken this a stage further, omitting wholesale the scenes involving Lord Suffolk, and representing 'Englishness' only, it seems, through the blurred memories and dreams of the central characters.

In the novel, the English patient's 'memories' of England appear to have been borrowed from his lover, Katherine. In the film, much of our sense of what is English comes from Katherine's idealised memories of the 'green and pleasant land' she longs for, or the platitudes and awkward humour which make Geoffrey, as played by Colin Firth, appear like a character straight out of P. G. Wodehouse. The other main source of reference is Kip and his experiences of English colonialism – the worst excesses of national identity exaggerated and packaged for ease of transmission. This 'Englishness' may be overtly mythic, as in the writings of Kipling who is much quoted in the novel. But it is also covert, in the stock phrases and trite reference points which always somehow seem outdated and superimposed. As Homi Bhabha has written, 'What is "English" in these discourses of colonial power cannot be represented as a plentitude or a "full" presence; it is determined by its belatedness.'[35]

In the film, many of the strongest images of 'Englishness' are extremely mundane or trivial. Almásy and Kip, neither of whom is English, find great delight in the phenomenon of condensed milk, that quintessential emblem of the tuck-shop and the public school. In another scene, the 'English abroad' celebrate Christmas in the stifling heat with the buffoonish Geoffrey insisting on dressing up as Father Christmas, while his compatriots sit down to a formal meal with all the trimmings. Yet even here we are not allowed the luxury of an uncomplicated response. While we might sneer at the English as they suffer in the heat, one of the trappings of this absurd ritual is transformed into a highly personal and poignant symbol. For we discover that the remains of the Christmas cracker appropriated by the lovers has become embedded amongst all the other fragments which interleave the patient's copy of Herodotus.

For the filmmakers, it was clearly important that there should be some demarcation between the different locations. This is achieved through subtle variations in lighting, sound/music and colour, not only signalling *where* we are (North Africa, Italy) but also, as we shall see in the next section, *when* we are (pre-war, post-war). As was mentioned earlier, much of the action set around the villa takes place in the half-darkness, the main exception being the English patient's room, which is often bathed in golden light. This contrasts sharply with the desert scenes, where darkness falls abruptly, and where the sunlight is blinding and unrelenting. Minghella also uses intertitles to provide some orientation in time and place and to underline the fact that much of the story is taking place in a past distant enough to be so framed. However, these are largely confined to major shifts in place or time. When the narrative jumps backwards or forwards a matter of days or weeks, or within the same setting, Minghella relies on the dialogue and on the audience's powers of interpretation to follow these shifts.

As Philip French has argued, the Second World War is a period which both novels and films have made familiar through frequent revisitation.[36] But in setting the action in the desert, and in concentrating more on the immediate pre- and post-war periods, *The English Patient*'s perspective might be described as off-centre, or even decentred. To some extent, the opportunities to indulge in 'toothsome' displays of cinematography influence both the content and structure of the narrative. It is evident that much of the epic quality of Minghella's film comes from the sheer scale and visual splendour of the landscapes he portrays. However, this is combined with an attention to detail, and a sensitivity to the dualities of these complex landscapes, which invites exploration and contemplation as well as sensuous enjoyment.

Time

Through formal experimentation, Ondaatje's novel often serves to disrupt our sense of the relationship between past and present. Ondaatje has stated that

I don't believe stories are told from A to Z anymore ... We discover stories in a different way. I discover something about you after knowing you X number of years, and then after 30 years I will find out some other changes that occurred 5 years earlier. That sense of discovery, of memory, and how we reveal ourselves to each other – none of that is chronological.[37]

He has also spoken of his admiration for his contemporary and fellow Booker Prize winner Graham Swift.[38] Swift is a writer who frequently experiments with narrative voice, as in *Waterland* (1983) where the narrator appears to be suffering some kind of breakdown, or *Last Orders* (1996), where each of the main characters takes his or her turn at narrating. Swift also experiments with chronology and with different ways of telling, and dealing with, the past, whether this is a publicly validated 'history', or the personal memories of fallible individuals.

Like Swift, Ondaatje appears to revel in experimenting with syntax and grammatical tense in his narration. From the very beginning *The English Patient* veers seemingly at random between past, historic present and present tenses, the characters' tales often gaining immediacy and drama as they appear to be relived vicariously through the retelling.[39] For example, much of chapter five, entitled 'Katherine' is narrated in the historic present, as a fragment of the past intimacy and torment of the lovers' relationship is laid before the reader. It might be argued that this device is reserved for such intense moments, but this would be to over-simplify the sensation of disorientation and, sometimes, pure shock, that we experience as we are shunted around in time and place. Like Swift, Ondaatje is also fond of surprising the reader occasionally with an unexpected future tense ('There are villages he will travel into with them ...'[40]) so that the narrator's knowledge appears momentarily to gain another dimension. Frequently, sentences appear without any main verbs – 'The faint glass noise and the diverse colours and the regal walk and his face like a lean dark gun'[41] – so that it appears impossible to locate the images or give them order, forcing us instead to dwell on, but also veer between, the pictures and the sounds that they evoke.

As we shall see in the next section, the novel presents us with a mosaic of narratives told by the different characters. These individual narratives are often full of gaps and time-jumps, so that the impression created is one of disjointedness. As the narratives jump around in time ('a few months later'; 'a year later'), like the English patient listening to Hana's erratic readings, we come to expect that they should have 'gaps of plot like sections of a road washed out by storms'.[42] Particularly with the narratives recounted by the English patient and Caravaggio, the ability to provide an order to events is disrupted by the impact of the morphine they are addicted to, which is constantly 'imploding time and geography'.[43] However, since this is compared to 'the way maps compress the world onto a two-dimensional sheet of paper',[44] it is clear that while the 'map' may be distorted, it may also have its own validity and function.

At times there is almost a sense of impatience with language as the various narrators explore its boundaries in an attempt to find expression. Caravaggio muses that 'The word should be thinkering ... another syllable to suggest collecting a thought as one tinkers with a half-completed bicycle'.[45] This reflects how the characters' memories are represented as a constant struggle to try and recapture the sensations they have had or the emotions they have felt, but one which is inevitably distant from, and prone to distort, that which they try to recover. For the reader, perceiving these images through the 'lens' of the characters, the effect is very much like that of the mirage, making them appear remote and unreal.

In his discussion of the representation of time in film and fiction, Bluestone argues that 'language, consisting as it does of bounded discrete units cannot satisfactorily represent the unbounded and continuous. We have a sign to cover a thing's "becoming", and one to cover a thing's "having become"; but "becoming" is a present participle, "become" a past participle, and our language has thus far offered no way of showing the continuity between them.'[46] Ondaatje seems especially fascinated by this gap in language, leading several critics to argue that we must attend to the techniques of poetry in appreciating the language of his novels. As Smythe puts it, Ondaatje has the 'capacity to provide a linguistic density that evokes an almost physical response – writing that can tingle the senses'.[47] His fascination with borders and boundaries clearly extends not just to the physical or geographical, but also to the temporal, including the boundaries between past, present and future, between lived experience, memory, dream and hallucination.

Ondaatje's novel begins at a languorous pace, with a present-tense description of Hana's movements around the garden, and the routines into which she and her patient have settled. Again, this illustrates the extent to which Ondaatje is intent on taking us into the heart of the experiences he describes. Minghella's film also seems to start at a gentle pace, with the image of a hand delicately painting a swimming figure as the opening credits roll. However, we are soon thrust into the realm of the spectacular, with the image of the plane flying across the desert taking the viewer's breath away. And it is not long before the pace is stepped up once more. Tom Shone has noted how

> At the start of the film, Minghella bowls you over with a bomb-disposal scene that flays your nerves bare: the perfect, tenderised state to take in the love story that follows, which you watch as if a bomb were stashed beneath your seat.[48]

This illustrates the extent to which Minghella is committed to the techniques of counterpoint and juxtapositioning of scenes, producing a mosaic effect on film to match that which is created in the novel. The stories *are* separate. We *do* need to appreciate that they take place at different times and in different locations. But how much more effective, and rich, is the impact when we are flung from one intense experience to another.

Flashback is used extensively by Minghella to juxtapose the piece of 'burnt toast' with the youthful, 'whole' figure of his former self. The account of Katherine's death begins with the patient's voice-over, excruciatingly forcing out each breath in order that the tale be told. As Fleishman has argued, the voice-over can create a disjunctive effect since the person 'behind' the voice appears to exist in two time-zones: that of the story being told and that of the narrating activity:

> We take the mature voice and the youthful image to be the 'same' person – a plausible enough view, but one that is not without its unsettling dubieties in some philosophical and artistic accounts of the continuity of individual existence.[49]

In Minghella's film, the voice-over brings home to the viewer the extent to which the patient is still struggling to come to terms with Katherine's death – because he is still the same person who experienced this tragic loss. But it also has a disorientating, eerie effect: while in some senses it is his voice which acts as a bridge between the past and the present, he is in many ways more 'real' in the past.

The patient tells Caravaggio at one point that "'*Death means you are in the third person*'",[50] and there is a sense in which his 'presence' throughout the scenes in Italy, but especially when he remembers the past, is insubstantial – he is like a spectre, a figure from the mirage who might fade away completely at any moment.

The English patient is not, however, the only link between past and present in the film. The copy of Herodotus which is still in his possession is full of fragments of his 'history' and that of others – for example Katherine's sketches, or the spent Christmas cracker which becomes yet another token of his love for her. Thus while the sheer survival of the classical text might attest to the universality of some of its images and meanings, it becomes a kind of highbrow scrap-book wherein the fragments which increase its significance ultimately threaten to burst its seams. In terms of the film's treatment of time, one effect of this is to overcome the sense in which 'pictures have no tenses',[51] since the 'scraps' that fill the historical text cannot but take the viewer back to the 'histories' of the various characters who handle them.

Ondaatje has spoken of the absence of any chronological order-ing in his construction of the novel, claiming that instead it was 'pieced together' from fragments of ideas and images on which he had been working.[52] Consquently it is clear that our sense of time in the novel is often surreal, as it is far from clear whether the char-acters are recalling or dreaming about their pasts. But this should not blind us to implausibilities or inconsistencies where they occur. In the novel the time between Almásy's departure and his return to the Cave of Swimmers, where he finds Katherine's body, is set at three years.[53] This scarcely seems to tally with his description of how she appears to him in death, and in the film Kristin Scott Thomas is positively radiant. It could be argued that the conditions in the cave are such that her body is preserved, but since neither the novel nor the film makes any attempt to hint at this, the implausibility remains.

In the novel, we learn of Katherine's death before we have been offered a full insight into her relationship with Almásy. We are told of the plane crash twice,[54] once in the third person and once in the first person. In the second instance, which occurs in chapter nine, the narrative works backwards from the scene in the cave to the plane crash, and intersperses the English's patient's attempt to recount how he first fell in love with Katherine, prompted by frequent injections of morphine. Katherine's death is reserved until much later in the film – in the opening shot of the plane flying over the desert it appears as though she is just sleeping. Minghella, therefore, exploits to the full the emotional impact of her death, and ensures that we are fully aware of the intensity of her relationship with Almásy before it is represented.

At the end of the film we return again to the doomed flight of the lovers, creating a loop-like effect, as though, like Kip trying to leave the war behind him, the film is 'rewinding the spool' of its own narrative.[55] Ondaatje has stated that he began the novel with the image of a man, burning, falling from the sky, drawing on mythic parallels with the figures of Icarus or Lucifer. Therefore, Minghella's decision to begin and end the film with this image represents an attempt to highlight these mythic overtones.

Through *mise-en-scène*, Minghella is able to avoid some of the overt 'gear-shifting' between past and present that is characteristic of the style of the novel, but which might seem clumsy if transferred to film.[56] Minghella succeeds in creating vivid snapshots to provide a flavour of the periods and places with which he is dealing – the strains of an Irving Berlin song, the foxtrot, Shepheard's hotel, the muezzin – without descending into the sepia-tinted sentimentality of the period piece or succumbing to the temptation to erect superficial links between these images and reduce them to a predictable linearity. Moreover, by keeping the use of intertitles and voice-over to a minimum, and maintaining a sense of disorientation through the often abrupt cutting between scenes, Minghella shows that he is not afraid to test his audience's 'patience' and disrupt their absorption in the fragments of events and lives which are being depicted. Some of his reordering of events does result in a diminution of the suspense which drives Ondaatje's narrative. But, like the novel, the film is continually challenging our preconceptions about time, whether this is 'historical', 'mythic', 'psychological', and so on. By constantly deferring closure, and dislocating our sense of beginning, middle and end, the film draws us into the worlds of the different characters with an immediacy which can be disconcerting as well as rewarding, but which is unrelenting in its intensity and its profound impact upon us.

Point of view

Ondaatje's novel opens with a description of the movements of two anonymous figures – a woman who appears to be fulfilling the role of carer, and her charge, who is passive and totally reliant on her. The perspective is that of an omniscient third-person narrator, so that we appear to be in familiar territory and can wait 'patiently' for the stories behind the two characters to unfold. At this stage, we feel some detachment from the characters, and this feeling is reinforced by the tendency of the narrator to subordinate his subjects within the sentences which introduce them: 'moving as if part of a glass curtain, his body enveloped within that sphere'.[57] Such sentences are again notable because of the lack of main verb, conveying the impression that the characters, and especially the patient, are almost in a state of suspended animation.

Ondaatje's stylistic experimentation, therefore, has a defamiliarising effect, so that the 'demarcation' between individuals, which might provide order and clarity, is denied. The narrative slips from third- to first-person narrative without any overt 'gear-shifting' as Ondaatje dispenses with quotation marks for his characters' dialogue. At first this has a disorientating effect as we have to work backwards to try and fathom who is speaking/narrating. In addition, Ondaatje dispenses with the tags 'he said', 'she said', so that we have to rely on the sequencing of utterances and the framing comments of the third-person narrator to work out who is saying what. In the opening sections this is not so difficult as we only have the two characters, Hana and the English patient. But the effect is nevertheless to 'make strange' the fictional world unfolding before us.

Such experimentation with the representation of speech has a long tradition. Writing in 1956, the French novelist Nathalie Sarraute castigated speech tags as 'symbols of the old regime', claiming that 'they mark the site on which the novelist has always located his characters, that is, at a point as remote from himself as from the reader'.[58] In Ondaatje's novel the stylistic experimentation seems at first to distance us from the characters and make them seem remote. But as the boundaries between first and third person appear to collapse, or at least become blurred, there is a sense in which we are drawn into their mental worlds, however confused or unstable these worlds might be.

The characters' utterances often seem broken and disjointed, especially the English patient's, since for him each word demands considerable physical effort. The style of the third-person narration appears to compound this sense of disjointedness, the present tense serving to create the impression of spontaneity and immediacy ('he wakes ... he remembers'). Short, broken sentences abound, appearing simply to record the movements and thoughts of the characters. But then we are surprised by a moment of lyricism, or an image which we cannot readily dismiss or digest before moving on ('cliff of skin', for example[59]).

Through the memories of the patient, we are soon moved on to a different world, a different time. This shift is marked initially by the use of the past tense, but as the patient's narrative unfolds it is far from clear how much is being told to Hana, and how much is simply his tortured thoughts. The patient and Hana between them share the bulk of the storytelling in the first half of the novel. Sometimes their tales are relayed directly, sometimes indirectly as reported by the third-person narrator. The reporting of a character's tale may occur where a particularly traumatic or emotional event is related, for example the narration of Katherine's death.[60] But even where we are aware of the narrator's hand shaping and organising these stories, we may be denied certainty or clarification, as when he acknowledges 'how much she is in love with him or he with her we don't know'.[61]

Only on one occasion in the novel does the narrator seem to refer to himself in the first person, and the effect is quite startling, as this occurs near the very end: 'She is a woman I don't know well enough to hold in my wing, if writers have wings, to harbour for the rest of my life'.[62] This might be dismissed as a kind of coda to the novel, a signing off by the narrator. But this would appear to be belied by the very lack of certainty which is being expressed, and by the fact that the narrative has an almost mystical quality in this section, bridging as it does the divide between Hana's and Kip's worlds. It is also left uncertain as to whether this is a direct address to the reader, or another of the many echoes of other people's words in the novel, as the sentence could also be seen as a quotation from the patient's 'commonplace book' which Hana has been thinking about.

The role of the narrator also seems evident in the aphorisms which punctuate the novel from time to time: 'When sunlight enters a room where there is a fire, the fire will go out'.[63] However, it is far from clear whether these sayings reflect the views of the narrator, or those of a character, in this case Kip. Once again, no 'gear-shifting' is evident between this seemingly impersonal comment and the expression of Kip's feelings ('he didn't fully

understand it ...'; 'he had loved Lord Suffolk ...'). The difficulty of
locating the perspective from which the narrative is coming can be
very disorientating. But we become aware of how even the most
straightforward of utterances may contain echoes of other people's
words, and other people's worlds (such as the English patient's
aforementioned 'memories' of England, which owe more than a
little to Katherine's). And often the words used by a character are
those of a source 'outside' the text, whether this be in the form of
an aphorism or a quotation, as when Almásy tells Caravaggio
'"*Death means that you are in the third person*"'.[64] Here, the italicisa-
tion and quotation marks ensure that we recognise the sentence as a
quotation but, as so often, the source is not cited and we are left to
fall back on our own resources to trace its origins.

The characters also quote one another. In one dizzying instance,
Hana remembers the English patient quoting someone else's words
to her: 'The Englishman once read me something, from a book:
"Love is so small it can tear itself through the eyes of a needle"'.[65]
As he is dying, the patient claims that 'We are communal histories,
communal books', conveying once again the sense that the identities of the characters are not fixed, sealed units, but constantly
shifting, permeable positions which they occupy for a time. [66] This
is reminiscent of Bakhtin's view that

> our speech, that is, all our utterances (including creative works), is
> filled with others' words, varying degrees of otherness or varying
> degrees of 'our-own-ness', varying degrees of awareness and
> detachment. These words of others carry with them their own
> expression, their own evaluative tone, which we assimilate, rework
> and reaccentuate.[67]

Thus while we might not be able to claim ownership or possession
of the words we utter, we are able to invest them with our own
creativity, and use them to construct or discover our own meanings
and truths.

The English patient's is perhaps the perspective with which we
feel the closest affinity in the novel, because of his wit and percep-
tiveness, but primarily because we are intrigued by him. At times his
detachment borders on the cold, even the inhuman, as when
Caravaggio wonders at his ability to speak of himself in the third
person: 'He wrote down all her arguments against him. Glued into
the book – giving himself only the voice of the watcher, the listener,

the "he".'[68] The patient also refers to those who are close to him in a cold, detached manner. The narrator reports that he refers to Katherine as 'the woman who bit into his flesh'[69] and in the notes inserted in his copy of Herodotus, he refers to her as 'Clifton's wife'.[70] Scobie has argued that the patient acts as a kind of blank screen on to which the other characters project their own passions so that 'patient, passive, he receives the identities they desire him to have', and in many ways this is just as true of how we as readers respond to the enigmatic figure at the heart of Ondaatje's novel.[71]

As we learn more about the patient's past, it appears that this aloofness and isolation persists even when he has learned to trust and love another. What he fears most is being betrayed, or himself betraying another. When Katherine breaks off the affair, and chooses to return to the mirage of conventionality and duty which is her marriage to Geoffrey, his fears appear to be confirmed. His response to this apparent betrayal is to militate against conventionality, becoming, as Ondaatje has put it, something of a 'heel'.[72] Yet in many ways this is merely an extreme manifestation of the frustrations and fears that underlie the polite veneer of other characters in the novel. The impression that we can never really 'know' other people is shared by many, for example Hana and Kip, who, in some senses, remain strangers to one another. Especially in wartime, perhaps, where emotions and allegiances between people are constantly shifting, or liable to disappear altogether, the predictability and familiarity of others often proves to have been nothing more than a mirage.

The English patient takes refuge in his role as the enigmatic outsider. But it also affords him an acute sensitivity which marks him out from the other characters. This is evident, for example, in his response to the sounds of words which he has learnt – words such as 'propinquity' which he delights in pronouncing.[73] When he loses Katherine, the patient feels that 'he has been disassembled by her',[74] but in his memories and in his relationship with Hana, there is still a realisation that in some senses he can only ever be '(re)assembled' by the care and love of others. In the desert he asserts that he becomes 'his own invention', but there is also the suggestion that this is a deceptive fiction since 'he knew during these times how the mirage worked, the fata morgana, for he was within it'.[75] Like many of the characters in Conrad's novels, a writer whom Ondaatje has acknowledged as an influence,[76] there is the fear that once you strip away the mirage of personality and individuality 'assembled' by others, all that is left is an empty core.

One of the challenges involved in bringing the character of the English patient to the screen is depicting his suffering and scarring without turning him into some kind of freak. Minghella does not shy away from bringing home to his audience the full horrors of the experience the patient undergoes, especially in the early scenes where the burnt flesh and the open sores are depicted very graphically. But at the villa the patient's appearance is one of stoic mummification rather than gross disfigurement. At times we are encouraged to share directly the perspective of the patient (during the segments of voice-over, for example). In addition, the camera sometimes represents Almásy's subjective perspective – when he is interrogated by the English the camera blacks out as he is knocked unconscious. Thus in many ways Almásy/the patient acts as the focaliser, or 'angle of vision' through which we perceive much of the action of the film.[77] Minghella gives his patient a certain amount of charm, engaging with the others in humorous exchanges, and retaining some pleasures, such as his singing or the taste of a ripe plum. As played by Ralph Fiennes, even Almásy's awkwardness and lack of social graces is engaging, so that we can come to believe that the stiff intellectual of the desert explorations, and the man who walks across a desert to bury his lover, could be the same person.

But Minghella's patient is much less of an enigma than Ondaatje's . From the moment he speaks in the film, we know that the patient is *not* in fact English. In addition, Caravaggio's knowledge of the patient's past is revealed fairly early on. This means that the focus is much more on the relationship with Katherine (or latterly, with Hana), than on protracting the viewer's curiosity and desire to crack the riddle of the man. In so doing, Minghella sacrifices the opportunity to tease and tantalise his viewers with the 'truth' about Almásy.

The other main focaliser in the film is Hana. As was mentioned earlier, Kip thinks of Hana 'as if a camera's film reveals her, but only her, in silence'.[78] In many of the scenes in which she is present, we share her perspective, but silently as she gazes on or is witness to events. For example, in the scene where her friend is blown up by the land-mine, we perceive the event, in part at least, through the window of the jeep in which Hana is travelling. Juliette Binoche's Hana is a complex woman who is harbouring great pain. When she first arrives at the villa, she hacks off her hair in a manner which at once conveys both defiance and self-loathing. Her solicitude for the patient is similarly complex, at once both a genuine outpouring of sympathy for his suffering, and a means by which she can begin to heal herself. She is portrayed throughout the film as an edgy, nervy individual who has a paranoia that those she becomes close to are bound to be taken away from her. However, we are also given an insight into a lighter side to her character, as when she plays hopscotch in the moonlight or dances with Caravaggio, so that we cannot fail to be delighted by her exuberance and vitality.

The viewpoint also wanders to accommodate the perspectives of other characters, such as Caravaggio's flashback to his interrogation by the Germans, in which the full horrors of the physical and psychological torture are conveyed. But Willem Dafoe's character is more often in the shadows or on the margins of events, a rather seedy figure who hardly inspires confidence or trust in his viewpoint. Although both the English patient and Caravaggio are dependent on morphine, it is Caravaggio who has to scurry around stealing his supply from under Hana's nose, and who is depicted performing all the rituals of the hardened user. As the patient's accuser, therefore, Minghella's Caravaggio has even less moral stature than he does in the novel. Since Minghella also portrays the relationship between Hana and Caravaggio somewhat differently, Caravaggio again seems a much more remote, even unpleasant figure.

Minghella's script brings to life much of the storytelling which takes place in the novel, through dramatisation of scenes and, more specifically, the dialogue of his characters. In the exchanges between Katherine and Almásy he subtly hints at the growing bond between them through their development of a shared, private language, again tinged with humour. Both the characters use the word 'absolutely' with great irony, meaning 'absolutely not', and Almásy playfully echoes Katherine's haughty assertion, uttered in the bazaar, that 'I don't care to bargain'. It is in the dialogue that he constructs for Katherine and Almásy that Minghella comes closest to reflecting the dissection of language, its joys and its limitations, that is so much a feature of the style of the novel. In one of their first exchanges, Katherine upbraids Almásy for the sparseness of his prose in a monograph of his which she has been reading. They subsequently engage in a discussion of the extent to which adjectives function to illuminate the meanings of the sentences in which they occur, with the discussion left unresolved as Geoffrey intervenes clumsily with a typically banal contribution.

The portrayal of Katherine is perhaps more problematic. In the novel she is in some ways a figure of legend, brought to life only in Almásy's reminiscences. In the film, she seems to be totally objectified as the gaze of the audience is invited to rest on the various parts of her body which Almásy (and the camera) map out. As in so many films, we are positioned looking over the man's shoulder and gazing on the woman's body as she reclines or is pushed back into a corner during their love-making. For all his contempt for 'ownership', Almásy is not immune from the impulse, and the audience seems to be invited to follow suit from the very first shots of the film where the contours of the desert landscape appear to be sculpted into the curves of the female form. But Kristin Scott Thomas's Katherine is hardly demure or passive. In the novel, the relationship between Katherine and Almásy is seen as being precariously balanced on the boundary between passion and violence. In the film the audience is often startled by Katherine's acts of random violence, as when she slaps Almásy both prior to and during their love-making.

Minghella departs from Ondaatje's novel in prolonging the courtship of Katherine by Almásy. Yet Katherine remains a remote figure. In the novel, Almásy reveals that he fell in love with her when he heard her tell the story of Candaules around a desert camp-fire. The choice of story is particularly resonant. It tells of the foolish Candaules who, in seeking to prove the beauty of his wife, allows another man, Gyges, to spy on her naked. When the wife discovers this, she instructs Gyges that he must either kill her husband and marry her, or die himself. Gyges chooses the former option, kills Candaules, marries his wife and ascends the throne. In both the novel and the film, much is made of Geoffrey's boasting about his new wife, encouraging us to see obvious parallels with the story from Herodotus. But the endings to the two stories are very different, as in Ondaatje's tale it is the husband, Geoffrey, who tries, unsuccessfully, to kill his rival and his wife.

In the film Katherine narrates the story framed by a halo of light from the camp-fire, while the rapt group of men sit in the shadows. The camera pans to reveal first Almásy's intent gaze, then Geoffrey's flippant comments, made in a futile attempt to laugh off his humiliation. Katherine appears to be in supreme control here, but in the film the narrative is shared between Katherine and Hana as the latter falteringly reads the same story in the ruined villa. This effectively creates a bond between the two women, bridging the distance between them. But it surely must also cast Katherine as a rather ethereal, almost spectral figure – a figure from the past who still 'haunts' the patient, but whose memory he can only cling to piecemeal as it threatens to fade altogether along with him.

Willem Dafoe has commented that during the filming of one of the scenes, he found himself asking, 'What kind of story can hold all of these characters in the same room?'[79] This reflects the extent to which the perspective wanders between the characters, so that we only appear to catch sight of them in glimpses. Moreover, our response to the characters is constantly shifting because their roles within the narrative become blurred or change completely. For example Dafoe's character is variously both interrogated and interrogator, as well as being portrayed as petty thief, spy and morphine addict. Scobie has written of Ondaatje's characters that they are 'each of them a strongly drawn individual, yet each of them also balancing, mirroring, and complementing the others, so that their total seems greater than the sum of their parts.'[80] This underlines the fact that the cutting between scenes, the blending of perspectives, leaves us not so much frustrated that we never get to know the characters, as enthralled by the ways in which this fragmentation provides us with an enriched insight into their many facets. As Barbour has argued, 'Ondaatje's great generosity as a writer … is his willingness to let them [his characters] go in the end , to allow them their human silences'.[81]

At times, visual imagery is employed by Minghella to imply links between characters or events. One of the most striking of these is the link between the glass bottles carried by the Bedouin healer who first tends to Almásy, and the bottles Hana places in her 'garden' at the villa to scare off the birds. Such images effectively complement the witticisms and neat turns of phrase of the dialogue, and provide the viewer with visual food for thought. The soundtrack by Gabriel Yared is also vital in setting up the mood of the film, and reflects the mosaic patterning of the narrative, juxtaposing as it does Hungarian folk tunes, Baroque music and popular songs from the period in which the film is set. But if the disparate elements of the film may be said to 'fit' in some sense, this does not mean that they are easily reducible to a composite reading or overall meaning. Instead, Minghella has the vision and the patience to keep positioning and repositioning the disparate fragments, celebrating the colours and wonders of the 'mirage' without rushing to find a way out of it.

Tom Shone has noted that the film opens with a bird's-eye view of the desert, but ends with a close-up on a human face – that of Hana as she embarks upon a new life.[82] But it is also the case that the last we see of Almásy and Katherine is a 'bird's-eye' shot of them still flying, as if into eternity, across the desert. This would seem to suggest that psychological insight and a sense of intimacy with the characters sit comfortably alongside the epic and the grandiloquent. It also appears to confirm that Minghella's narrative ends on a more positive, final note than Ondaatje's. But the lovers' 'resurrection' is presented very much as a kind of dream sequence, since it mirrors the manner in which the film opens. Thus the complex mixture of emotions that their story has produced is scarcely diminished by this ending.

Conclusion

Edward Said has claimed that in the postmodern age, 'narrative which posits an enabling beginning point and a vindicating goal, is no longer adequate for plotting the human trajectory in society. There is nothing to look forward to: we are stuck within our circle.'[83] But perhaps it is possible for a novelist such as Ondaatje to exploit this apparent impasse, to take the time to explore the ramifications for those who have 'nothing to look forward to' and assess the possibilities of discovering meaning and purpose within the mirage he constructs. As Kertzer has argued, Ondaatje's central character in *Coming Through Slaughter* (who, like Almásy, is partly based on a historical figure) is represented as abhorring any kind of certainty, associating it with finality and with death.[84] As a jazz musician, he delights in exploring the boundary between form and chaos in his music, resisting the impulse to reduce it to manageable forms, and revelling in the opportunity to experiment and improvise. In many ways, Ondaatje may be said to display some of these qualities in his writing, but Kertzer goes on to claim that 'images which first strike us as disjointed and disturbing gradually take their place in a mosaic the total design of which is the argument of the book'.[85] Scobie makes a similar point about Ondaatje's technique, arguing that as a writer, Ondaatje is drawn to the moment when balance collapses, the moment when his characters lose their fine control; but of course he himself, in the precision of his work, always maintains his own balance, his own control.[86]

The implication is therefore that Ondaatje's is a controlled chaos, a mirage which might entice and intrigue, but which ultimately we know has been pieced together and which, therefore, may be 'disassembled' to examine its mysteries and its contours. The impulse to reassemble and reconstruct is one that is shared by the main characters in *The English Patient*. Each of the four characters at the villa has been disassembled by the process of war, their sense of their selfhood and identity shattered by the experiences they have undergone. The characters are forced to re-examine themselves because many of those by whom they defined themselves previously – friends, family and loved ones – have been taken away. In addition, they are unable to fall back on the myths of national identity as boundaries are redrawn, and they find comradeship and empathy with peoples and races they had previously encountered only through books or songs. No solutions are offered, and not one of the characters re-emerges 'whole' from their experiences. The impulse to narrate represents a continuation of the need to try and 'piece together' their own personal histories, but this is a tortuous, fragmentary process in which their narratives may never attain any perceptible closure.

Consequently Ondaatje's novel might be said to present the ending of the Second World War as a crisis point for the modern sensibility, a period in which the old certainties and truths appear to have been destroyed with an immense force like that which is unleashed on Hiroshima and Nagasaki. But the idea that there could be such a thing as a composite 'modern sensibility' itself comes under question as the boundaries between different time-scales and different cultures are constantly being eroded by the characters' memories and by the intertextual references which punctuate the novel.

My analysis of Minghella's adaptation has shown that some concessions are made to the need to piece together fragments of the mirage. Thus some aspects of the novel are foregrounded at the expense of others, and the film achieves a kind of closure which is denied in the novel. What is missing, if anything, is the power of Ondaatje's prose to create effects such as the 'implosion' of time which may be impossible to convey visually. Minghella's film fleshes out the characters for the audience in a manner which makes their suffering and their joys impact on us with great emotional force. But in so doing the novel's depiction of the characters' (and the narrator's) ongoing struggle to find the language in which to discover and 'map' themselves as well as others is perhaps inevitably lost. With any adaptation of a literary text, some elements of the writer's style will always remain beyond the scope of translation into a visual medium. And Ondaatje's style(s) may present more challenges than most in this respect. However, Minghella's adaptation of *The English Patient* has shown to a wide and diverse audience that the 'disassembled' text, like the disassembled individuals which it places before us, can be both engaging and moving.

Minghella's film may be said to end on a more optimistic note than that struck by the novel, since the aforementioned images of Katherine and Almásy continuing their journey, and of Hana about to embark on her new life, seem to speak of beginnings rather than endings. For many viewers, myself included, seeing the film provided the impetus to read (or reread) the novel. At first I was struck by how much the film had omitted, especially as regards the relationship between Hana and Kip. But on seeing the film for a second time, I came to appreciate the task faced by Minghella, and the considerable lengths to which he goes in attempting to capture the novel's main themes and images. Surely there can be no greater praise for an adaptation of a literary text than that it encourages debate, but also that it exists in interaction with the novel from which it derives. Such an interaction is perhaps more a feature of the contemporary 'classic', given that the precedence, both temporal and cultural, of the written text is less firmly inscribed. Ondaatje's novel alludes to, and draws upon, some of the techniques associated with the cinema. It is also the case that in Minghella's film we are constantly reminded of the power of the written text to inform, to entertain, to move, and to provide comfort, as the characters draw strength from quoting from texts they have read, or escape from suffering into a world of fantasy and make-believe.

To return, finally, to the motif with which I began, it could be said that the film adaptation of *The English Patient* relies for its success on a 'mirage' of romanticism, sweeping its audience along on a 'grand emotional tour' centring on the relationship between Katherine and Almásy.[87] Yet this would be to do both the film and its audiences a great disservice. Through the use of flashback and cutting between scenes, Minghella conveys the impression that each of the four central characters occupies his or her own mirage both as an escape and as a protection from the realities of war. But at the same time, the film powerfully dramatises the ways in which the mirages of national interest and just causes are shattered for the characters, for example through Kip's response to the nuclear bombings, or the brutish treatment of Almásy at the hands of the British. The most memorable image from the film is that of the shifting sands of the desert with which it begins and ends. This encapsulates the extent to which the characters' lives, and the worlds in which they live, are in a state of flux, the boundaries between the sexes, between different races and different nationalities, always shifting and realigning. The consequent decentring of individuals and of groups of people leaves us with some feelings of unease. But there is also a sense of celebration that intense emotions and cherished memories can provide some kind of anchor for the individual – something on which to try and build one's own, unique, mirage. Circumstances may change and memories may fade, but the intense feelings Almásy has for Katherine, or which Kip feels for his friend Hardy, may provide some glimmer of the enduring, the immutable.

'Piecing together a mirage' is ultimately a gradual, tentative process. Like painting a figure on a cave wall, the image with which Minghella's film begins, a delicate and a 'patient' artistry is required. It may be that such a process is begun only with the belief that, ultimately, the whole picture will be revealed. However, for both the artist and the observer, there is great pleasure involved in each painstaking stroke of the brush, and in anticipating what will emerge from the 'piecing together' of these strokes. Perhaps such a pleasure is only attainable if one is prepared to be immersed in the mirage oneself.

NOTES

1 Derek Malcolm 'A Fiennes Romance', 'Friday Review', *The Guardian* (14 March 1997), pp. 6–7.
2 R. Brooks, 'Real-life English Patient Adored Africa, Cigarettes, Guns – and Men', *The Guardian* (17 August 1997), p. 3.
3 J. Atiyah, 'Read the Book, see the Film, Do the Holiday', 'Travel and Money', *Independent on Sunday* (16 March 1997).

4 Throughout this chapter, references to Michael Ondaatje's novels are taken from the following editions: *The English Patient* (London, Picador, 1993); *Coming Through Slaughter* (Toronto, Anansi, 1976); *In the Skin of a Lion* (Toronto, McClelland and Stewart, 1987).

5 The three films made by Michael Ondaatje were: *Sons of Captain Poetry*, Mongrel Films, Canada, 1970, 35 mins; *Carry on Crime and Punishment*, Mongrel, 1972, 5 mins; and *The Clinton Special*, Mongrel 1972, 71 mins.

6 B. Testa, 'He Did Not Work Here for Long: Michael Ondaatje in the Cinema', *Essays in Canadian Writing*, 53, Michael Ondaatje Issue (1994), pp. 154–66.

7 Ondaatje, *English Patient*, p. 300.

8 P. French, 'Review', *The Observer* (16 March 1997), p. 12.

9 A. Billson, 'Hearts Crashing and Burning in Epic Style', 'Review', *Sunday Telegraph* (16 March 1997), p. 9.

10 Film Night Special, 'The Making of *The English Patient*', Channel 4 (1 March 1997).

11 Film Night Special.

12 Throughout this chapter I will be referring to the central character as 'Almásy' in those scenes which take place prior to the plane crash, and as 'the English patient' when denoting the figure who is emotionally and physically scarred by that crash.

13 Ondaatje, *English Patient*, p. 119.

14 Ondaatje, *English Patient*, p. 121.

15 Pico Iyer, 'Mapmakers and Magic Carpets', *Time*, 46 (16 November 1992), p. 74.

16 Ondaatje, *English Patient*, p. 286.

17 Ondaatje, *English Patient*, p. 301.

18 Billson, 'Hearts Crashing'.

19 T. Shone, 'An Affair to Remember', 'The Culture', *Sunday Times* (16 March 1997), p. 4.

20 K. Jackson, 'Never Mind the Hype, Prepare to Be Seduced', 'The Critics', *Independent on Sunday* (16 March 1997).

21 S. Scobie, 'The Reading Lesson: Michael Ondaatje and the Patients of Desire', in *Essays on Canadian Writing*, 53, Michael Ondaatje Issue (1994), p. 97.

22 Billson, 'Hearts Crashing'.

23 Ondaatje, *English Patient*, pp. 95–6.

24 Film Night Special.

25 Ondaatje, *English Patient*, p. 158.

26 Ondaatje, *English Patient*, p. 43.

27 Ondaatje, *English Patient*, p. 117.

28 Ondaatje, *English Patient*, p. 218.

29 Ondaatje, *English Patient*, p. 18.

30 Ondaatje, *English Patient*, p. 170.

31 Malcolm, 'A Fiennes Romance'.

32 Shone, 'An Affair to Remember'.

33 Film Night Special.

34 Scobie, 'The Reading Lesson'.

35 H. Bhabha, 'Signs Taken for Wonders', in H. L. Gates Jr (ed.), *Race, Writing and Difference* (Chicago, University of Chicago Press, 1985), pp. 168–9.
36 French, 'Review'.
37 E. Wachtel, Interview with Michael Ondaate, in *Essays in Canadian Writing*, 53, Michael Ondaatje Issue (1994 [1992]), pp. 250–61.
38 E. Wachtel, *Essays in Canadian Writing*, pp. 250–61.
39 The 'historic present' is defined by Katie Wales (*A Dictionary of Stylistics*, Longman, 1989) as 'The special use of the present tense in oral or written, anecdotal or literary narrative, where the past tense might be expected, the shift creating a more dramatic or immediate effect. The listener/reader is "drawn into" the account.'
40 Ondaatje, *English Patient*, p. 21.
41 Ondaatje, *English Patient*, p. 10.
42 Ondaatje, *English Patient*, p. 7.
43 Ondaatje, *English Patient*, p. 161.
44 Ondaatje, *English Patient*, p. 161.
45 Ondaatje, *English Patient*, p. 37.
46 G. Bluestone, 'Time in Film and Fiction', J. S. Katz (ed.), *Perspectives on the Study of Film* (Little, Brown, 1971 [1961]), pp. 91–8.
47 K. E. Smythe, '"Listen It": Responses to Ondaatje', in *Essays on Canadian Writing*, 53, Michael Ondaatje Issue (1994), p. 3.
48 Shone, 'An Affair to Remember'.
49 A. Fleishman, *Narrated Films: Storytelling Situations in Cinema History* (Baltimore, Johns Hopkins University Press, 1992), p. 77.
50 Ondaatje, *English Patient*, p. 247.
51 Bluestone, 'Time in Fiction and Film', p. 96.
52 Film Night Special.
53 Ondaatje, *English Patient*, p. 171.
54 Ondaatje, *English Patient*, pp. 172–3, 256–7.
55 Ondaatje, *English Patient*, p. 290.
56 The term 'gear-shifting' has been employed by Norman Page (*Speech in the English Novel*, London, Longman, 1973) to describe shifts in perspective in a novel, such as might occur between an 'objective' narrative voice (past tense, third person) and the direct speech or thought of one or more of the characters (present tense, first person).
57 Ondaatje, *English Patient*, p. 9.
58 N. Sarraute, 'Conversation and Sub-Conversation', in *Tropisms and the Age of Suspicion* (London, John Calder, 1962 [1956]).
59 Ondaatje, *English Patient*, p. 4.
60 Ondaatje, *English Patient*, p. 170.
61 Ondaatje, *English Patient*, p. 127.
62 Ondaatje, *English Patient*, p. 301.
63 Ondaatje, *English Patient*, p. 195.
64 Ondaatje, *English Patient*, p. 247.
65 Ondaatje, *English Patient*, p. 288.
66 Ondaatje, *English Patient*, p. 261.
67 M. Bakhtin, *Speech, Genres and Other Late Essays*, trans. V. W. McGee, ed.

C. Emerson and M. Holquist (Austin, University of Texas Press, 1986), p. 89.

68 Ondaatje, *English Patient*, p. 127.
69 Ondaatje, *English Patient*, p. 96.
70 Ondaatje, *English Patient*, p. 97.
71 Scobie, 'The Reading Lesson', p. 98.
72 Film Night Special.
73 Ondaatje, *English Patient*, p. 127.
74 Ondaatje, *English Patient*, p. 155.
75 Ondaatje, *English Patient*, p. 246.
76 Wachtel, Interview with Michael Ondaatje.
77 Focalisation is defined by Rimmon-Kenan (*Narrative Fiction: Contemporary poetics*, London, Methuen, 1983, p. 71) as 'the mediation of some "prism", "perspective", "angle of vision", verbalized by the narrator though not necessarily his'.
78 Ondaatje, *English Patient*, p. 300.
79 Film Night Special.
80 Scobie, 'The Reading Lesson', p. 93.
81 D. Barbour, *Michael Ondaatje* (Twayne Publishers, 1993).
82 Shone, 'An Affair to Remember'.
83 E. Said, *Culture and Imperialism* (London, Chatto and Windus, 1993), p. 29.
84 J. Kertzer, 'The Blurred Photograph: A Review of *Coming Through Slaughter*', in S. Solecki (ed.), *Spider Blues: Essays on Michael Ondaatje* (Montreal, Vehicule Press, 1985), pp. 296–300.
85 Kertzer, 'The Blurred Photograph', p. 299.
86 Scobie, 'The Reading Lesson', p. 102.
88 Billson, 'Hearts Crashing'.

Index

Index

Index

Ferretti, Dane 166
Festival of Britain 47, 48
fidelity 2, 15
fidelity criticism 3
Fiennes, Ralph 203, 222
Film Weekly 60
Finch, Nigel 127
Fires were Started (1943) 47
Firth, Colin 21, 211
Fisher, Terence 124
Fitzgerald, Walter 43
Flaubert, Gustave 165
Fleishman, A. 215
Flint, Kate 58, 62
Forster, E. M. 61, 160, 164
   Aspects of the Novel 149
   Howards End 148, 149, 150,
     157
   Longest Journey, The 149
   Passage to India, A 147–60
   Room with a View, A 149,
     150
   Where Angels Fear to Tread
     150
Fort-da 17, 19, 22, 24
Foucault, Michel 4, 5–7, 8, 10,
   48
Four Weddings and a Funeral
   (1994) 10
Fowler, Harry 42
Frampton, James 102, 103
Frampton, Mary 102
Franco, Jesus 124
Frankenstein 125
French Lieutenant's Woman, The
   150
French, Philip 198, 212
Freud, Sigmund 6, 17
Fumed Oak 43
Fussell, Paul 189

fuzziness 3

Gainsborough Films 46
Garnham, Nicholas 15
Garson, Greer 179
Gaskell, Elizabeth 75
   Cranford 42
Gauge, Alexander 42
Gelder, Ken 122, 125, 128
General National Consolidated
   Trades Union 103
Genette, Gérard: *Narrative
   Discourse* 135
Gesamtkunstwerk 26
Ghost 198
Gielgud, John 181, 186
Gingold, Hermione 44
Gish, Lilian 67
Go Between, The 45
Goldsmith, Oliver 37
Gone with the Wind (1939) 71
Goodbye Mr Chips 45
Goodfellas (1990) 163, 167
Gounod: *Faust* 164, 166, 170
Grainger, Percy 106
Granger, Derek 180, 181, 192
Grant, Cary 144
Graphic, The 37, 104
Grave, Nickolas 187
Graves, Robert 185
Gray, Thomas: 'Elegy written
   in a Country Church-yard'
   89, 96
'Great Debate' 32
Great Expectations (1946) 31, 32,
   38, 46, 47, 148
Greeks had a Word for It, The 43
Greenaway, Peter 81
Greene, Graham: *Brighton Rock*
   43

Index

Grenfell, Joyce 44
Grierson, John 47
Griffith, D. W. 54, 55
Grillo, John 187
Guardian, The 160, 197
Guinness, Alec 155, 158
Gunning, Christopher 86

Habermas, Jürgen 15
Hall, Peter 8
Hampton, Christopher 132
Happy is the Bride 45
Hard Times (Granada, 1977) 32
Hardy, Robert 83
Hardy, Thomas 11, 164
  Far from the Madding Crowd
    93–4, 96, 104, 105
  Jude the Obscure 93
  Mayor of Casterbridge, The 99
  Return of the Native, The 93, 99
  Tess of the d'Urbevilles 93, 94,
    105–11
Harnay, G. J.: *London Democrat*
  36
Harper's Bazaar 104
Harrison, Kathleen 44
Hart, James 119, 120, 125
Hart, R. 202
Hartley, Hal 72
Havers, Nigel 153
Hayter, James 42
Heart of Darkness (1994) 131
Heartbeat 185
Heckerling, Amy 71, 72
Heiress, The 165
Hepton, Bernard 181
Herodotus 10, 199, 202, 209,
  212, 216, 221, 224
Herzog, Werner 124
Hewison, Robert: *Culture and*

Consensus: England, Art and
  Politics Since 1940 48
High Noon (1956) 137
Hill Street Blues 126
Hitchcock, Alfred 131–45
Hodge, Douglas 86, 103
Hogarth, Mary 61
Homicide 20
Horace 32
Hordern, Michael 86
Horror of Dracula (1958) 124
Houston, Penelope 149
Hoyle, Martin 127
Hughes, Thomas: *Tom Brown's*
  School Days 41
Hunter, Mrs Leo: *Fancy Dress*
  Dejeune 44
Hunter, Lew 137, 138
  Screenwriting 133
Huntley, Raymond 44
Hurst, Brian Desmond 31, 38
Hutchins, John 103
  History of Dorset 101
Huxley, Aldous 55, 62
Hypnotist, The (1927) 123

I was a Male War Bride (1949)
  42
infidelity 17
integrity, right of 4
Irons, Jeremy 181, 184, 185,
  186, 191
Irving, Henry 124
Irving, Washington 37
Ishiguro, Kazuo 164

Jackson, Kevin 203
Jakobson, Roman 23
James, Clive 185
James, Geraldine 181

237

Index

Index

Index